THE REAL DEAL

THE REAL DEAL

The Autobiography of Britain's
Most Controversial Media Mogul

RICHARD DESMOND

BUSINESS
BOOKS

1 3 5 7 9 10 8 6 4 2

Random House Business Books
20 Vauxhall Bridge Road
London SW1V 2SA

Random House Business Books is part of the Penguin Random House group of companies
whose addresses can be found at global.penguinrandomhouse.com

Penguin
Random House
UK

Picture acknowledgements: 'International Musician and Recording World cover', by permission of the British
Library (P.433/102); 'Northern & Shell Building, Crossharbour', Paul Harmer Photography; 'Prince Philip
opens new N&S building', Glenn Harvey/Camera Press; 'David and Victoria Beckham on their wedding day',
'With Jade Goody', 'With Hollywood royalty', 'With Joy, David Cameron and Simon Cowell', 'With Joy, baby
Valentine, Angel', Mark Moody; 'Proud owner of the Express', Stuart Clarke/Rex Features; 'Relaxing with a
good newspaper', Dan Chung/The Guardian; 'With Katie Price', 'My mother makes a speech', 'A meeting with
the queen', 'Me and my beloved Ludwig drum kit', 'Health Lottery speech', Jonathan Buckmaster/Express
Newspapers; 'With Air Commodore Malcolm White', Tim Merry/Express Newspapers; 'The Crusaders in
concert', 'Proud owner of Channel 5', 'A revived Dallas', Tim Clarke/Express Newspapers; 'The Richard
Desmond Children's Centre', Rosie Hallam; 'Royal Television Society speech', Paul Hampartsoumian.

First published in Great Britain by Random House Business Books in 2015

www.randomhouse.co.uk

A CIP catalogue record for this book is available from the British Library

ISBN 9781847947482

Typeset in Roos SemiBold by Palimpsest Book Production Ltd, Falkirk, Stirlingshire

Printed and bound in Great Britain by Clays Ltd, St Ives plc

Penguin Random House is committed to a sustainable future
for our business, our readers and our planet. This book is made from
Forest Stewardship Council® certified paper

To my parents, without whom I would not have been here, to my dear Joy, without whom I would not want to be here, and to Angel Millie the most beautiful daughter in the world, Valentine the world's best little son and Robert the world's best big son.

CONTENTS

FOREWORD

My advice to friends over the last year has been: when you get to the age of 62 spend some time getting your life down on paper. It will jog your memory about all sorts of things you had forgotten, and give you the opportunity to swap reminiscences with people who've played a key part in your life. It will also help you understand yourself a bit better. In my case, it has the additional advantage that in future, instead of endlessly retelling the tales of my early days in business, I can simply give people page numbers. What's more I now have a record for my children and their children of my history and the family history, and my son Robert will have something to remind him that our immigrant grandparents were not buried in Ukraine, as he seemed to think, but Streatham.

I want to thank about a thousand people for helping me with this project but most directly Paul Ashford who has been with me for most of my working life and Martin Townsend who has been with me for many of the most exciting bits, both of whom after all this time are able to finish my sentences for me. I'd also like to thank my publishers Nigel and Gail for their input and their enormous cheques which will go to my charity foundation to help the needy.

In fact my wife and my board directors are thankful, too, because this account was put together during the time I was waiting for EU approval of my Channel 5 deal, so it did something to distract me from driving everyone mad a hundred times a day asking when I would have the cheque. Instead, I only drove them mad fifty times a day. That sale was, for me, the defining deal of a lifetime in business and the first time I felt secure in financial terms and accepted it was now unlikely I would end up on a park bench. It was the achievement that helped make sense of everything that had gone before, and it helped set up my next business ventures. Meanwhile my wife Joy was pregnant for the second time, so I felt I could now rely on at least four readers: herself, my daughter Angel and new son Valentine, plus grown-up son Robert. And – as I write – now five, God willing, because Robert and his partner Basia are expecting their own child which will make me – amazingly – a grandfather.

So already in 2015 my future isn't the same as I thought it would be in 2014. Meanwhile, business-wise, the media is being transformed by big digital players and the trend for 'programmatic selling' which means the whole process is conducted by computers and databases. It's all very different from when I started out. Still, if any would-be Richard Desmond in the digital generation or indeed any generation can take something from this book and apply it to their business or their life, that will make me happy. In fact, despite all the changes that are going on, I strongly suspect that the basics of business will remain as they always have been.

I have a strong suspicion that a third of my readers will like me and my story, a third will hate me, and a third won't care at all. Well, I should thank the first third for their support and the other two-thirds for making me try harder – and I'd also like to thank all the great one-off characters who appear in this book for making my life more interesting and more colourful.

Enjoy, be happy, and be lucky.

Richard Desmond
London, April 2015

PROLOGUE

I do not notice the motion of the hospital trolley. I expect this is an effect of the drugs that have been administered to prepare me for the operation that I hope will save my sight.

As my consciousness starts to fade I notice I am wearing a name tag on my wrist. The thought occurs to me that I am being taken to play another concert, like those I have done with Roger Daltrey, Robert Plant and Greg Lake. I hope the bass drum pedal will be OK and will not collapse when I put my foot on it.

Then I hear a voice that I know comes from within my head, even though it appears to originate among my surroundings at the hospital, somewhere just out of sight.

'So, you idiot, you've worked 18 hours a day and seven days a week. You've ignored most things other than getting to where you've got. I hope you're pleased with yourself.'

I do not quite know how to answer this, but as I search for a suitable response the image of my workplace comes into my head. The voice persists: 'Do you like your office – overlooking the Thames at the Tower?'

'Well, yes, I would say it's the best office in London.'

'And your newspapers and your magazines and your privileges and going to Downing Street to see the Prime Minister?'

'Yes.'

'Well, you'd better decide whether it's all been worth it.'

'What do you mean?'

'You'd better decide whether all your material achievements are really the most important things in life, and if they're not, just exactly what you're going to treat as your priorities from now on . . .'

The voice appears intent on teaching me some kind of lesson, and I suddenly feel I am about to face the toughest choice of a career which has had its share of tough choices. But before I can answer, the drugs take their full effect, and I know nothing more until I awake surrounded by my medical team at Moorfields Eye Hospital, and am told the procedure has been a success.

My condition is called acute angular glaucoma, a malfunction of the eyes which characteristically affects those of Far Eastern origin. Since my family originated in the Ukraine some will speculate about a distant relationship with Genghis Khan and his invading hordes.

It seems unlikely because this Genghis Khan was a very aggressive fellow, and I always do my best to be agreeable.

But perhaps I should start at the beginning.

1
RICHES TO RAGS

My earliest memory is of sitting on the pot, in my mum and dad's bedroom, looking at the walnut wardrobes. Those wardrobes seemed very grand to me, and I suppose at the time we Desmonds were quite a grand family. Unfortunately we were not going to stay that way.

We lived in a nice detached house in Dorset Drive in Edgware, which is a suburban corner of Middlesex. I used to like getting on my tricycle and pedalling along our road pretending I was a bus driver, stopping at all the houses around the little cul-de-sac where we lived.

At the age of 3 I even rode my tricycle to my school, Fernhurst Junior, which was a mile and a half away. Mrs Porter there used to make us lunch, and she always singed the puddings, giving me a taste for burnt food, in particular burnt custard, that has stayed with me ever since.

In many ways we were a typical enough Jewish household of the period, in touch with our roots, keeping the Sabbath and the High Holidays, and looking to make our way in the world. Both sides of my family originated from eastern Europe. My father, the grandson of Latvian immigrants, had grown up in Stamford Hill. His mum and dad had died in the flu epidemic at the end of the First World War, so he and his sister were brought up by their grandparents who were in the fur business and apparently very tough. They sent my father to school at what is now known as the Sobell Centre, but which used to be run by nuns. I don't think he can have enjoyed it much because in later life, whenever he saw a nun, he would spit.

When I think of my mother back then, I always think of her smiling, which is remarkable because she, too, had gone through some hard times. Her family came from Ukraine, from an area that up until the Second World War had a Jewish community numbering some hundreds of thousands. Few survived the Holocaust and I have to say that when I went back to the town of our origin a couple of years ago with my son Robert, we didn't exactly feel welcome either; nobody refused to serve us, but they did tend to say things like, 'Oh I'm afraid the food you want is going to take two hours. Do you *really* want to wait?' You can understand why my family left when they did.

My mother's parents originally landed at Liverpool, before coming down to London and settling in a house on the Mile End Road in Whitechapel. My mother would always say we came from Mile End, because that was posher than Whitechapel. There was no pretending to be posh inside the house, though: the family had to sit on orange boxes because they couldn't afford furniture.

My maternal grandfather, Louis, made money selling tyres and records, either from a market stall or a cart. He and my grandmother had nine children. Two of them became doctors, one died from cancer, two were with the RAF and got shot down, another was a bit of a Jack the Lad and was in Cobham's Flying Circus: an amazing aviation display team. Yet another went to America and opened a garage in Los Angeles in the 1930s. My grandfather was very orthodox and constantly at synagogue. But all the daughters other than my mother married non-Jews; one of them even became a Catholic and acquired a posh accent, which broke her father's heart. One way and another, they were an adventurous family, and, when I look at the photographs now, always very smartly dressed.

As she grew up my mother wanted to help her parents out by getting them a flat in Hendon, but it was not to be. When she was 20, my grandfather died suddenly (she was always upset that she went out that night and never got the chance to say a proper good-bye to him). A few years later her mother passed away too.

As for my father, Cyril Desmond was a proper character. He was also, during his early career, a high-flying media executive, who started out on the *Daily Express* as a circulation manager (the *Daily Express*, then, has always been part of my life), before moving to a new paper in Whitechapel called the *Jewish News* (a challenger to the *Jewish Chronicle*, it modelled its offices on the *Daily Express* building). And it was at the *Jewish News* that he met my mother, who was working there as a typist. They duly married and settled briefly in Mile End. Because publishing executives don't live in that part of town, however, they moved to Stoke Newington, then to a flat in Regent's Park which had rats, then to Mill Hill, and so, eventually, to Edgware, to the house with the grand wardrobes.

While all these moves were going on, my dad took a new job at Rank, the big theatre group. And there he met two other Jewish boys, Dickie and Ernie Pearl, who were to play a big part in his life. The two brothers were originally from Swansea but had come down to London first to sell balloons on Hampstead Heath, then to sell advertising on those balloons. They were clever and entrepreneurial, so it was always on the cards that if the right opportunity arose they would set up on their own. The opportunity duly came when they met Bob Dean, a smooth, debonair Christian from Yorkshire. Together, the three of them set up a new company, Pearl & Dean in the Finchley Road, to sell advertising into cinemas, and when they set up an overseas division shortly afterwards, they invited my father to run it. They even offered him a share in the business, but as he had two children at the time he felt it was safer to take wage and commission rather than be a shareholder. I won't say that was his ruin, but it's why he didn't ultimately benefit from his association with them to the extent he could have done. His decision provided me with Business Lesson Number One – where you can, take ownership.

The Pearl & Dean team worked well together. Ernie Pearl was the visionary, the real brains behind the company. Dickie Pearl was the schmoozer. He would travel to somewhere like Wigan, where he'd come across a man showing films in a church hall, and ask him if he'd like to make an extra shilling a week. Dickie would then give the shilling, guaranteed, for two years, if the man agreed to show three minutes of advertising during screenings. Bob Dean was good with the big advertisers, because he was very smooth. And finally there was my father: the master salesman. As the business grew they all moved to a very smart building in Dover Street, in central London, with uniformed commissionaires on the door. Each year they would have a Christmas party, not just for the adults but for the kids too. It was very formal. The adults enjoyed whisky in crystal glasses, cigars – and cashew nuts! Those nuts seemed a very expensive luxury back then.

Eventually, in the early fifties, Pearl & Dean decided that they fancied opening offices overseas. Quite cleverly they avoided America in favour of places like Greece, Singapore and Africa. It became my father's job to go out to whichever country it was, open up a local office and get it going. I did not see much of him during those successful years: sometimes he would be away for three months at a time. All my memories of him are of sitting in the back of his car on the way to or from the airport and being choked by the fumes from his cigar. Yet I was happy enough. Life was good. My mother had an account at Selfridges, which we all thought was a big deal. On occasion, the Pearls would come round to our house, Dickie in a Bentley, Ernie in his Rolls-Royce. One of the African heads of state visited us too, the first black man I'd ever seen, and the boss of Shell dropped in for tea! As for me, I played cricket with the bloke across the road whose father owned the All

Weather Garage in nearby Burnt Oak, and I'd play cars with Michelle Mortner, of whom I was very fond. We'd play in the woods in Edgware, by Canons Drive.

My brother was 15 years older, and he was excited because he was engaged to be married to the daughter of Mr Austin of Austin Suite Furniture. They were one of the big Yiddisher furniture companies but my father would never give them any respect. To him they were 'f***ing cabinetmakers'. My father, you see, was Cyril Desmond of Pearl & Dean worldwide screen advertising – a media person and man of the world.

Then, when it seemed nothing could go wrong, disaster struck. Out of the blue, my mother called me in. I knew, from the look on her face, that something was badly wrong.

'Richard,' she said, 'I've got something to tell you and there's no easy way to say it. I've got to go to Africa because your father . . . well, he could be dying.'

I couldn't quite believe what I was hearing. I felt like I'd been hit with a hammer. Apparently, my father had contracted a terrible illness through drinking contaminated water.

My mother flew to Africa with Dickie Pearl, and they brought my father back, by air ambulance, to Hammersmith hospital. He was told there was an antibiotic that might save his life, but that it might leave him blind, deaf or even paralysed. That day he was a Savile-Row-suit-wearing 45-year-old executive who jetted round the world. Everything was great. But he took the antibiotic and the next morning he woke up completely deaf.

It must, of course, have been a real personal ordeal for him to find himself in that condition. What struck me most at the time, though, was that all of a sudden his friends either disappeared or made disparaging comments. 'After all,' they would say, 'he can't hear, silly old bastard.' One minute they were all chummy with my father; the next, because he had lost all his influence, they didn't want to know.

The only real friends that my father was now left with were us, his family. And we really wanted to do our best for him. But we struggled with a far more serious problem than his deafness: his addiction to gambling.

I knew, even at my young age, that this was something he'd always struggled with. In his earlier Pearl & Dean years, I can recall him taking advertising clients to Sandown Park, complete with his top-of-the-range binoculars in a smart leather case (everything he owned had to be top quality), and showing them what a big man he was by placing some huge bet. Of course in those days he could afford it and it was part of the sell.

But after the illness, it was another story. The Pearls tried to look after him financially. Dickie Pearl took my mother up to Dover Street in his Bentley to discuss the future. He offered £100,000 in 1954 so that my father could start a shop of some sort and so earn an income. My mother, however, was horrified at the idea of giving my father such a huge lump sum because she knew he would just gamble it away. Instead she asked that he be given a wage for the rest of his life and they agreed to £3,000 a year – perhaps the equivalent of £500,000 now.

It was a sensible strategy so far as it went but, sadly, it was to no avail. Because of my father's setback his gambling addiction grew steadily worse. My mother went back to the company and asked if he could be given something to do. They suggested he collect debts. He tried that, and hated it. Eventually he went to see Ernie Pearl and said, 'Look, I am a salesman, not a debt collector.'

Ernie agreed and so my father went back to selling, perhaps at a lower level than previously but at least that was his first love. I remember once going with him to a very big agency whose clients included brands like Domestos. Of course his deafness made negotiations very difficult, but because I was able to make him understand me, I was able to interpret for the buyers. Years later Dickie Pearl said to my wife: 'Do you realise your husband was selling advertising when he was five years old?'

I often accompanied my father on his selling trips, and if the company gave him, say, Felixstowe Cinema for the summer, I'd be able to go to Charlie Manning's amusement arcade while he was working. More often than not, though, I'd be sitting in his Triumph Herald pretending to drive it, while he was in the bookmakers. I sat outside a lot of bookmakers. Spicers in Finchley Road, William Hill, Corals. Eventually, he would emerge, having lost heavily. 'Bastards!' he would say. 'That Joe Coral's a crook!'

About this time I moved from my private nursery school to Edgware Junior School. Fernhurst, it turned out, would be my only encounter with private education. From then on it was the state sector all the way. Thanks to the grounding I had already had, I found that I was ahead of the rest of the class, but it didn't exactly make me popular. Nor did my origins. The other kids, from council flats in Stanmore, would make comments like: 'Oh well, you must be rich, because *all* Jews are rich.' Things were not helped by the fact that sometimes I would have to be taken out of school to attend various Jewish functions.

By the time I was eight my father's gambling debts had become so heavy that we were becoming very hard up indeed. I had to find a way of raising cash. I used what little money I could scrounge or borrow to buy quantities of cheap bubblegum, which broke all my teeth, collected the cards inside and sent off for various things like a camera or a rugby ball. Then I sold them, saved the money and took my mum out, at Christmas, to see a show and have a meal at a Berni Inn.

But of course it wasn't enough. Things gradually got worse until eventually my father lost everything, including the house. This was the final straw for my mother. I used to wonder whether she left my father because he'd gone deaf or because he'd gone broke. But the heartbreaking truth, I now think, is that she left him because she wanted to save *me*. She wanted to try and give me a better life.

I can understand that, yet as I've got older I've also come to feel increasingly sorry for my father. It's almost unbearable now to imagine what he went through and the frustration he must have had to endure. He was trapped in what had become a loveless marriage, he couldn't hear, he couldn't even really have a conversation. On top of it were all those endless and hopeless trips to the bookies, making a bad situation even worse each time.

My mother found a flat for the two of us to move into and she sold the idea to me by saying that it had very nice cupboards – much bigger than the ones we had in Edgware. Then she met me after school one day and took me on the bus to see it. I remember arriving at a block of very old flats. We walked up the stone stairs to No. 16 and opened the door. It was dark inside. One bedroom, a lounge, another bedroom. And a balcony that looked over the backyards of all the shops so you could see the deliveries arriving, and, beyond that, a main road with buses and cars going up and down. You couldn't open the front windows because they were all rusted up.

Suddenly I felt very alone. I knew nobody. My friends Nigel Sloane and Michelle Mortner were gone, along with David Kestelhaut, with whom I used to play cricket in Green Lane.

By now I was 11 years old and starting at my secondary school, Christ's College. It was a grammar school, which was supposed to be a good thing, but I thought it was a terrible place. The sort of teaching they did meant nothing to me. Not only did I not know what the capital of Egypt was, I didn't *care.* Then you had the woodworking class. I liked maths and history, anything that had a purpose to it. But woodwork? Jews don't do woodwork. To make matters worse I felt isolated. The kids at Christ's College were like the ones at my nursery school: they all lived in detached houses in Woodside Park, Finchley Central and Hampstead Garden Suburb. They'd go out for fish and chips at lunchtime at the Three Brothers restaurant round the corner, but I could never afford that, so I felt lonely and excluded.

In fact we could not even afford the uniform for Christ's College. We were, however, allowed to sew the badge on to a plain blazer my mother found. I had to wear the same blazer to synagogue on Saturday, which led to a lot of teasing and laughter at my expense. Many years later I met one of my tormentors, who by this time was the accountant for my PR man Alan Edwards. He said, 'Hi, remember me? We used to go to Woodside Park together. We were friends.' I told him we were never friends and reminded him he used to tease me about the blazer.

My attempts to fit in at school were a failure. I was poor, lonely, a bit fat, and an outsider. I had my talents, but even those failed to help me.

On one occasion they wanted to raise money for a church fête or something similar and they gave all the kids programmes to sell. The one who sold the most programmes would get a pound, and win his class a trip to Southend. So off I went, Saturday and Sunday, up and down Finchley selling programmes. I worked hard at it and it turned out that I was a good salesman. What's more, it turned out to be great fun because sometimes people would give you a pound and not even take a programme.

Anyway, I raised more money than anyone else, and so won my class the trip to Southend. I felt so proud of myself. When we arrived, I fancied going to the amusements. Unfortunately I was a bit late coming back. I thought they might be understanding but, no, I got the cane from a teacher who looked just like a Nazi when I saw pictures of him in later years – plus a thousand lines: 'I must not be late'. I couldn't believe it: without me they wouldn't have even *been* in Southend.

By this time my mother and father were divorced. My mother started working for Orlik, a famous company in Archway which made pipes for the gentleman smoker. My father, meanwhile, clearly feeling guilty about what had happened, bought me a bike. It didn't do him much good: I suppose I'd taken my mother's side and felt he was to blame for everything. My brother, however, made me go round to see him in his new flat in Finchley Court, which was halfway between where I lived and the school, and my visits there became something of a regular fixture, especially when my mother was working. When I arrived at his flat, my poor dad would invariably announce proudly that he was cooking a chicken for me. He'd be standing there, in his little kitchen, in his Savile Row jacket, with his hearing aid whistling and his cigar ash tumbling on to the food. The chicken was always undercooked. It's taken me nearly 60 years to come back to eating chicken again.

Far more enjoyable were my Hebrew classes at Woodside Park, where I could meet other Jewish blokes, where the cantor was very warm and friendly, and where there were bagels on a Sunday morning. For a while I thought I might even become a cantor myself. Indeed I went so far as to visit the United Synagogue headquarters in Woburn Place to find out about the training. That's when I discovered the problem with my plan. They told me I'd have to learn all this stuff, book after book. I, however, just wanted to sing the songs.

So my ambition to be a cantor quickly ceased. But my attraction to music did not – it simply took a different direction. One of the people I became friendly with at Woodside was called Jonathan

Portner who had an older brother who was into music. So Jonathan came along every Sunday with a little tape recorder and he played me the Animals and Georgie Fame. Around that time everyone was listening to Beatles songs, but I never much liked the Beatles. They seemed terribly manufactured to me. But when I heard the Animals with Eric Burdon's voice and the Vox organ I thought they were fantastic.

Jonathan said I should start reading the *Melody Maker*, too, which was great advice and probably why I still go to him as a dentist.

All in all, it was the beginning of my lifelong love affair with music.

And then I came across live bands. Strangely enough, I had a French exchange student to thank for my first encounter with them. I had been to his home in Paris, where his father had taken me out for an opulent lunch of *moules* and oysters. When the boy came for the return visit to stay with me, he clearly expected me to reciprocate, but I knew we couldn't afford to take him out to the country for a roast beef lunch. Instead I decided to take him to see John Mayall's Bluesbreakers, featuring Eric 'Slowhand' Clapton. We took the 221 bus to the Manor House, walked up the stairs, paid our 7/6 each, and found ourselves in a crowded room, on a warm summer's night, with about 30 other people. I went back to the Manor House recently and it's only a small room, but it seemed big back then. There were windows along one side with curtains, I remember, that didn't quite fit the windows. A projector was beaming through a piece of plastic and you could smell the plastic melting.

Then this group with 'John Mayall's Bluesbreakers' written on the organ appeared. They started playing and I forgot about French exchange students, family problems, money problems, everything.

I had to hold on to the radiator.

I had never heard anything like it.

2
GOD GAVE US ROCK AND ROLL

When I was 13 I forged my date of birth so that I could get a Saturday job at Woolworth's, earning £1 3s 6d for the day. But my real ambition was to do something in the music world – or, at least, close to it.

One evening I went along to the Manor House to watch Zoot Money play, and got chatting to the cloakroom attendant. He told me that he was leaving and asked if I knew anyone who wanted to take over. I didn't think twice, especially when he told me that I could earn a pound just for the evening, plus tips, and that if I left the door open, I could hear all the music. I could also meet the musicians when they walked past to get to the toilet – and after all, everyone has to go to the toilet.

The first night I was there my predecessor came up and asked if I'd do him a favour. Apparently, he had been charging people sixpence each to leave their coat, but his uncle, who owned the pub, thought it was only threepence. If I took ten coats and gave his uncle ten times sixpence he would probably give his nephew the taste of his belt. If, on the other hand, I stuck with the existing system, I'd earn an extra threepence a coat and the former office holder would be saved a lot of unnecessary pain.

At the end of that first evening I went down to see the boy's uncle, who was sitting in the pub having a drink, with his Alsatian dogs around him. The Manor House was not in the East End but it was still pretty rough. He asked me how many tickets I had sold, and I told him: 42.

'And how much is it a ticket?' he asked me. 'Sixpence, isn't it?'

He knew exactly what his nephew had been up to. I agreed that it was sixpence.

However, later on I learned a good trick. If a couple of punters came up I'd say, 'Oh you're together, aren't you? You'll only need one ticket.' I'd then charge for both coats, but put them on one hanger. So far as the pub was concerned, we'd just made sixpence rather than a shilling, and I was therefore able to keep the difference. Later still, I put the price up to ninepence a ticket, pocketing the extra three-pence, and eventually, when I realised I was doing all the work and the landlord was having a drink inside, I even introduced my own tickets, which I purchased from a sweet shop in Friern Barnet. They were raffle tickets in green, pink and blue just like the ones the land-lord used, which meant that I could control exactly how many of his I gave out and so decide how much money he should get.

I have to confess that I didn't feel bad about doing any of this. My mother and I really needed the money; I was acutely aware that my family could not afford to do the things others were doing. Other kids were having lavish bar mitzvahs, for instance, but there was to be no bar mitzvah party for young Richard and since I couldn't invite people to mine, I couldn't expect invitations to theirs. Today I sometimes think to myself, 'Remember that, Mr Desmond', if it happens that one of my daughter Angel's friends doesn't invite her back to their home: you never know, maybe it's because that friend lives in a one-bedroom flat.

My other reason for needing the money was that, by now, I had discovered that listening to music was not enough: I wanted to play, too, and in particular I was desperate to learn the drums. I think I acquired this desire from my brother who was an enthusiast – and from some bongos my father had once brought back from Africa.

Of course I couldn't afford the £40 I needed to buy a proper drum kit, but – as luck would have it – one of my classmates, whose father worked for a music company, got a new drum kit for his bar mitzvah. I asked him what had happened to the old one and when he said he'd thrown it out the day before, I went round to his very nice house in Finchley Central and gave him £5 for it. It wasn't much of a drum kit to be honest: a couple of cymbals, a hi-hat and a bass drum. I think it was a blue Broadway, which was made by Rose Morris. But it was something to hit and I like to tell my eldest children, Robert and Angel, the story of those first drums, because when I think today about how many things they have, it's funny to remember how grateful I was to get something that had been thrown out!

With my job in the cloakroom bringing in a bit of cash, much of my life at this time centred on the Manor House pub. Upstairs at the pub was a club called Bluesville which was run by a couple called Ron and Nanda Leslie. She was a little Greek woman with black hair, who used to shout at all the gangsters who came in: 'You know I don't allow you in here!' They would then look a bit sheepish and mumble, 'Oh all right, Nanda, all right.' Ron (who had once been, I think, a drummer) had grey hair in the sort of style favoured by the famous jazz musician turned club owner Ronnie Scott, and always kept a very smart E-type or Mercedes car parked outside. He'd show his cars off to all the groups who played at the club but would then have to go on to say what great bargains they had been, because he couldn't admit to how much money he was making.

Ron not only ran his Bluesville club at the Manor House but also one at the Fishmonger's Arms in Wood Green, and others at venues in Brentwood and in Ipswich. All the groups he engaged were signed to a company called the Rik Gunnell Agency. And the way that this company did business fascinated me. Rik and his brother John would sign up Rod Stewart, Zoot Money, Georgie Fame, John Mayall – everyone – and pay the leader of each band £30 a week and the rest of the musicians £20. The reason they could be so confident about their outlay was that alongside booking them at places like Bluesville they also knew they could guarantee bookings at the other clubs they ran, including the Ricky-Tick club at Windsor, which featured in the famous 1960s film *Blow-Up*. It resembled a little cartel and I thought they were clever.

Eventually, because they liked the way I handled things down-stairs in the pub cloakroom, Ron and Nanda asked me if I'd work Sundays and Wednesdays too. I pointed out that I had to be home by 11pm so Nanda arranged that the commissionaire would take me back to the flat on his moped. Now, it seemed, the cash was coming in and I was rocking and rolling. Even so, I was still keen to earn more because my family experiences and our money difficulties left me with a keen sense of what it means not to be financially secure.

The one day of the week I was reluctant to work was a Saturday because that was the night that Ron and Nanda weren't there to run the club in the evening; instead it was organised by some people from Highbury. And that was the night when things could get quite rough. All through the week the club was full of blokes in reefer jackets, but on Saturday everyone wore smart 'tonic' suits and instead of bands they had a soul-music disco, the sort of stuff the girls who hung around with the tougher crowd could dance to in their miniskirts and see-through tops.

However, I happened to be in the cloakroom one evening when some of the Highbury guys came in and asked if I would do a Saturday stint for them. They had heard I was reliable, they said. They would pay me £2 a night, and were prepared to let me carry on with my little fiddle with the ninepence, which they knew all about. So I agreed.

For the first two weeks, everything went fine. But then on the third Saturday four blokes came into the cloakroom, closed the door behind them, pointed at one of the coats, and said, 'We want that sheepskin jacket.'

I said, 'What do you mean you want it? You haven't got the ticket.'

Before I could even think of trying to stop them they jumped over the counter and simply grabbed it. At first I didn't know what to do. Then I decided to go and tell Wally, who was one of the guys in charge, what had happened. He listened to my description of the thieves, and informed me that they were the Smith brothers, from a local gang called the Highbury Mob. When the owner of the stolen jacket came to collect it, Wally told him what had happened and on hearing that the Smith brothers were involved, the bloke immediately told him not to worry about it. He did ask, though, if I had been in on the theft. I didn't like that at all. I'd had enough and I told Wally that I didn't want to work on Saturdays any more.

Wally, however, tried to reassure me. In future, he said, I should keep the door open and blow a whistle he'd give me if there was any trouble. If for any reason he didn't come straight away because he hadn't heard the whistle, I should smash the little bottle of cider I normally had by my side, and hold it under the chin of the one who was doing the talking.

'They'll all soon back down,' he said.

I didn't really like the sound of this at all, but as I was still keen to carry on earning I nodded.

A few weeks later, the gang came strutting into my cloakroom again, closing the door behind them and demanding another expensive coat, a Crombie.

'Look, you're not having it,' I said.

They started arguing with me.

I didn't reach for the whistle, instead – Smash! – I waved a broken bottle at the one who was doing most of the talking. 'You're not getting the coat,' I yelled. 'You might take me down, but I've got you – now fuck off.'

And guess what? They backed down. I told Wally I thought we should call the police, but he shook his head: 'No one really cares.'

'Yes, but *I* care.' I said.

I insisted that he call the police, and a Black Maria duly came and arrested the troublemakers. I was told that at some point I would have to go to Caledonian Road police station to give a witness statement.

A few days later, a fellow came into the club, informed me that he knew not only where I lived but where I went to school, and warned me that if I gave evidence against the bloke who had tried to take the coat 'they' would kill me. Apparently, the would-be thief was already on probation and would certainly go to prison if convicted. A day or two later, I noticed a big 3.5-litre Rover parked outside Christ's College. There were four blokes inside.

'What am I going to do?' I wondered.

As instructed, I went to the police station, where I told them about the unwelcome visit I had received. Their response was that I had managed to get tangled up with a very dangerous crowd. Obviously, said the inspector, when asked in court who had taken the coat, I should tell the truth. But, he added, looking me straight in the eye, I had to be absolutely 100 per cent sure. If I was even only 90 or 99 per cent sure I could identify the culprit, that would not be enough, and I'd have to say as much.

On the day of the trial I took the bus with my mum to Stamford Hill magistrates' court. As we walked in, I noticed that all the gang who had come into my cloakroom were sitting there, staring at me. I was asked my age and when I said 13, the place went very quiet: the assumption was that I'd have to be 18 or 19 at least to be working in that club. The magistrate said, 'Well, son, before you is Mr Smith. You have said he took the coat. Are you 100 per cent sure?'

My heart was pounding. I said: 'I'm pretty sure . . . but I can't be 100 per cent sure.'

The judge told Mr Smith he was free to go, much to his obvious relief. He came up to me afterwards and said that he and his brothers really appreciated what I'd done and that if there was anything they could do for me in return, I should call them – and he handed me his card.

Of course there was no way I was ever going to call them. However, our paths did cross once more. Seven years later, I bought a second home in Wood Green, and one of the people who came round hoping to rent one of the rooms turned out to be Mr Smith, the thief from the Manor House. He obviously didn't recognise me, and because he only used the room as an occasional bolt-hole I never saw him again. However, he did replace all my horrible old furniture with brand new stuff. It's funny how everything goes round.

By now I had managed to save enough money for a set of new drums, so I bought a white kit with German-made Trixon fittings (proof, if it's needed, that I'm definitely not anti-German!).

Whenever Zoot played at the club, I chatted with his drummer, Colin Allen, in the tiny little dressing room. He taught me how to play paradiddles and showed me how, if you put bicycle chains on cheap cymbals, it gives them more of a ring. He also told me I should get drumming lessons.

I looked in the *Melody Maker* and rang one of the drum tutors who advertised there, whose name was Max Abrams. Max Abrams (originally Max Abramovich) was a very famous drummer, originally from Glasgow, who had played with many of the biggest bandleaders from the thirties and forties including Ambrose and Jack Hylton. The story I love about him is that every night he'd put on his black tie, turn up at whatever function was going on at the Hilton, sit down at one of the tables and have his dinner.

'Max, you always seem to be in there,' I said to him years later.

He replied, 'Well there's always a spare space, and no one ever asks for your ticket. I have my dinner, have a drink and go home!'

When I approached him for drum lessons, though, Max was unable to help me, so instead I went along to a guy called Frank King who told me that he'd charge me £1 2s 3d for half an hour – *exactly* what I earned at Woolworth's for a day's work. (I always thought of money in those days in terms of the pay for a day in Woolworth's or a night at the cloakroom.)

I agreed to his terms, started lessons, and found that he and I got on quite well. When I wasn't having lessons I would practise and practise at home. It must have been terrible for the two old girls who lived in the flats above us. Eventually, I agreed to move my drums to my father's flat. Obviously he couldn't hear them, and when his neighbours complained he couldn't hear *them* either!

One day I was trying to get to my drum lesson, which took place in a room above Footes drum shop in Piccadilly's Denman Street, when both the bus and the Tube were badly held up. I eventually struggled in an hour and a half late. 'What are *you* doing here?' Frank asked. 'I'm teaching another bloke now.' The bloke he was teaching was Trevor Morais from a band called the Peddlers.

'Look, Mr King,' I said, 'it's not my fault,' and I told him about the transport problems.

'Well, time is money. I'm teaching someone else now.'

'But I've worked so hard. I'd tell you if it was my fault. But it wasn't my fault.'

Then, out of the blue, Trevor Morais said he'd be happy for me to sit in with him.

I couldn't believe my ears. What a wonderful gesture! Trevor was one of my heroes. With all due respect to Ringo Starr and Bob

Henrit, Trevor Morais was the top bloke at that time. He was a great drummer, and the Peddlers, who were like an early Emerson, Lake & Palmer, were a brilliant band. But I have another reason to be grateful for meeting Trevor that day. The simple truth is that if I'd been turned away from my lesson, if Trevor hadn't let me sit in with him and taken the time to practise paradiddles with me, I might well have said 'fuck this', and given up. After all, drumming was, and is, grief.

Now I started meeting musicians at different gigs or from *Melody Maker* classifieds and playing in various bands, the first of which was called Rebellion and was a cross between Zoot Money and all the jazzy stuff – which I liked – and Jimi Hendrix and the Who – which the other members preferred. It offered a great excuse to bash around on the drums. We used to go and see Pink Floyd at the Roundhouse and were very impressed with the fact that they broke milk bottles in a dustbin and then played the sound through a PA. We also liked their brilliant light show. Consequently, when we happened to be in Southend a little later, we cut the wires and nicked the lights from the seafront thinking that if we used them they'd make us look like the Floyd. It was shades of the business motto 'Get on, get honest, and get honourable.' Unfortunately, on this occasion we didn't get on because the lights operated on a different voltage so we couldn't make them work for us.

Our biggest problem was the perennial one that all bands face: getting people and stuff around. Our first manager had an American car, a huge thing that kept breaking down. We used to drive around in that as a 'superstar group'. He also made use of a waffles van, which was less impressive. Our second manager had a Vanden Plas, but it was always being taken back by the hire-purchase company because he hadn't made the payment that month. Sometimes we'd come out of a gig and it would be gone.

Over Christmas 1966, we managed to get a four-night residency at the Hercules pub in Holloway Road for the massive sum of £40.

To make sure we didn't eat into our fortune, we'd leave our gear at the pub between gigs and would then walk home, every night, from Holloway Road to Friern Barnet – a long way.

The driver of the rental van who took us to the Hercules on the first night suggested it would be a lot cheaper if we bought our own van, rather than renting one. He recommended a bloke called Mr Goldstein, who ran a business in Liverpool Road. He also offered to look the van over for us.

When we got there, we found Mr Goldstein sitting at his desk, smoking his little Manikin – people like him were always smoking Manikins. He pointed his cigar at a van and said: 'You can have that one if you like: how much you got?'

We told him: '40 quid.'

'Oh,' he said, 'I wanted more.'

'Well we haven't *got* any more.'

'All right,' he said, 'give me the 40 quid. I'll get it delivered to you.'

After what seemed like a very long wait, and not before we'd phoned his place several times, the van appeared. Unfortunately it was being towed.

We were very excited to get our very first set of wheels, of course, but the fact that we couldn't get it to start was a bit of a problem. I went to see Mr Goldstein, first with my brother, then with his brother-in-law, the cabinetmaker's son, Robin, who was a lawyer. Mr Goldstein, though, was adamant that he would not take the van back. 'Sold as seen,' he insisted.

Then my father said he would come with me. Confronted by a man of stature, Mr Goldstein reluctantly agreed that for £20 more, which we could pay in instalments, we could have another van – and one, moreover, that worked. This was a huge relief, except for the fact that we hadn't actually got £20.

To drum up some cash, we found a cabaret agent, changed our

name to the Rick Desmond trio (which sounded quite slick) and secured some bookings. At a stroke, our fee per gig went from £3 to £30. On the minus side, we had to play songs like 'Tie a Yellow Ribbon' and 'Congratulations'. This, I realised, was where we and bands like Pink Floyd differed. They played their own music. We, on the other hand, had to play pop stuff people already liked in order to buy a van. We were getting nowhere.

So I joined a band called Canterbury Glass, who, like Pink Floyd, wrote their own songs. Their members included Steve Hackett (who went on to play guitar in Genesis) and a bass player called Toad (whose father owned Marine Ices, an ice-cream parlour in Chalk Farm).

Toad told me, 'You're uncool, man,' and gave me a very tight, green floral shirt to wear, so that I would be cool and not let the others down.

Shortly afterwards, there was a change in personnel. Hackett left, a guy called Les came in and we also acquired a singer called Jill, who we called Jill The Pill From Muswell Hill. She was a Jewish girl whose parents had a ladies-wear shop.

Canterbury Glass, like Rebellion before it, were on at least one occasion less than respectful of others' property. One night at a university gig we nicked a big barrel of beer. Unfortunately, we didn't realise that you have to tap a barrel and do this and that to it in order to get at the beer inside. I was beginning to realise that crime really doesn't pay.

All through this period I was still struggling on at school, not wanting to learn. My studies — if you can call them that — consisted of playing drums in the cadet hall and then sitting under the cadet corps hut, smoking a fag.

One day, when I was nearly 15, the headmaster called my mother in and told her that I wasn't learning anything and that I was disruptive, both of which charges were true. He also complained that all I did was drum on the table and talk about groups and music, which was also true. Finally he suggested that I should go off and become a drummer for a year and if it didn't work out I could either come back to the school or go to a technical college and learn a trade.

Learn a trade? I was horrified! Before, whenever they had asked me at school what I wanted to be when I grew up, I would say – at least before I considered becoming a superstar rock-and-roll drummer – that I would go into 'the medium'. OK, the word was not quite right, but for the son of the managing director of Pearl & Dean, the ambition was clear enough. Now they wanted me to learn a trade? I did know, though, that drumming wouldn't be easy – after all, in the time I had worked in the cloakroom and performed in bands I'd only been able to save up £50. But I still wanted to try it.

To this end I joined a group called Winston G & the Soul Set, whose music was easy to play. I thought Winston G was a fine fellow, but it turned out he was quite tight with money and always seemed to think that it was my turn to stump up for the petrol. It came to a head one night, when, after driving back from a gig in Bournemouth, Winston again insisted it was my turn to pay to fill the van up. I refused – at which point he said that he would dump my drums right there on the road.

We were in Finchley by the time he said this, and I knew my friend Jonathan Portner lived just around the corner, so I managed to persuade Winston to leave the drums there instead. Next day Jonathan called me up. 'There's only one person who could've left a drum kit in front of my house at three in the morning, and that's you! But don't worry. My mum's going to bring them round for you!'

Was it time, I wondered, to put the drums aside and think about what I was really going to do with my life? If I was not going to be the world's greatest drummer (even though I am, perhaps, the world's greatest drummer), I needed to find something else to do instead.

The question presented itself one more time when, at the age of 18, three years after I had actually got a proper job, I went to the Regal in Edmonton with Russ Ballard and Bob Henrit to see the Who. Russ has since told me that Eric Clapton was in the dressing room that evening but I don't remember seeing him. What I'll never forget, though, is that after the gig, John Entwistle invited us to go down to the Playboy Club in Park Lane with him. We all got into his stretch limousine, and I remember thinking how strange the whole experience was as we sped through the Manor House and Holloway to get there.

During the course of the evening I met a young blonde, Samantha Juste, who was a presenter on *Top of the Pops*. And she made me an offer which would force me to make one of the big decisions of my life. She knew all the bands who hung out in California, she said; why didn't I go there with her to pursue my drumming career? What a moment! My head was spinning. I knew that if I went to California, my whole life would change, irrevocably, and that I might well never come back. On the other hand, I couldn't help remembering, I'd just taken out a huge mortgage of £7,250 to buy a house for my mother and me. I knew that if I went to America she would not be able to afford to live there on her own.

In fact Samantha would end up with another drummer, Micky Dolenz from the Monkees. She lived life to the full, and I was very sad to learn of her death in 2014. Me? I kissed her goodbye that evening.

Then I walked home, on my own, to Southgate, because I didn't have the money for a taxi.

3
LUNCHEON WITH MR HILL

So at the age of 15 I gave up my dream to become a rock star, and started to cast around for a proper career. And as I found myself wrestling with the issue of what job to go for, something happened to remind me that I'd once thought of working in newspapers and magazines.

It started with an encounter at the club with an important cloak-room customer. In the course of our conversation, I talked about my career dilemma, and he suggested that I should call Tommy Tomkins, who was in charge of the post room at Thomson Newspapers, the then owners of *The Times* and the *Sunday Times*. Apparently there was a job going in the post room where all you had to do was walk round handing the post out. There was a canteen and lots of beautiful girls in miniskirts, this being the Swinging Sixties.

When you're 15, of course, young girls in miniskirts cannot be ruled out as grounds for a career choice, but clearly there was more to it than that because that mention of newspapers reminded me of my father. Aha, I thought, this sounds just the way I had always visualised 'the medium'. I probably did not think of myself in those days as an entrepreneur in the making, and still less a media entre-preneur, but I had to find something I could take pride in, that would lead somewhere, and where my talents would be appreciated. I might not have known in full what my talents were, but I already knew I had focus and determination – and that a job with a newspaper might play to my skills.

Thomson at the time was located in the Gray's Inn Road, where ITN is now, next door to Elm House, home of Northwood Industrial Publications – also part of Thomson. My brother offered to drive me down there in his silver mink Ford Zephyr, and the night before my interview I worked out with my father exactly what I was going to say to Tommy Tomkins in order to get the job. Unfortunately, when I got there, it turned out that it wasn't entirely within Tommy's power to employ people – as he explained to me, they had a personnel manager who dealt with such things. I couldn't work this out at all. Tommy was the bloke who needed the post-boy, so why did I need to see anyone else? (My incomprehension may explain why I have never liked having too many management layers in my own business.)

While I was waiting to see the personnel manager, a woman, passing by, asked me if I had a cigarette. I always used to buy a packet of five Guards so I handed her one of those and she asked me why I had come.

I told her my story and she asked me what my mum and dad did for a living: a question I always ask people myself because it's a very revealing one. She was very impressed when I mentioned Dickie Pearl and Bob Dean – both of them big names at the time – and amazed that Dickie was my godfather. It even turned out that she knew my father.

Our encounter proved to be an incredible stroke of luck for me – and a demonstration of the advantages of smoking – because it transpired that this woman was Ros Tew, the worldwide classified manager for Thomson. She immediately told the personnel manager that I wasn't going to be working in the post room but that I should be sent to something called telesales instead. I had never heard of telesales, so she had to explain that it meant selling advertising on the phone. When I looked slightly worried, she told me that there was a book I could read about it and that, in any case, they would provide training. She then called down the classified advertising manager, Mr Richard Vince – who was a really cheerful sort of character – and off I went to telesales.

The training, which included little tips like not saying 'actually' on the phone, avoiding negatives, and so on, would seem very basic now, but back in the 1960s it was pretty revolutionary. Of course, technically I should not have had the job at all because I was under 16, but nobody had woken up to my real age at that point, and even if they had nobody was going to argue with Ros Tew.

What's more, I turned out to be a bit of a superstar at telesales. First I was put on *Construction News*. Then I moved to *Hotel & Catering Times*, and tried to help it in its circulation war with a publication called *Caterer & Hotelkeeper*, a beautifully produced 200-page magazine that made my publication look rubbish by comparison. Music-mad as I was, I decided to introduce an entertainment section. After all, hotels offer entertainment, don't they?

I called up my old favourites the Rik Gunnell Agency and said, 'I'll get you a whole new market outside of the blues – the cabaret market.' They loved the idea. Like me, in my brief Rick Desmond trio incarnation, they realised there was more money in cabaret than rock 'n' roll.

Barry Dunning, the boss of one of the other music agencies we managed to secure, the London City Agency, rang me one day, amazed at my chutzpah. 'Anyone who can convince my partner to take an ad in the fucking *Catering Times* should be working for me,' he said. 'Come round and see me immediately.'

The job he offered me – managing a band – might sound like the sort of thing I'd have loved at that time, but it turned out that it mainly consisted of getting petrol for vans that had broken down (which really didn't appeal to me) and bailing members of the group out after they'd been arrested by the police (which appealed to me even less). Worst of all, in order to rescue bands from tight situations you needed to be able to drive, and I was too young to do that without ending up in a police cell myself.

Even the fact that they told me I wouldn't have to wear a suit didn't impress me because I liked wearing a suit – I had two from Burton's and had even gone a bit upmarket and bought a herring-bone one from Hepworth's.

I was in the medium and being a manager wasn't medium, it was vans, oil and drugs.

So I carried on getting ads for *Catering Times* for just about everything from one-armed bandits – because hotels have slot machines – to organs, because they have those too. I signed up Lowrey and Hammond organs, unwittingly making contacts that would turn out to be very useful a few years later. In fact, I secured advertising for just about everything except catering.

Eventually my success was noticed and I was summoned to lunch with Mr Peter Cable, managing director of Northwood Publications. It took place at the very posh RAC private gentleman's club in London's Pall Mall and I had to ask my friend Richard Vince what to do because I'd never been to a place like that before. He told me to smile and be myself, which would have been good advice except that I was 15, fat, and now smoking so many cigarettes that my fingers were all stained.

Of course Mr Cable, having seen my sales record and my smooth call to action in the magazines ('To advertise, call Rick Desmond'), was expecting someone much older. And probably someone who looked a little more like that handsome 1960s TV star Jason King.

We had a slightly frosty lunch. Mr Cable was very reserved and English. However, he offered me a job managing a whole raft of magazines, with a salary of £20 a week, basic, and a brand new Morris 1100 which, it turned out, was parked outside. He jangled the car keys at me. I didn't want to admit that I wasn't old enough to drive it, because that would probably have been the end of my job. Instead I said that I hadn't passed my driving test yet so perhaps he could put it back in the garage for the time being.

I went to see my friend Mr Vince and admitted my dilemma: I'd have loved to have earned £20 a week but I was only 15, I couldn't drive and if I did I'd probably end up in jail. It was one thing to drive a van to a gig without a licence, but quite another to glide around unlicensed in a brand new Morris 1100.

He understood completely. What's more, he told me that he'd just been offered a job in sales at another company and there might be one there that would be perfect for me too. He had met an Irishman who, he said, was a bit of an oddball but had made an absolute fortune starting various magazines dedicated to the Beatles. Now he wanted to launch a new publication called *In-Plant Printer*.

I had no idea what that might involve, but I nevertheless agreed to meet the chap at his offices at 32–34 Westbourne Grove.

At this point you have to think of the movie *Telstar*, about the maverick 1960s record producer Joe Meek, because the Irishman, who was called Sean O'Mahoney, looked exactly like the dapper gent who provided Meek's financial backing. He was like a big, gangly John Cleese figure. He wore a smart suit that was not quite Savile Row, handmade but not tip-top, and was ex-Army rather than RAF.

'Now Richard has told me you're a really great salesman,' O'Mahoney said to me. 'Why do you think you can do this job?'

'Well,' I replied, 'I'm not sure I can . . .'

'That's not the right answer!' he shouted, 'that's not the right answer at all!' He added, 'Look, we're going places and this magazine is going to be huge, HUGE!'

He went on and on in this sort of vein. I hadn't got a clue what he was talking about, until at the end he offered me the job at £20 a week (and, more crucially, told me that I wouldn't have to drive). I couldn't believe it. I was, after all, only on £8 a week at Thomson.

And so I became the classified manager of *In-Plant Printer*. When I suggested that I get involved with the Beatles magazines, too, however, he turned me down flat.

Luckily for me O'Mahoney was just about to move his operation to Parker Street in London's Holborn, which was nice and easy to reach from my home in Friern Barnet. On my first day I walked to the new office thinking, well, at least I can have my two pints a week and my five cigarettes. It's interesting, when you are a kid, that you think that you can live on not very much a week for ever.

Reaching Parker Street, I walked up the stairs to the office. There was no sign of Richard Vince, just O'Mahoney, with his feet sprawled across the table in his oak-panelled office. It was not a very big office and it was not very good oak but he'd covered everything in it. He even had an oak record player.

'Ah, right,' he said. 'I was waiting for you. I suppose you want to see your office?'

The office, which was entirely lime green and smelled of paint, consisted of a partition, a desk and a card index. There was no window.

I asked Mr O'Mahoney to remind me of the title of the magazine I was working on.

'*In-Plant Printer*,' he snapped.

'Do you mind if I write it down?' I said.

He snorted and walked out.

Suddenly I felt ill. I was beginning to regret giving up the job that I'd liked so much, with all those lovely girls in miniskirts. Now I was on my own in this bizarre place with this off-the-wall and eccentric character.

The first company I called from the file index was Aerostyle of Sunbeam Road, NW10. The phone was answered by a Mr Frank Webb, and I decided to try a novel approach. I asked him why he thought his products should be advertised in *In-Plant Printer* magazine. He told me and then booked six and a half pages.

'Now,' I said, 'could you explain to me what in-plant printing is all about?'

What he said was that it was for people who had small Rotaprint machines which could do little bits of printing – a few thousand copies at most. What I heard, though, was that it was for people who did printing – so I assumed that meant that all printing companies were potential advertisers.

I went on to ring up a company called Tapp & Toothill. They agreed to book a half page and went on to take half a page for ever. It was only when their first advert appeared, and people burst out laughing, that it became apparent I hadn't quite understood Mr Webb. Tapp & Toothill, apparently, was a large gravure printer (gravure is the method used for large print runs on glossy paper) whose lowest print run would be 100,000 or 200,000 copies.

But ultimately I had the last laugh. The bottom line, it emerged, was that people who bought a few thousand copies might, from time to time, want a lot more, and since Tapp & Toothill were the only big gravure printers in the magazine they'd get all the business. It showed me the dangers of being too clever. Those in the know would never have called the 'wrong' people. I had, and had ended up with a good bit of new business, and a very happy advertiser into the bargain.

When I started at *In-Plant Printer* there was one client that nobody could get: Goodhale guillotines. I was 17 by now and desperate for a car.

'If I can get Goodhale,' I said to Mr O'Mahoney, 'could I have a car?'

There were other salesmen working in his office who were earning three times what I was earning and they had silver mink Ford Cortinas, so O'Mahoney agreed that if I got the ad I could have a Cortina. But I persuaded him to promise me a Mini instead, because Colin Allen, Zoot Money's drummer, had a Mini, and if I could get one of those I'd feel as if I was part of Swinging London.

I called up the head of Goodhale guillotines, who were based in Croydon, and when he asked me why I wanted to come down, since he'd already seen six people from my company, I told him I was the boss of *In-Plant Printer*. Then I drove down in my old Thames van, and parked it by a pub up the road from his office. When I arrived and he asked me where my car was I said that I had asked my chauffeur to take my mother out for a spin for the afternoon.

'What car have you got?' he asked.

'A Jaguar XJ,' I said, because I'd seen one of those in the car park and guessed it was his.

'Oh, I've got one of those too,' he said. 'Best cars. Let me take you to lunch.'

He took me to the local Conservative Club and as we talked it emerged that his company dealt in vending machines as well.

I said that I couldn't guarantee anything but that if he agreed to advertise in *In-Plant Printer* I thought I could speak to my procurement officer and get him the contract to supply vending machines to our offices.

'OK, fine!' he said, 'let's have a game of snooker.'

I had never played snooker in my life, but whatever it takes to sell an ad . . .

Just before I left I asked him to call O'Mahoney for me and tell him that he'd booked 12 half-pages from next month and that he would like the opportunity to provide our office with vending machines.

'Fine, fine,' he said, 'but where's your car?'

'Oh,' I said. 'I told my chauffeur I'd walk up and meet him. I like a walk after lunch.'

When I got back to Parker Street, O'Mahoney was standing outside. He could not believe I'd got the ads. 'OK,' he said, 'you can have your Mini. *Done!*'

Taking advantage of what I thought was his good mood I asked him if I could now get to work selling advertising on his music magazines, because I thought that there was an opportunity there if we did some instrument reviews, too. He wouldn't hear of it. He insisted that he made all his money from the cover prices of the magazines, that he made nothing from advertising, and that we were all 'overhead'.

I explained that I understood that. However, I asked if I could still have a go. If I was able to secure £100 extra, I said, and was allowed to keep £5 of it in commission, that would be £95 towards his overhead.

'OK,' he said, 'if you think you can do it – do it!' And he set me to work on selling ads for *Beat Instrumental*.

I knew I could do it because all the potential advertisers were like me – young and unconventional. They were people like Mr Mercer from Carlsbro who had a shop in Mansfield and made amplifiers in his bathroom with his wife.

The ads began rolling in and very soon, at the age of just 18, I was earning £3,000 a year basic and another £3,000 in commission. I tried to move out of the flat where I had lived for the last eight years but everyone kept turning me down for a mortgage because they couldn't believe someone so young was earning so much money. Eventually the Nationwide was persuaded, but it was a tough job.

I was hugely ambitious. At the same time, though, Mr O'Mahoney was driving me so mad that I developed ulcers on my hand. I didn't realise until later, when I left, that I probably wasn't the only one who had ulcers either inside or out! Given that his style of management was a little unusual – he would, for example, have Monday meetings where he'd throw cups at us – it wasn't that surprising.

O'Mahoney was ambitious, too, and constantly coming up with new ideas. One day, for example, he came back from lunch after a few drinks and told me that we would be launching a magazine called *Property Price Guide*, and that it wouldn't need any advertising. What did I think of that?

Unfortunately, it turned out, people don't move house very often so the magazine didn't sell. After a few months O'Mahoney asked if I could get him some ads after all. I went to all the property people including Wimpey, whose boss just liked to talk about train sets, and Lyon Homes in Colliers Wood whose boss was in a band. He told me he'd heard I was a good drummer and would only take an ad if I played some gigs with him. Which is how I ended up in a pub in Colliers Wood on a Friday night nodding through Kris Kristofferson songs! It might not have helped me make it through the night but it certainly helped me get a page.

After another boozy lunch with our distributors, O'Mahoney announced he'd come up with another buyers' guide, this time for motorists. It was basically a copy of the famous *Glass's Guide*, and the suggestion was we call it *Parker's Car Price Guide*, after Parker Street where we were based. O'Mahoney said, 'Great – like Elvis's manager, Colonel Parker!'

Meanwhile, he continued to drive everyone mad with his concerns about overheads, complaining, for example, about the cost of employing people to produce the artwork for the ads we ran. My response was to launch a little sideline of my own called Mr Badger design and print, with artists who would do the work at weekends. It gave me some extra money and stopped at least some of his criticism.

I had another sideline outside work hours, too: promoting groups on a Friday night at the Alan Pullinger Youth Centre in Southgate. I was fed up with drumming by this time, but I still wanted to carry on being involved in music, so when the guy who ran the youth centre suggested the idea, I jumped at it. Among the bands I booked were the Average White Band (at a cost of £65 a time) and Thin Lizzy (who, at £100, were a bit more expensive). On my very first night I watched as Screaming Lord Sutch emerged from a coffin! My dad came along to see that one. He turned his hearing aid down.

One Friday, we had booked the Pink Fairies to play. Then we got a phone call to say they couldn't come. That left me with a problem. The Pink Fairies were a big band at that time and I had a huge queue at the door. I could hardly cancel because I'd already incurred a lot of expense, hiring the venue, printing posters, advertising and so on. So all I could do was to send on the support band I'd booked. I thought that, with a bit of luck, people would have such a good time they wouldn't mind about the main band not playing.

I was wrong. As soon as I announced the Pink Fairies were not coming everyone in the room wanted their money back.

The girl who usually looked after taking the tickets at the door for me had taken the night off, so it was left to the girl who worked behind the coffee bar to give them all their ticket money back. Then, feeling sorry for me, she took me out for a Chinese. That girl was Janet, a mother of one child, Darren, from a previous relationship, who in due course became my first wife.

One Friday night O'Mahoney turned up at the Alan Pullinger centre in his (by now) Savile Row suit, accompanied by his wife in her fur coat and jewellery. He was not in a good mood. He didn't like the fact that I was promoting groups without him being involved, and even though I explained that I was doing it outside working hours he suspected that I was using some company time to make the arrangements. 'I should be getting a cut of the profits from this,' he suggested.

He kept on and on about it. In the end, he insisted that he should give me a contract so that I would be a shareholder in his company.

'After all,' he said, 'remember Andrew Oldham . . .'

'What about Andrew Oldham?'

'He is managing the Rolling Stones,' said O'Mahoney, 'but *I* should be doing that.'

What had happened was this: as a publisher of music magazines we often had people from the industry coming to our offices and, a few months earlier, one of these had been Andrew Oldham, who had once been the PR man for the Beatles, and who now approached O'Mahoney to ask him if he would like to manage the Rolling Stones. O'Mahoney declined, and referred him on to a bloke called Eric Easton, who looked after the pianist Mrs Mills: a huge act at that time.

The deal that Oldham did with Eric Easton was that Andrew would do all the work, Eric would provide office facilities, and they would be 50–50 partners: as a manager, Eric had much better connections than Andrew. I doubt that there was ever a contract, because there rarely was in those days, but they shook hands and the deal was done. That's how Eric Easton got 50 per cent of the Rolling Stones. That is also why O'Mahoney felt so sick at missing out – and why he was determined not to do so again with me.

O'Mahoney played me a record that he said had been written by a friend of his called George, from Liverpool. It was called 'Mr Teaser' and it was quite good. His plan was that we should do what Robert Stigwood did and turn kids from stage schools into pop stars. We therefore went along to the Barbara Speake acting school in Acton, run by Phil Collins's mother June, listened to various students being put through their paces, and found a girl called Lorenza Johnson. We put her into a studio to record 'Mr Teaser' and the Phil Spector song 'To Know Him Is To Love Him'.

The studio, in Denmark Street, was called Regent Sounds, and it was owned by a guy called Freddie Packham. I got them to agree to give me two or three hours of free recording time, in exchange for advertising space in our magazines. Then I made the record and took it to Pye. I told them that I could promote the record through our various magazines – *Beat Instrumental*, *The Beatles* magazine and *Rolling Stone* magazine – but that I wanted an advance of £1,000 because the production had cost a lot of money. They gave me the £1,000 and agreed a royalty of 10 or 11 per cent which apparently was very good.

O'Mahoney was pleased, and made it clear that he was even more determined that I should go into partnership with him. On the eve of my 21st birthday, he invited me out for lunch.

'Well I suppose we could get a sandwich,' I said.

'No,' said O'Mahoney, 'I'm taking you to Simpson's in the Strand!'

As we were walking up to the restaurant he said, 'There's just one thing I want to ask. Would you mind calling me Mr Hill in the restaurant. When I'm out I am known as Mr Hill.'

'I'm sorry,' I said, 'I'm a bit confused.'

He explained that people in magazines wrote under different names so he didn't see why he shouldn't use a different one sometimes.

We went in and ordered our food and the waiters busied round us saying, 'Yes, Mr Hill, no, Mr Hill.'

Finally I had to ask, 'Why do you call yourself Mr Hill?'

He looked at me and said, 'Well, people might think I'm Irish.'

At the end of the meal he told me that he had some good news for me. He had decided that the two of us were going to form a new music company called Bear Music and I would get 1 per cent of the profits. He also told me that, even though it cost a lot of money to get records made, I wouldn't have to put any of my own money into the venture.

I pointed out that, so far, he hadn't put any money in either. After all, I'd got Lorenza Johnson's record made for free, in return for advertising, and, on top of that, had landed a £1,000 advance.

He countered by saying that he'd had to spend £1,000 on advertising the record in *Music Week*. He also reminded me that, to promote the record, I'd flown up to Manchester to do a radio interview – and that had cost money too.

I wasn't particularly in the mood to argue, and once we'd got back to the office I didn't think any more about it. I was, in any case, starting to come to the view that I was more interested in the publishing business than the record business. It was around the time Branson was making a name for himself with Virgin. I knew him slightly, and remember bumping into him in Cannes where I was selling ad space at one of the annual industry gatherings. He said, 'Hey, Rick, let's take off all our clothes and run naked down the seafront to cause some excitement!' I knew that wasn't my style – I didn't want to cause excitement. Branson went for his run and got lots of publicity. I stuck to selling and got lots of pages. We both achieved what we wanted.

During this period many of the editors moaned about O'Mahoney. For my part, though, I was so busy I just ignored him, and I didn't really care what he got up to. I was succeeding, making money, I had a second house I was renting out, a red Rover V8 3500 with a sunshine roof, I could have a curry anytime I fancied. I was *happy*.

Then, out of the blue, a contract turned up for the new music company O'Mahoney wanted to start with me. I gave it to an employment lawyer we used, called Tony Russell, who worked for Sheridan & Partners, a top firm, and I also gave a copy to my mum who took it to Walter Jennings in Kentish Town, for whom she was working at the time.

Within a couple of days Tony Russell summoned me to his office and told me that under no circumstances was I to sign the contract. It was absurdly one-sided. Exactly the same advice came back from Walter Jennings. I decided to try and stay out of O'Mahoney's way.

And now another opportunity arose. Around this time there was an amplifier maker called HH, who had started making solid-state amplifiers when everyone else's were valve models. They were cosmetically smart amplifiers, with a nice clean sound and with a control panel that lit up, which was a bit of a novelty at that time. Marc Bolan was among the musicians who used them.

In distribution terms, HH didn't really have expertise in that specialist market. Mr HH, Mike Harrison, had brought in a furniture salesman called Malcolm Green as his partner, to set up their franchises, but Malcolm didn't really know a great deal about the musical instrument industry either. For some reason he decided to restrict their sale to 100 shops at a time when the market leader in amplifiers, Marshall, had 300.

One of my friends, at Carlsbro sound equipment, who advertised in *Beat Instrumental*, couldn't get an HH franchise and asked me to help him. I knew that another friend of mine was about to lose his HH franchise because he wasn't selling enough of their amplifiers so I collected them from his shop in Hertfordshire and took them up to Carlsbro in the Midlands.

Unfortunately Malcolm Green at HH was also an advertiser. He called me up and asked me if I knew where Carlsbro had got their HH amplifiers from. He was very strict with the franchises, he said, and Carlsbro made their own amplifiers so, in fact, they were hated rivals.

It was all very awkward but I decided to be honest and tell him that I had supplied the amplifiers. I told him I had done it to try and keep Carlsbro's advertising and hopefully get some more.

Instead of having a go at me he asked me how much it would cost to get a photograph of Marc Bolan using HH amplifiers made up into 10,000 posters! I told him that it would be £400, and he asked me to deliver them to his house personally.

I thought that was very odd: I'd messed up the fellow's business and he was not being aggressive with me. Then I met him and found I really liked him. He was a little bit older than me, a Catholic, very pro-Jewish with a lovely French wife, Babette.

It turned out to be the start of a very useful friendship, not least because Malcolm and I had something important in common: we weren't happy with our current employment set-ups. He didn't get along well with his partner at HH and I was finding my relationship with Sean O'Mahoney increasingly unworkable. Within months we had got together and opened a record shop in Barnet, which we called White Rabbit Records. A little while later Malcolm came up with a proposal that would change my life forever.

'Why don't you start your own magazine and I'll back you,' he said.

Meanwhile, Ray Hammond, O'Mahoney's editor at *Beat Instrumental*, was also contemplating his own music magazine, and we discussed it at a memorable lunch at the Pizza Express near the British Museum — as one does. Every idea has its time.

International Musician was about to be created. It was November 1974, in fact the year and month my second wife, Joy, was also born, but more about Joy later.

4
PAGES
PAY
WAGES

The launch of my first magazine, *International Musician and Recording World*, was not easy. If the start of that magazine had been one of the celebrity childbirth stories we later came to do in *OK!* magazine, we'd have called it a miracle baby. Nearly everything that could go wrong did go wrong, and also some things that couldn't. But when you're launching your first major business you're starting from nothing, you have nothing to lose, so the only way to go is up.

I began with the principle that has served me well in publishing ever since – if I produce something that I like, then others will like it too. For me, the key point for a musicians' magazine was to get inside the heads of the guys who really knew how to play, to find out how they did it and to review the gear they used. Better still, to persuade those same top rock stars to do the reviews themselves.

But before we could begin on the content of the magazine I had to decide on some practicalities, the most basic of which was where would I get offices and staff? It would be easiest, I decided, to work with O'Mahoney, who had all of those things already. But before I could do that O'Mahoney made a decision of his own. I was walking past his office one afternoon when I saw a guy outside whom I recognised. He worked for *Studio Sound* magazine, one of the rivals of *Beat Instrumental*.

'What are you doing here?' I asked him.

'I'm here for the group advertising job,' he said.

At that moment the door opened and O'Mahoney came out. He looked shocked that my rival and I had bumped into each other, and that I knew him. But seeing that the game was up, he didn't mince his words with me.

'Right,' he said. 'Now you know. I am going to get rid of you and he's going to get your job! He'll be half the price without any aggravation.'

The reality was that O'Mahoney's ego had been dented because some people were starting to treat me as the man in charge, which, of course, I wasn't, though I was doing a great deal of the work. What's more, I got on with the other staff by and large, while O'Mahoney could upset them.

The meeting with my would-be replacement therefore went ahead and the following day O'Mahoney sent for me, confirmed I was out, and paid me up to date, no more and no less. He demanded my car keys but I insisted on taking out the eight-track player, which I had paid for myself. He escorted me up the road to supervise its removal and take possession of the car.

I called Malcolm Green and told him: 'If you want to do this magazine, I'm no longer with O'Mahoney now, so let's get on with it.'

Malcolm and I became joint managing directors of our new venture, and we appointed Ray Hammond as the editorial director. We gave him a 15 per cent share of the company, which was more than Malcolm would have wished, but Ray said if there was ever a dispute he would always vote with me. Ray was a chameleon. He was two or three years older than me with hair so blond it was almost white and piercing blue eyes. He'd convince you, and himself, that he was whatever he needed to be at that moment – an accomplished sound engineer, the former manager of Dave Lambert of the Strawbs, whatever. He'd convince everyone that he'd done everything. Maybe he had.

Of course as soon as O'Mahoney got wind of what we were doing he served writs on all of us, accusing us of conspiring against him, stealing his staff, soliciting his clients, and generally trying to undermine his business. I responded that I had just been fired and I ought to be allowed to make a living, which, indeed, turned out to be the legal position. With right on my side I was able to go to all the advertisers who had been paying £200 a page in *Beat Instrumental* and offer them a page in *International Musician* for £165.

This was December 1974 and we needed to publish our first issue in time for the big Frankfurt music show the following February. We therefore needed a distributor fast. Of course Ray reckoned he knew all about distribution, or at least he convinced both me and himself that he did. He put me in touch with a company called Spotlight Publications, who agreed to take our business. There wasn't much paperwork involved: I believe at one point Malcolm may have asked if we should have a contract, but that was about it. As so often in those days, it was assumed that everyone would behave properly.

We made all the other necessary arrangements. For offices we found some very down-at-heel premises in Covent Garden, which at that time was still a fruit and vegetable market. No problem with our five a day, at least. We worked pretty much 24/7 in that shabby room, and what time I had left over was spent selling advertising. If I did not reach the number of pages I set myself on a particular day, I did not go home until I had.

Then, just days before the launch, we got a telephone call. Spotlight had decided not to distribute us after all. They had their own music paper, *Sounds*, and were also friendly with O'Mahoney, so perhaps they had never intended to in the first place. Desperate for help, I tried Argus and IPC, who both said no, and then, when I was almost at my wit's end, I came across a company I had never heard of: Independent Magazines in Great Victoria Street, run by a husband-and-wife team, Rowlie and Beryl Vickers. I was so distraught when I met them that they offered me a whisky. They listened to what I had to say, calmed me down and took on the business. Job done. At least so I thought. I went back to selling pages.

The magazine launched at the beginning of 1975 with Ritchie Blackmore of Deep Purple on the cover – and was well received. I was also lucky because Ivor Arbiter, who owned the rights to the world-leading Fender guitar brand in the UK, decided he liked the idea of a young Jewish guy having a go and offered to send a letter to all his shops telling them that they had to sell ten copies of *International Musician*. He also gave me some advertising and a free Fender plectrum to give away on the cover of the first issue.

I had filled the book with advertising in a matter of weeks, but there was a good chance our first issue might also be our last. I had nothing for the second issue. So the Frankfurt music fair, which now loomed, became something of a make-or-break affair for us. We booked a single hotel room there for three of us. I had to share the bed with Ray. Malcolm got the couch because he was rich.

During the day at Frankfurt everyone wandered around the stands, and in the evening they went to the Kaisterstrasse, the red-light district famed for its sumptuous rooms full of naked women which looked like the cover of Jimi Hendrix's *Electric Ladyland*. But I couldn't care less about the women. I was there for the advertising. I had my order pad out all the time. The second night I was there a lady propositioned me and told me she would only cost £30. I told her she had to be joking: £30 was the profit on a page and a half! That remark followed me round for years.

Eventually at Frankfurt I sold 40 pages of advertising for six months' worth of issues. That meant an income of £8,000. The problem was that £8,000 only just covered the cost of producing a 60-page magazine, it didn't help with our overhead. Within six months we were out of cash and Malcolm had to put in £5,000 to keep us going. Even so, at least everyone in the industry was familiar with Mr Page, as I had become known, and they respected us for having a go. We could even see a time when all the hard work would pay off.

Then – disaster. Our kindly whisky-offering distributors suddenly went bust, knocking our company for a whopping £46,000. It might as well have been £46 million. We were out. We had no cash. We could not go on.

I was desperate. I even made a call to my friend Ivor Arbiter to ask whether he could think of any way to get the debt repaid. Now, Ivor had had his share of taking liberties with the law. He narrowly escaped a murder rap during an incident while fighting a bunch of Mosleyite fascists and his businesses were prone to burn down at opportune times. I told him that he must have experience in getting out of tight spots. These people had bankrupted me and lost Malcolm Green a fortune. We were finished.

Ivor, in his inimitable way, put me right. 'Let me tell you something,' he said. 'As you know I've had a few fires, I've had a few things. You know I was done for murder, although I was never convicted. I was lucky but I also learned: I should never have stepped over the line. Because I'm telling you, son, you might be aggravated today but you'll get over it. You'll get through it. Do not do anything rash. That's my advice to you. And I'm not going to help you. It would only come back to haunt you. You'd be paying for years . . .'

It was good advice. As I discovered, there is always another way. Something always comes up. Later that same day a man called Peter

Treadwell from Thames News Distribution rang me. They had been the London distributors for Independent Magazines so they'd lost that business but they thought they could distribute *International Musician* nationally for us. I explained that I'd lost £46,000 and couldn't actually afford to produce the magazine, so unless he could pay that to us as an advance he would have nothing to distribute. He agreed to help. We were back in business.

Soon the magazine was going from strength to strength. After 18 months it even showed a profit of £80,000. Malcolm and Ray went to Harrods and bought us all hampers to celebrate. I was not amused. Perhaps I knew how many ads you had to sell to pay for those hampers. Perhaps I am not a hamper person.

We were not making big money, but *International Musician* was *there*: it was *the* magazine. Bob Henrit, from Argent, came to do drum reviews, Rod Argent did keyboards, Jim Rodford covered bass guitars. It was the magazine the guys in the top bands were reading – and writing for. Phil Collins used to feature in our subscription ads and turn up at our anniversaries to cut the celebratory cake. Paul McCartney used to share the secrets of his songwriting, revealing, for example, that the original version of 'Yesterday' was 'scrambled egg' because he thought up the words during breakfast. Keith Moon gave us what was to be his last interview. Obviously, he did not know that at the time, but we appreciated it. The reviewers had a panache that anticipated *Top Gear*: 'This mixing desk is tough. No matter what we did to it, we couldn't break it. In the end we took it outside and backed a Volvo over it. It still worked.'

I learned in those days what I later understood to be called editorial integrity, although at the time I could probably not have spelt it. Essentially, you have to play it straight with your readers.

My first experience of this came when we managed to bring in Marshall as an advertiser – although we almost lost them again straight away. Marshall is even today the leading worldwide brand in amplification but like us they had modest beginnings. Jim Marshall was a small, aggressive bloke, a good old-style drummer who ran a music shop. He wanted to build amplification equipment and teamed up with an ex-RAF mate called Ken Bran, a radio operator. Being a radio operator rather than a sound engineer, Ken built an amplifier with slightly distorted sound, but it proved to be an attribute that gained great favour with a number of rock musicians including, in the early days, John Entwistle of the Who. John, however, wanted bigger speakers so Marshall built him a huge speaker cabinet, 4ft by 8ft. It was so big, in fact, that when he came to collect it, they couldn't get it out of the door. Ever-resourceful Jim, who was a bit of a carpenter, rolled his sleeves up and sawed it in half, unwittingly inventing the Marshall stack, probably the most famous speaker set-up in rock history. Getting Marshall to advertise with us was a real coup.

Now, I entrusted equipment reviews in *International Musician* to Malcolm, who, because he knew nothing about most of the gear, drew in turn on the services of experts who knew everything about it. The result was that certain sections of the magazine would consist of pages and pages of technical know-how and graphs that seemed as though they had been provided by a boffin from Cambridge. Some of them were. So it was a big deal when one of our reviewers introduced Jim Marshall's new solid-state amplifier – designed to challenge Malcolm's old company HH – with the headline 'This Amplifier Will Electrocute You'.

I was mortified. I could imagine Jim Marshall breaking my legs. But Ray Hammond was insistent it should run, arguing that if we were going to be different from *Beat Instrumental* we could not shrink from the truth. So we published it. Jim Marshall exploded on the phone to me – and cancelled his advertising. Six months later he withdrew that amplifier from the market. And from that date on, while still as aggressive as ever, he became one of our biggest advertisers. It just goes to show that if you tell the truth in editorial people will respect you for it – and for a specialist magazine such as ours, the respect of the reader and the industry was vital.

Soon we became known nationally and internationally. It helped that we included among our number musicians and ex-musicians – including a drummer. I have probably made enough jokes about good and bad drummers and good and bad businessmen in my life. Yet it's a fact that some of the attributes of a good drummer are well-suited to running a business: you need to set the pace, lay down the structure, and hit the cymbals at the right moment. Many of my own achievements in business have been less about doing the right thing than about doing it at the right time.

I remember having this discussion with a number of music industry types at dinner during one Frankfurt music fair, and discovering, as I went from person to person round the table, that just about everyone had played drums. This being the music industry, quite a few of them were Jewish too. Which is why it caused a stir when the very German Gottholt Meyer, the founder of Musik Meyer and a generation older than most of us, announced, 'You perhaps do not know it, but I, too, was a drummer.'

We all looked at him with respect. This was, indeed, new information. We asked him who he had played with.

He cleared his throat and proclaimed, 'Ze Hitler Youth.'

It was a good thing we were all so tolerant.

Trade shows are central to an industry, and our industry was emphatically international, so we had to make regular trips not only to Germany, but also to America. Our earliest expedition to the NAMM (North American Music Manufacturers) show was done in the days when we were financially desperate. Indeed, we were so short of money that Ray had to offer to pay for me to go on his Access card. On the way out to Chicago, with all the big players like

Mr Marshall and Mr Arbiter on the plane, I spent the entire ten hours selling them advertising, with the result that I'd got all the pages I could from them before I even reached America. I then spent the entire fair seeing American manufacturers.

On the same trip I stopped off to see General Media, who published *Penthouse*, but who had expressed an interest in bringing out *International Musician* in America. We did ultimately launch there, though not with them, but I made some contacts that would prove useful a few years down the line. I also made vital connections with some young American music entrepreneurs, offering them help with distribution in the UK in return for handling their advertising and catalogues in my magazines. They included inspirational businessmen like Hartley Peavey who looked like Jesus, with his 'vertical integration' (doing all functions in-house) and his 'three-legged stool' of manufacture, distribution and marketing: Hartley made cheap high-quality instruments and amplification in Meridian, Mississippi, a town which he basically owned. Then there was Larry DiMarzio, the sharp operator who convinced the world (helped by me) that everyone needed to take the original pickups and hardware off their guitars and replace them with DiMarzio gear. Well, I leave it to guitarists to debate the merits of doing that.

On the plane back all the music manufacturers I'd signed up on the journey out took the mickey out of me for my advertising zeal. Ivor Arbiter even walked up and down the aisle saying, 'Come on, buy a page.' He then actually managed to sell a page for me – to Farfisa organs.

And that happy accident led to a new departure for us. Of course, getting involved with home organs would be a total sell-out for someone based in rock and roll, wouldn't it? A bit like going on stage to play 'Tie a Yellow Ribbon'. Yet following Ivor's successful deal on my behalf, Ray Hammond happened to wander into a shop in Dunstable called Jerry Allen Organs.

'Rick,' he told me on his return, 'these organs: there's *millions* of 'em, and there's no magazine for them!'

I was a bit sceptical at first, but I nevertheless went to see the Hammond organ company (no relation to Ray) to check out the lie of the land. They, it turned out, were incredibly enthusiastic at the prospect of a dedicated magazine: they wanted home organs to be considered a leisure activity, they said, like caravans, hi-fi and videos. If I brought a magazine out, they assured me, they'd take pages of adverts *and* the back cover. Then I went to see Kemble Pianos, a company run by an old Jewish family from Hampstead Garden Suburb who had picked up the distribution for Yamaha, and they were even more enthusiastic. Not only did they offer to take six pages a month, they also gave me the contract to produce the artwork for those pages for six months and paid in advance: I went away with a cheque for £36,000.

So *Home Organist* magazine was born and in its way became just as popular as *International Musician*. In its early issues it featured many interviews with celebrity home organ lovers including Dudley Moore and the snooker star Steve Davis, and an exclusive interview with Edward Heath during the period when he was PM.

There was more good news to come. I was just getting ready for bed one evening in our flat above White Rabbit Records in Barnet High Street, which I was still running with Malcolm as a sideline, when Ray Hammond rang up to tell me that he'd wrested the £3 million advertising account for Yamaha away from a mainstream ad agency called Lansdowne.

'But we haven't got an agency,' I pointed out. After all it was one thing doing a bit of artwork for advertisers; it was quite another handling their entire consumer advertising business.

'I told them we did,' said Ray.

And from that moment, it became true. Now we were a publisher and an advertising agency. Ray, who had worn jeans to be editor of *International Musician* and a suit to be a publishing executive, was now to be seen in a red shirt and white tie and held meetings from which I was excluded with the words, 'Fuck off, Rick, you only sell advertising, you don't create it!'

As DeMonde Advertising we spearheaded the home organ boom via magazines, national press, and TV campaigns like Yamahappiness, and More Smiles per Hour. We were aided and abetted by Yamaha's ebullient managing director Carl Spencer, a big, energetic man who looked a bit like the comedian Jimmy Edwards. It turned out he had once been in a jug band called Carl Spencer's Washboard Kings managed by the same London City Agency who had once offered me a job.

We were also now, thanks to a sort of hippy called Paul Ashford we'd taken on, running a sidcline producing catalogues and supplement magazines worldwide for music brands like Aria, DiMarzio, Gibson and Fender. Since these were the days before faxes and email, Paul was editing such publications by telex and so used to walk around festooned in ticker tape. When Ray departed to pursue his own career as a writer and futurologist, Paul stepped up to take charge of the creative side of the magazines. Around the same time we were joined by Martin Ellice, who would in due course become joint managing director. He started as junior credit controller on the sales ledger from A to L, but in fact it turned out that Martin could control more or less anything from print costs to distribution trucks, provided you let him take it away and think about it.

Soon, *International Musician* was taking so much advertising – 200 pages in some issues – that the printers were complaining they had problems binding it. And by the end of the 1970s we'd launched in Germany, Japan, Scandinavia, France, Italy, Spain and Australia. Thanks to all this, and to all sorts of cross-charging (a bit like Google today), we were making £750,000 to £800,000 a year.

We were even approached by Jacob Rothschild, who wanted to merge our company Cover Publications with Boosey & Hawkes, believing incorrectly that we were a sheet music publisher. I decided to remain independent, but it was a valuable early connection with someone who would remain friendly for decades to come. With *Home Organist* also proving successful, we were doing well.

We still had one big challenge to overcome, though: to establish *International Musician* in America, a crucial territory that had, so far, caused us nothing but trouble.

The deals I had made with my young music entrepreneur contacts in the USA had initially been followed through by a shrewd operator called Julius Graifman, whom I had first met when I worked for *In-Plant Printer*, and whom I had then taken on to ensure that we had some American advertisers in our British edition. Now, he undertook to form a US company on our behalf and publish an American version of *International Musician*. The company had to be in his name, however, because in those days an American corporation could not have an overseas owner title.

The problem that reared its head, though, was that he couldn't get sufficient advertising to make sense of the venture. And then just before Easter 1979, a huge pile of paper arrived from a lawyer called Walter L Kantrowitz, to the effect that unless we paid his client Graifman $40,000, Graifman was entitled to exclude us from the company and pocket the $40,000 or so that was in its bank account. I went to my own lawyer, who recommended a hot-shot American entertainment attorney called Dennis Ardi. I flew to New York, found new premises at 1500 Broadway, moved offices and was legally reinstated in the company, and then settled with Graifman – all over the holiday weekend. Only in America.

We had rescued the American company. But we had no one to

run it and no staff to work for it. We tried an English salesman, then an American who sold guitars. Finally we tried a bloke from a company called Unicord which distributed Marshall in America and which was part of Gulf & Western. His name was Mitch Haber, and I really liked him. He was a Jewish accountant and lawyer who wore smart suits and always smiled. Luckily he didn't like his boss and so was happy to come to work for us. I told him that I wanted to make $30,000 a month from America. It was just a figure plucked out of the air but Mitch, being a corporate type, took it literally and decided to run a very tight ship. Instead of employing a rat-catcher in the building, for example, he borrowed a cat from his neighbour, thus saving $30 a week. Instead of giving free coffee to the staff, he got them to pay for their own, adding another $100 to the bottom line. The business started to tick over.

But more importantly our American venture led to an inspirational meeting that gave me an insight into how it is possible for a small company to become big, and how we could reach out beyond the boundaries of the comparatively small industry we served. It was typical of many of the journeys I have made in my career: not a straight line but a zigzag, as I tried a new idea that might not work directly but that had a way of leading me to something else.

Now, it may have been Mitch who made me aware of Gulf & Western, but it was one of my music show contacts from the Swedish guitar company Hagstrom who said I would really get on with its boss, Charlie Bluhdorn. He undertook to set up a meeting and I went to the Gulf & Western Building at 15 Columbus Circle in New York.

Charlie was a very laid-back fellow, so I was interested that he had achieved so much and I asked him how he got started.

'Well,' he said, 'I had an office in the Empire State Building and from there I would offer to do share swaps. Basically, that meant that I would swap a share in Gulf & Western for a share in someone else's company. Because I'm a public company, *they* could be a public company too.'

I didn't get it, I told him. Why would people just agree to share swaps? And what about the name of his company, Gulf & Western? I assumed it must be something to do with Gulf Oil. Charlie said that was what I, and others, were supposed to think. That was why he had picked the name.

'What I thought,' he explained, 'was this. Everyone has heard of Gulf Oil and Western Telegraph Company. So I reckoned people would like shares in something called Gulf & Western. Young guys like you would come along, be impressed by our company name, and agree to a share swap. I got lucky on the third company I did a share swap with. It was a company that made "gas-filled fenders" [in English, a kind of shock absorber, I believe] and just as we did the share swap the government changed the law so that everyone had to have these fenders with gas in them. The fender company became huge. With the money I made from that deal I bought Paramount – which led on to bigger and better things.'

I thought it was an incredible story, and I thought his office building was pretty amazing, too.

'Oh, we don't own it,' he told me. 'We just rent the air rights.'

What that meant, he explained, was that he was allowed to put his name on top of the building.

I was inspired by the meeting. If Charlie could seize opportunities, create an image and manoeuvre himself into becoming a mainstream blue-chip corporation, why shouldn't I? In fact, hadn't that, really, always been my intention? As soon as I got back to London I changed the name of our company from Cover Publications to Northern & Shell: 'Northern' as in Northern Rock or Northern Songs, and Shell as in Shell Oil. I also found out that if you filled in the right bit of paper you could make yourself a plc, so we became Northern & Shell plc. When it came to designing a logo, we launched a £50 staff competition which was won by the assistant art director of *Home Organist*. For good measure we adopted the motto *Forti Nihil Difficile,* which means 'nothing is difficult for the brave'. It was suggested by the editor of *Home Organist*, Phil Baldwin, because it was the motto of his old school.

People would ask us if we were the Shell oil company and I'd say, 'We are whatever you want us to be.'

So there we were, publishing editions of our music magazines across the world and visiting international news trade shows equipped with large colourful bags that declared that more than 100 million people worldwide read our titles. Of course, as every ad salesman knows, readership is not the same as circulation. Advertising was really paying the wages.

At the same time the music industry, on which our entire business was based, was heading for some tough times. It was Mitch Haber who worried most that we were in a contracting industry and that we had not diversified. Did we, he asked, have a five-year plan?

At the time, we were lucky if we had a five-day plan. But I was beginning to have a vision of what it was to be a major player. It was clear we would need to expand our horizons. What the consequences of that thought process would be, nobody could have foreseen.

5
LICENSED
TO
THRILL

You could say the story of publishing *Penthouse* under licence from Bob Guccione began at the Frankfurt music fair in 1982. For our *International Musician* party that year my people hired a band called Depeche Mode, whose drummer was a computer. It was a sure sign that the music business I knew and loved was changing. And not only was it changing, it was in decline. Maybe people making electronic keyboards were doing reasonably well, but the traditional market of guitars, amplifiers and drums was collapsing. Music shops were going bust. Admittedly Fred's Music Store would go broke only to be replaced by Fred's Music Shop UK (no connection with Fred's Music Store that went down owing lots of money except that the owner was, once again, Fred). But the signs were ominous.

Home Organist began to struggle as the stately Yamaha home organs lost out to little Casio keyboards that cost a few pounds in Dixons. In due course we changed the title to *What Keyboard?* But unlike organs (love them or hate them – and for the record, I hated them) the little Casios were not a way of life, they were just a throw-away consumer gadget. They were not really the kind of thing you would buy a magazine about, any more than you would buy a magazine about calculators or electric toothbrushes.

On one memorable occasion we organised a Home Organist of

the Year competition on behalf of Yamaha, to be attended by the Japanese owners and the Jacobs and Kemble families who owned the British distribution company. For us, these were clients to be taken seriously. The head of our advertising agency, Philip Bailey, who wasn't one for underselling, hired the Commonwealth Institute, and we advertised in *Home Organist*. Since we needed Yamaha to understand that we ran the most powerful magazine in the world, we had to have a packed house. On the morning of the event I asked how many people had bought tickets for the 300-seat hall.

'Er, 45.'

'Well, you'd better sort it out,' I said, trying to remain calm.

Time passed. The evening began. The hall was full, a great time was had by everyone and Yamaha were deeply impressed. Afterwards, I asked Bailey how we had got from 45 guests to standing room only in the space of a few hours.

'Well, basically we hired a couple of coaches and toured the local old folks' homes abducting the residents.'

We escaped that night, but the writing was on the wall. It was clearly time to explore more robust areas of business. We tried diversifying into different music magazines, including computer music ones, but we needed to do more than this.

It was Mitch in America who started the ball rolling. Mitch was not normally a man of ideas: he was a man of budgets, and he adhered to them religiously. Hence the cat as pest control, and the charges for the office coffee service. However, Mitch could see beyond music. He told us we were not, as we had thought, part of the music industry specialising in magazines, we were part of the publishing industry who just happened to publish music titles. We were, however, 'leesure' publishers, and could certainly do other 'leesure' magazines.

Now the main thing in leisure at that time, as Depeche Mode knew very well, was computers. If you can't beat them join them, I decided. We made plans for a high-technology magazine that would cover the new electronic products that were all the rage, the new generations of Sinclair, BBC, and yes, probably Apple computers, as well as video recorders, household electronics: anything for the geeky and the gadget-mad.

The magazines we came up with were *Innovations* in the USA and *Next* in the UK. The American title never really got off the ground, because Mitch was not much of a salesman. As for the UK magazine, everyone admired *Next*, which was edited by Rick Maybury (who now writes for the *Telegraph*), but very few actually bought it. We learned a valuable lesson about the importance of specialisation. People might have an interest in a general topic, but if you want people to spend money on a magazine, you need to focus tightly. Owners of Sinclair Spectrum computers wanted a magazine on Sinclair Spectrum computers, not about computers in general. Owners of video equipment wanted a magazine about video equipment, likewise camera enthusiasts or digital musicians. If you wanted generalised broad-brush treatment, you turned to the newspapers and the Sunday supplements, not to magazines. Not for the first time, we discovered that you had to be either very specialised, or very big. There was no halfway house.

Nevertheless these early enterprises were not a waste of time; they represented a foray into more mainstream publishing, and that was a step we needed to take.

Meanwhile, our efforts attracted some favourable attention, and brought us into contact with proper consumer advertisers. One of these was a fellow named Sidney Shepherd of Freeman Mathews and Milne, advertising agency for the top cigarette brand Rothmans. Sidney was fond of a sociable drink, and he was apparently also fond of me because he had 'never met a proprietor before'. I suppose I had never met an agency media buyer either. But as I was busy, I generally left Sidney to my publisher, Mel Lewis, whom I had brought over from WH Smith because he had the expertise in consumer magazines I felt we lacked.

One evening I received a call from Sidney, who said he had to see me personally to discuss an important business opportunity. I agreed to meet at the office but made sure Mel would be by my side so I could escape when I wanted to.

The meeting got off to a not very encouraging start.

'Big tits, big tits!' Sidney exclaimed. Hearing this didn't fill me with confidence either about the business prospect he wanted to discuss or his state of mind. Then he said, 'You know Tony Power? You know Bob Guccione? You know Paul Raymond?'

'What, the hairdresser?' I think I was thinking of Raymond 'Teasey Weasey' Bessone.

'No — the strip clubs! Look — I'm trying to tell you that *Penthouse* is for sale and Paul Raymond wants to buy it from Bob Guccione, but you're the one that should have it!'

I may have been slow on the uptake but I still didn't quite get the reference to *Penthouse*. It vaguely suggested to me the idea of an apartment in London and I explained that I had a very nice house in Southgate to which, in fact, I wouldn't mind getting back.

He explained about the magazine, and he wouldn't shut up.

'Look — if I call my lawyer in New York — then can I go?'

I called Dennis Ardi on the spot and asked him if he knew Bob Guccione. He said he did.

'Well, Dennis, tell Mr Guccione we'll take his *Penthouse* in the UK. Now — Sidney, can I go home?'

That was that, and I did not give it much more thought. I had more pressing issues. The next few months were a depressing time for us. It was all Depeche Mode and we were still Ritchie Blackmore. Yamaha cut their advertising spend as the Japanese moved in to take control of the business from the Kembles and the Jacobs, and meanwhile Casio continued to destroy the home organ market.

Then, out of the blue, I received a call from someone calling himself John Evans, the head honcho boss president of everything international on *Penthouse* magazine. He came from Romford.

'I'm coming to see you.'

Without Sidney to egg me on, I was reluctant to pursue the interest that Dennis Ardi had indicated on my behalf. I explained that to John. 'Honestly it's not for me, mate. I'm a drummer. I can't do porn.'

'No, it's not porn – it's Men's Lifestyle. It's the vanguard of lifestyle.'

Somehow he persuaded me to meet, and turned up with the *Penthouse* group's international lawyer, Ben Baker. Ben, it tran-spired, was not a Harvard high-flyer but came from Southgate, just down the road from me.

'Listen, Richard,' said Ben. 'This could be the deal of a lifetime because Bob is one of the richest men in the world, and at this moment he needs you.'

Apparently Guccione had had something of a disagreement with the bosses of WH Smith, Sir Simon Hornby and Malcolm Field. He'd said that he was not prepared to operate within the regulatory environment they sought to impose, that he didn't need them and that they could f*** off. For good measure, he also pointed out that he was an artist: he was Michelangelo. Since they did not see him in exactly that light, he had found it impossible to get *Penthouse* into Smith's retail shops. And what Ben Baker said was that if we could get that magazine into Smith's we could write any deal we wished.

I may not have cared for the title but I do like a challenge, and I had a useful weapon in my armoury: Mel Lewis, my trusted ex-Smith's man. We made some calls and Mel persuaded me to go and see Malcolm Field in person. Malcolm, it turned out, was a smart, straight-up ex-military type, a proper businessman.

'Are you going to live the lifestyle?' he asked.

I replied that I published *Home Organist* magazine but did not play the organ. I also pointed out that I had been with the same partner since the age of 20. I was just a publisher who needed to expand.

'As long as you don't live the lifestyle and bring us into disrepute, and provided that if we want changes made to the magazine there's no argument – we'll take it.'

His reference to changes was because in those days Smith's and Menzies would approve in advance every picture in magazines of that type, using criteria infinitely more modest than the laws of the land required. For us, that was scarcely a problem.

With Field's blessing, therefore, I accompanied my lawyer Dennis Ardi to a posh hotel in New York, which *Penthouse* paid for, and I again met John from Romford and Ben from Southgate, since Bob was painting the ceiling of the Sistine Chapel or photographing models. Apparently his practice was to take them to dinner on the first day, to photograph them on the second day, and then on the third day to . . . But then, he, unlike me, lived the lifestyle.

We got round the table and started discussing terms. I was still having serious doubts. Did I really want to get into this? How would I tell my mum I'd started publishing such a magazine? I had got through the first seven years of my business career without killing anyone or making compromises. And now this. I was uncomfortable. I started being difficult, asking, for example, for two years 'rent-free'. Yet John from Romford and Ben from Southgate looked respectable enough. Plus Smith's and Menzies were in, and the magazine was, in its way, respected. Sean Connery would give you an interview, or Denis Healey when he was Chancellor of the Exchequer; it was the *FHM* of its time.

Even so, I stuck to my preposterous terms. We had a punch-up, although not of the physical kind, and I threw them out of the suite. Their suite. Dennis Ardi came round the following day and thought he could 'resurrect the deal'. Ben Baker had confided to him that anyone who could swear at them and throw them out of their own hotel suite must be the right person to do business with. So we went back again and sorted out the details of what from our point of view was a highly advantageous deal – this time without any explosions on my part. The only condition, as Ben put it, was we had to 'keep Bobbie happy'.

'Once a year you come to America and whatever he says you agree. He'll say black is white, and you say – yes, I'd never thought of it like that before, Bob, you're right!'

So that is what we did. In 1983 I became the UK licensee of *Penthouse*. And I would never be allowed to forget it. There was an existing operation at premises in West London which Bob went on to sell us as a side deal (a slightly problematic deal, it turned out, as he did not actually own them), but we quickly brought everything into our cramped offices in Drury Lane. We then proceeded to put together our own British edition, mixing Bob's photographs from America with celebrity interviews and reviews from the UK – and making sure that we kept our promises to the news trade.

As for Bob Guccione, once a year we would go to see him and his wife Kathy Keeton (who had started out as a stripper at the Windmill Theatre and was proud of the fact), carefully negotiating our way past his six Rhodesian ridgebacks (which are large dogs bred to kill lions). Bob had actually begun his business in the UK after an unlikely initial career managing launderettes, and my first impression of him was that for a sex god he was a bit fat. That said, he did live in the biggest town house in New York with rooms that looked like sets for the film *Caligula* and with young girls all around and old masters on the walls. He also had security fit for a president. His rival Larry Flynt had been shot for publishing 'men's sophisticate' magazines and Bob did not want to be next.

Our conversation would go something like this.

'So you're Desmond. You fucked my magazine up. I don't like what you're doing to it. Has anyone told you?'

'Yes.'

'What have they told you?'

'That you'd like a cleaner layout, Bob.'

'Then why haven't you done it?'

Ben would then intervene and try to defuse things a bit ('Oh – have you seen that painting over there? It's a Magritte – isn't it marvellous?') and things would calm down. Bob's people had persuaded him that he was selling 4 million copies a month even when he wasn't, that he was making a fortune even when he wasn't, and that he was a genius and could do no wrong. Being surrounded by people who never told the truth or said 'no' turned out badly. Bob embarked on a number of ill-advised adventures, generally accompanied by lawsuits and always carrying crippling costs, while the US edition fell in circulation and became unsustainable on the extravagant budget Bob set for it.

I, meanwhile, settled into a more workaday routine. I ran my music magazines, continued to acquire small specialist titles, published my new *Penthouse* magazine in the UK, and did not live the lifestyle. In fact my lifestyle was spectacularly unspectacular. We still had problems with cash flow, and watched every penny. I did not know about leasing – my rule of thumb was if I couldn't afford it we didn't buy it. All our cars, for example, were left-hand drive Escorts bought from Brussels for £2,500 rather than purchased in England for £3,500. I can recall having a long and angry debate about the purchase of just one photocopying machine.

Anyone who thinks the licence to print *Penthouse* was a licence to print money should have been at my wedding, on 3 August 1983. Janet and I had been together for many years, but we very romantically planned our marriage so that it would coincide with the British Musical Instrument show: that way, we could invite all the advertisers who were in town for it and get a few pages of advertising, because, of course, pages pay wages. My best man was my best advertiser. It was very hand to mouth. *Penthouse*, like everything, required attention, determination and sheer hard work. I am probably still not contractually allowed to say what the circulation was when we took the licence, but believe me it wasn't very much. What money we made in those days came mostly from our music magazines and agency clients in the music industry – and even those sources were drying up. Looking back, my impression of that whole period is that all we did was to keep things going. It was, in fact, the beginning of nine years of grief, until we got lucky again in 1992.

Janet and I had our wedding at the registry office and then a lunch at the Selfridges Hotel. I was annoyed that Paul Ashford and Martin Ellice were late turning up from the office. Rude bastards. I pulled them to the side when I got the chance and told them they might at least have arrived on time. They explained that they had been delayed by the arrival of the bailiffs at the office in Drury Lane. Apparently we had been a little slow in paying for something, and they had come to seize our typesetting equipment.

This, incidentally, is why today I become concerned when, say, my driver tells me that he's planning an expensive wedding and three weeks in Cancún. It sounds unromantic but I'd say you don't know what might happen tomorrow. Spend the money when you've paid your house off. But, that's me. Some people go through life with that underlying fear of ending up on a park bench, and some do not. As I write this, interest rates are set at more or less zero, but at some point they will shoot up again and that makes me worry for any of my staff who are taking on high levels of debt. Many people are saddling themselves with up to a million pounds in debt, at a time when there's no longer an uncapped pensions tax break and payout. You could end up working all your life, wearing your white shirt, doing your best (never good enough, of course) and suddenly, at the age of 65, having a heart attack or going deaf and having no resources to fall back on. Well, perhaps that doesn't always happen – but it can.

Having said all that, when it came to my honeymoon we were persuaded to splash out a little (even though we only spent four days away). Previously our idea of a holiday had been camping in France, but John Evans said we should go to Villa d'Este on Lake Como. I still remember the bill. Or should I say bills. We paid the first one, and then as we were leaving someone came across to us and said, 'Here's your bill.' We replied that we'd paid. He said, 'No, this is your *other* bill.' This, incidentally, had to be paid in cash, for which we had to be taken into town to find a bank. Italian hotels can be fond of extras, a bit like printers, but I shall get to that in a moment.

Apart from allowing me to entertain advertisers on her big day, Janet also played a role in the business. All I knew was the music side – that would have been my subject on *Mastermind*. Janet's knowledge was rather wider. Her father had been an RAF squadron leader and had been killed in action, but her mother had managed not just to bring up two daughters but to put them through public school: Janet won a scholarship to Westonbirt. In spite of this, or because of it, Janet, like me, had an intense dislike of posh privileged people, since, even though she had been privately educated, her story was like my own. The other kids' parents would come each weekend in their Jags to pick up their children, while poor Janet would be left stranded there because her mother couldn't afford to get the train down. The good thing, though, from my point of view, was that it meant she understood people from the Establishment so she was not in awe of them: they were, after all, the people she had been at school with. Being educated also meant she could talk to Kathy Keeton, Bob's wife, about Isaac Azimov, which was what Kathy really liked to talk about, and why she launched *Omni* magazine, which was one of their more expensive failures.

. . .

Even Janet, however, would not have been able to get along with Paul Raymond, who was the next problem we were to encounter. We printed *Penthouse* with Hunter Print (no connection with today's company of that name). Mr Hunter was a smooth operator with very white teeth. On investigation it seemed to us that his price could be as much as 50 per cent more than everyone else in the industry. We called him in and told him he was sending us broke; he needed to match industry prices. He agreed at once. It then turned out that Mr Raymond, who owned the adult market, printed all his titles with Mr Hunter, who was his best mate.

There was another reason why Mr Raymond didn't like us. When the *Penthouse* deal had cropped up, he'd sent a creative genius by the name of Tony Power to secure it (this was why Sidney Shepherd mentioned the name when he first called, except I thought he'd said Powell). Power, however, was a drug addict who was so under the influence at the time that he failed to turn up, leaving us as the sole contenders. So now we had *Penthouse* and Raymond had a grudge. This fellow who only published music magazines had nicked a trophy title from under his nose and to add insult to injury got it for almost no money.

We reckoned that Raymond therefore used his commercial influence with Hunter to get at us. Having agreed to lower his prices, he proceeded to send us two bills the following month – rather like the hotel at Villa d'Este – one listing the charges we had been expecting, and the second with all the 'extras' on it. We could, of course, have repudiated the bill and refused to print with Mr Hunter, but that would still have left us with a major problem. When it came to *Penthouse*, we were the licensee, and if for any reason we failed to print, we would be in breach of our licence. My lawyer by that time was Ian Rosenblatt, who has remained with me right through the Channel 5 deals and up to the present day, and I asked his advice. He said: pay but don't agree, and ask for a negotiation. We did so, and then filed a claim about the spurious costs. In December 1983 we received a telex from Hunter: if you don't agree to drop your claims, he said, we won't print the next issue.

I was in a corner. Raymond was already calling Guccione and telling him I wouldn't be able to print. An alternative printer I found couldn't get the paper we needed. I was worried sick, so when I happened to be at our office in Germany that handled our German-language edition, I asked if they could help. The sales director, Herbie Katz, a very celebrated Finnish jazz guitarist in the Django Reinhardt style, pointed across the corridor to a sign saying FINNISH PAPER AUTHORITY (though in German, of course). We paid a visit. They liked jazz guitar, and Herbie was a god. They could get us paper, they said, but it would take 30 days. It was progress, but it did not solve the immediate problem. Then my friend David (Lord) Evans of Centurion Press very kindly told me he could 'borrow' suitable paper for the 30 days, but if we didn't replace it after that period he was a dead man. We gratefully accepted his offer. We had been saved from almost certain ruin.

Mr Hunter, however, was still owed some money. I did not like Mr Hunter. I invited him in to talk things over. I had our offices cleared, had rubbish strewn around the floors, and gave instructions to my secretary, who was a bit of an actress, as to what she was to say when the time came. I dressed in old slacks and a kipper tie I had.

When Hunter came in I offered him coffee and the girl spoke her line on cue. 'You ain't paid me for two weeks and I ain't paying for any more coffee for you, I need my money . . .'

I said, 'Please, not in front of Mr Hunter.'

I told him that he could see how things were with us, but I also said that I wanted to be honourable. I knew I owed £180,000 but maybe he would just accept £5,000 a month for a year: it would be better than getting nothing when we went bankrupt. He took my first cheque and signed a new agreement with us. I offered to take him for lunch. I said there was a very nice café at the Asda store opposite. He declined.

So that was Mr Hunter dealt with. However, we still had to deal with our distributors Comag, who, like Mr Hunter, were not immune to the Raymond effect, even though they were 'Condé Nast and the National Magazine Company'. To keep them onside, we would get up at six in the morning once a month to drive to their offices in West Drayton for a meeting which finished at one o'clock. We were never offered so much as a sandwich before we left for our two-hour drive back. I asked about this once, and was reminded that as well as handling our magazines, they also distributed Raymond's titles. 'You may have one Rolls-Royce but Paul Raymond has fifty.'

This was a bit unfair on their part because in fact the management at Comag owed their jobs to me. In the early days they had a senior member of staff who I discovered was planning to set up on his own and take all his employer's clients. I had telephoned the chairman Terry Mansfield, who was very supportive (and even used to come to our *Bicycle* magazine rallies), and told him, 'Terry, you have one fault, you are too trusting.' I had then explained what was going on. Terry had called his vice-chairman Nicholas Coleridge, the culprits had been confronted, they had departed, and the second tier of management had been promoted up. It was a pity therefore that, when push came to shove, they turned into loyal members of the Paul Raymond fan club. When Terry Mansfield tells this story he asserts that afterwards I told him he owed me a favour, and that two percentage points on our distribution margin would do the job nicely. I don't remember saying that, but it seems in character.

As for Raymond himself, I only met him once during that period, when he complained I had paid too much for some pictures and was therefore forcing up the prices for everyone. He said, 'Just remember – they're all just strippers.'

I thought that uncharitable, but it stayed in my mind.

If *Penthouse* taught me anything, it was that I needed to understand not just advertising revenue but circulation revenue – what made people buy things and carry on buying things. And, of course, how to 'keep Bobbie happy'. In this latter context, Guccione employed a very posh English fellow called Joe Brooks, who had been with him from the start. Joe's expertise was in an area I had never thought about: *Penthouse*'s brand appearance. He insisted on a very strict style and format in terms of how elements lined up on the pages, what the permissible layouts were, what the sizes of the photographs were, how the graphics and typefaces were used. His job was to go through every foreign edition to check these things. There was not a rule book but there was definitely a style to aim for. Joe would come over and stay at Blake's Hotel at our expense and say Bob didn't like this or that, or that the grammage of the paper was too low, and we would say, 'Yes, right.'

In reality, we sold 40,000 copies a month but the NRS, the advertisers' standard readership audit, gave us a readership in the millions, perhaps because of past glories, or because *Penthouse* was the top-shelf magazine people were comfortable to tell researchers they looked at. So in readership terms, we were up there with the consumer titles which could attract top advertisers. This was great, of course, but you do need circulation to build or else even the NRS research might notice that things are slipping a little. I was also concerned that the magazine was beginning to look a bit passé with its exclusive interviews with Stirling Moss and pictures of undraped American ladies shot by Bob who made them all blurred by putting Vaseline on his lens.

Fortunately, it was at this point that we discovered the cover star who would tick all the boxes for a British readership both as a model and as a celebrity.

Sam Fox, at the time, was contracted to a well-known red-top tabloid (not the *Daily Star*), so while she was prepared to speak to us she would not do exclusive photo shoots for us. That changed after I'd been to Australia to sort out problems with our local edition of *International Musician*. After I'd done that, I'd had a meeting with the editor of the Australian licensed edition of *Penthouse*, Andrew Cowell, who had previously been quite high-handed with us, but who now very helpfully explained that in spite of Joe Brooks's visits we still didn't understand the design structure of the magazine, and that for the price of a ticket he would spend some time in our office and sort out some templates. So he came and worked with us for two weeks, and while he was there he pointed out that we needed to talk to the guy who knew all the right models. Actually, he said, this guy already worked for us on a freelance basis. His name was John Kelly.

John was a wonderful old-school newspaper photographer. He had been married to Vivienne Neves, whose claim to fame was being the first topless model in *The Times*. They had a huge rambling mansion in Surrey which was at one point rented to Marlon Brando, and, for a while, they were probably Britain's coolest couple. Vivienne was very beautiful and John had the good looks of a young Jeff Beck. Later, however, Vivienne fell victim to MS, they split up, and John became almost a vagrant, living from hand to mouth and sleeping on people's floors.

I met John and asked, 'How well do you know Sam Fox?'

'I discovered her.'

Sam Fox's father, apparently, was a carpenter who had driven John mad insisting that he should take pictures of Sam, so they both owed him a debt for launching her career. Now he arranged for us to have an interview with her. When it came to accompanying pictures, though, we had nowhere to shoot. It was the day before the Christmas party I was due to hold at my house. Perhaps, suggested John, I could offer a suitable venue? My wife hated what that implied, but she fell for his charm and said she would go out to the sales and let us get on with it.

Sam came round. She was 4ft tall and ate all my Jaffa cakes. But she liked the Animals and blues, it was a great shoot featuring my new swimming pool, and everyone was happy. That month our sales more than doubled. We felt we had a formula, and John was able to repeat it with Linda Lusardi, Suzanne Mizzi, Maria Whittaker and other glamour models of that era, though not, after that first occasion, at my residence.

These 'Page Three girls' therefore became a fixture in *Penthouse*. We even went multimedia because the girls were happy to do comic messages for readers on pre-recorded phone lines. In this way we added something of our own to the magazine to go with the established style and format, the occasional world-class exclusive like Madonna's famous nude pictures, and the 'investigative journalism' which New York also insisted upon (an early UK example was an exposé of the work practices that killed hundreds of divers in the North Sea oil industry; our major source was the MP John Prescott, who at one point had been a merchant seaman and union official). The UK edition of *Penthouse* began to have its own distinct identity, evolving many of the elements that were developed further in *OK!* magazine: the celebrity angles, luxurious shoots with known stars who collaborated with the magazine, and writers and photographers who were rated the top of their profession.

We even had a politics and opinion column, Advise and Dissent, which lured me into my first declaration of political sympathy when I wrote 'Why I Am a Socialist' in the face of what Rupert Murdoch was doing at Fortress Wapping. I felt that the stand-off at Wapping and Murdoch/Thatcher's use of public law enforcement to support the operation was excessive and un-British. I thought Murdoch was doing what the old press barons had done, that he was erecting an edifice designed to keep the price of entry into the newspaper industry prohibitively high for any potential rivals. I cannot say whether at that stage I saw myself as a potential rival. I accepted that new technology was inevitable – we were early adopters ourselves – but I believed that Maxwell and the *Mirror* handled the transition much better. I expect that my article was widely read, since people bought *Penthouse* magazine mainly for its political commentary and, of course, the car reviews. I put the price up from £1 to £2.50.

John Kelly became a fixture. I gave him a car and a room in Crouch End, which he said was so depressing he thought of hanging himself. And as Sam Fox's UK pop career began to take off sales of the magazine rose to a dizzying 200,000. Bob Guccione, however, was not impressed, and proceeded to write me an eight-page letter in which he explained that Sam Fox was not a Penthouse Pet. A Penthouse Pet was 6ft 6in with long legs, perfect bone structure and perfect teeth. What's more, Sam had a pointed chin. This in my opinion was not what the readers were really focusing on but Bob saw it as grounds for terminating our licence. It just shows that England and America are divided not only by a common language but also by how men look at women, and for all I know how women look at men. England was always about Barbara Windsor and girl-next-door types. In the USA it was Hollywood and supermodels.

I replied to the criticism about the chin with suitable humility, Joe Brooks was sent over to bring us back into line, and life went on. Then a couple of years later Sam Fox broke America, and we received a very courteous letter asking us if we could get the US rights to our pictures of her for their front cover. Recognition at last. The Sam Fox incident was just one of the many occasions Bob wanted to terminate our licence, but John Evans and Ben Baker had managed such situations before and they also understood we needed a degree of latitude in the way we put our edition of the magazine together if it was to succeed in the UK. When I later became a licenser of *OK!* magazine, I remembered what had happened with *Penthouse*, and made sure that our local licensers were free to adapt the formula to their own territories and cultures; in recognition of that, they got the lion's share.

Brands, however, come and go, and Bob Guccione's company in New York was beginning to slide. His problem was that he was always right, and even when he wasn't the people around him told him he was. Instead of acting like a publisher, therefore, he now embarked on a series of ill-fated business ventures and picked a series of fights that would ultimately leave him with nothing. Among other things he decided to set up a rival to Hugh Hefner's mansion on the East Coast in Atlantic City, a gambling and leisure complex on a scale comparable to the Trump Tower. His company president/lawyer David Myerson took him to a bank to get a loan, with strict instructions that he was to keep his mouth shut, but being Bob he was soon banging the table and asking the bank manager how much he had made last year, because he, Bob, had made $40 million, and he didn't need their money and could fund the complex himself.

The new enterprise was begun, but it ruffled quite a few feathers and also brought Bob into conflict with the Mafia who had similar interests in the area. Bob somehow ended up in a lawsuit with them. It was his proud boast that this was the biggest lawsuit in history and, of course, he never lost a lawsuit. (Costs were something else.) Lawsuits, in fact, were a way of life with Bob. In any event Bob sued many of his rivals, and by the end he was suing most of his family, too, including his son Bobbie Junior over *Spin* magazine. When Bob's father died leaving a small legacy to be distributed amongst the relatives, Bob sued all of them on the grounds that he had given the old man the money in the first place, so it should all come back to him.

Of course he eventually got round to suing us as well, and tried to take our licence away. By now he'd got rid of his original team, which meant that there was no one to help him duck and dive his way through the shrinking business, or persuade him to move to a smaller house by telling him that it was actually a bigger house. The point of the story of Sam Fox's chin is that it shows that times change. Bob refused to change with them, and that destroyed him.

So as we developed our other businesses, the *Penthouse* brand gradually diminished and simply ceased to be trendy. James Bond cancelled his membership of the Playboy Club, and presumably his subscription to *Penthouse* too. Meanwhile a new generation of Guccione executives employed various lawyers and accountants who then busied themselves dismantling the relationships which Guccione's old guard had built up. They looked for reasons to start disputes, and when you look for trouble you can usually find it.

What followed was a series of spats between ourselves and General Media, Bob's company. The first concerned which European countries were included in our distribution rights – a debate that descended into a dispute as to whether Austria was in Germany or not. Then there was the matter of 'specials', which the Americans originally encouraged us to produce to augment the title's circulation but for which they suddenly starting billing us extra royalties. One way and another, being a *Penthouse* licensee became complicated, thankless and boring. Then it became litigious. In the early 1990s the management at US *Penthouse* formed a relationship with one of our ex-employees and ex-United Newspapers distributor Andrew Cameron, who wanted the licence. The dispute that followed was described by one of our advisers in the words first coined about the Falklands War: we were 'two bald men fighting over a comb'. Eventually we managed to reach a settlement whereby Bob got *Penthouse* back (which made no money but had a lot of his ego invested in it) and we kept *Forum. Forum* was an intellectual sex magazine for lords, bishops and so forth. It boasted among its writers Alastair Campbell, later Tony Blair's spin doctor, Karin Smith who became Elizabeth Hurley's agent, and numerous other illustrious names. It had a board of consultants headed by Chad Varah, founder of the Samaritans. It made a lot of money and, what's more, had none of Bob's ego invested in it.

Some years later, in 2003, when we had launched *OK!* in America, I thought I'd do the decent thing and visit Bob (despite the fact that it was the year of the big power cut and all the lights seemed to be out when I was there). He opened the door himself, and at first clearly didn't recognise me, perhaps because I was wearing jeans and a T-shirt. I reminded him who I was. 'Oh, yeah, Richard,' he said. He seemed pleased to see me. But he was ill with throat cancer, and he looked it.

I'd put my back out on the air journey, so I asked Bob if I could lie down.

He said, 'I think I prefer you like this.'

I looked around at the famous town house now stripped of its luxuries.

'Where are all your people?' I asked.

'They're gone. Everyone's gone.'

'And your furniture and your paintings, your art collection?'

'All gone.'

I could see the discoloured patches on the wall where the art treasures had been. In the last months of his business he had even sold Kathy's jewellery to pay the wage bills. As much as Bob may have been frustrating in the former years, I had to acknowledge the scale of the empire he once built, and it was sad to see how far he had fallen.

He said, 'Let me tell you something. Just stay clear of these venture capital funds!'

He had been involved with one called Cerberus. He explained

how he had faced immense tax bills because of a mistaken belief that losses in England could be set against profits in America. Rather than negotiating with the tax authorities or paying easy instalments on an $80 million tax debt, Kathy had wanted to repay the whole sum in one go – apparently, just so she could sleep at night. But this involved raising the money from outside investors, and clever ones at that. Personal guarantees were signed; an 8 per cent bond was issued; and when the interest rate soared to 14 per cent the company could not meet commitments. In the end everything went for $1 to Cerberus.

Bob said there might still be a chance I could take his business over. I said I had moved on, but I pointed to *OK!* and told him how much I owed to him: the attention to style and format, my under-standing of sales on news-stands – all from a learning curve that began with my *Penthouse* licence. The stupid thing is he could have sold for $300 million at one point, and lived happily for the rest of his life. After all, what he actually liked doing was painting, and what Kathy liked doing was writing about longevity, which was a pity because she died relatively young.

Seven years later Bob Guccione himself died in New Jersey in a rented flat.

For us, *Penthouse* was a step on the journey, a way of breaking out of niche publishing and into the wider market. Of course it gave us a stigma that was even harder to shake off than the damning assumption that we were 'just music publishers'. Then again, I have never minded being underestimated.

Penthouse was a part of an era. But it wasn't our route to the big time. Indeed it wasn't even a magazine that gave us our major break. It was a location.

6
I WASN'T BORN YESTERDAY

Back in the early days of the *Penthouse* licence, our overall business was certainly expanding, but we were also finding it quite tough financially. *Penthouse* needed resources, people, ability, determination, stamina, imagination, originality, courage; in short it was exactly like every other business I have ever encountered. True, our three music magazines and their various foreign editions were ticking over, we had *Next* magazine, and we were beginning to look at acquiring further specialist titles, but none of this was major league; and while our advertising agency was successful it relied very heavily on two or three big musical instrument clients.

And then there was the cost of running a 7,000 square foot office at 141/143 Drury Lane with its rent, services, rates and car parking costs. We were always being broken into because there was a shared lift, so we had to pay for special security gates. And because we had a full repairing lease, no alterations were possible and we had no room to expand.

Perhaps we could move out of London? Perhaps we could operate from Peterborough or somewhere similar, as our publishing rivals EMAP did? I began talking to my bank manager John Melbourne about moving to Milton Keynes, which he thought was mad, not appreciating that my music clients were there.

And then at about the same time I was contemplating life in Milton Keynes, I started to notice poster advertisements with pictures of cartoon crows saying, 'WHY MOVE TO THE MIDDLE OF NOWHERE WHEN YOU CAN MOVE TO THE MIDDLE OF LONDON?' I have since been informed that the crows may have been ravens, as in the Tower of London, but whatever they were, they were promoting the idea of business premises in the undreamed-of area of London's Docklands, which had been designated as something called an Enterprise Zone.

We tried to find out further details. I even went down to Docklands on a Sunday with my wife and my stepson Darren (he took his bucket and spade because we knew there was water there, so we might as well go equipped for the seaside). But we couldn't get in. The roads were barricaded and the vast empty site was boarded round. So we gave up. I telephoned instead, and was told that all the land was gone – whether sold, let or reserved they did not say.

I might just have let the matter drop, but shortly afterwards I happened to be travelling to visit our German *International Musician* colleagues when I came across a copy of *High Life* in the British Airways lounge in which there was an interview with the boss of Trafalgar House, Nigel Broackes. Nigel was a man who spoke very poshly (he had a partner Victor Matthews who spoke very unposhly), but despite the poshness he was actually a self-made entrepreneur who had started off buying bomb sites in Brixton and built up his huge conglomerate from there. Among other things, Trafalgar House owned Express Newspapers, for which Nigel had paid only £11 million because its then proprietors, the Beaverbrook family, thought it was going broke. Nigel proceeded to sell one building the next day for £11 million, leaving him with a multitude of other assets and buildings as profit. From my point of view, though, what was interesting about his interview in *High Life* was that in it he mentioned that he was now chairman of the London Docklands

Development Corporation, and that it was all going very well – though he would not take his Rolls-Royce down there.

I wrote him a note saying, 'Dear Mr Broackes [he wasn't a knight then because he didn't get his knighthood until I got involved in Docklands], I *did* take my Rolls-Royce down there, but I couldn't get in and they told me there was nothing left.'

He wrote a nice letter back inviting me over, and this time I did manage to get in. It was a complete wasteland, full of bomb craters and blackberry bushes. Everything was ruined and abandoned, a monument to the conflict between the dock bosses and Jack Dash and the dock workers' unions that ended with the closure of London as a shipping terminal and the removal of all operations to the deep-water facilities at Tilbury. The only intact building seemed to be an old warehouse, which later became the Docklands Arena. I was taken inside, and, much to my surprise, found that things were buzzing there. There must have been some 300 people with computers. In 1982 you didn't see computers. I was impressed. A scruffy fellow introduced to me as Reg Ward came up and started telling me how they would have an airport here and a monorail there and a tower somewhere else.

After ten minutes of this I said, 'You're fucking insane! With respect, Mr Broackes, I don't know what you are doing associating yourself with this – it's mad.'

Broackes replied, 'Mr Desmond, Margaret Thatcher is putting in £1 billion a week and I can assure you once the Link is built under the water, this is going to be the new City and if you turn your back on it you will regret it for the rest of your life.'

I had been on the point of walking out, but now I turned round and asked, 'What's the deal?'

'What do you want to build?'

'An office block.'

'Are you really going to build it?'

'Yes.'

'You're not just going to sit on the land?'

'No.'

'If you build it we want £70,000 for 2 acres of land: a third on signing documents, a third on completion of the build, and a third 5 years afterwards. But don't forget that you will receive 100 per cent allowances from the government, so if the building cost is £1 million it will only actually cost you half, and you won't have to pay rates for 12 years.'

In effect, they might as well have given the land free. As it happened I had just bought a house off The Bishops Avenue (for £301,000) and had engaged an architect called Stanley Trevor to do some work there. I phoned him straight away, in front of Broackes and the others, and asked him if he could design office blocks. He said he had been design-ing office blocks for hundreds of years and that he was the best office block designer in the world. I told him he'd better jump into a car straight away, and half an hour later he was with us (it was possible to make the journey from Hampstead to Docklands that quickly in those days, because no one wanted to). Stanley sketched a solid traditional brick building with classic lines and curved corners. They liked the curved corners. We were in. A million pounds for our own premises on a prime waterside site a couple of miles from the City of London. I confirmed to Broackes that I would be, in effect, his first customer.

There was then the question of finance. I could provide £649,000 if I put my house up, but I needed a further £450,000 from a bank. Back in the office again, my first call was to Rothschild's, but they didn't exactly fall over themselves to help. They did agree, though, that I could probably let the offices to myself for ten years and that if the building ultimately proved worthless I would at least have enjoyed a period of cheap rent. Unenthusiastically, they said I could have the money, provided I could give a personal guarantee.

Of course. But it's nice to have a bank that shares your vision rather than just demands that you put yourself on the line. So I called John Melbourne, my bank manager at NatWest, outlined the project and offered to come over and show him the plans. I explained I was putting £649,000 of my own money into it, which was everything I had in the world, and I needed a further £450,000. He agreed to the loan but asked me not to show him the plans: a technicality meant they could not take a charge on the freehold until I fully owned it. The arrangement therefore was that I would meet Melbourne every month on a Sunday at the site so he could see the building going up and assure himself that the project was on schedule and the asset growing in value, and then we would have a beer together. That was the paperwork. And that was proper banking.

In fact the Enterprise Zone culture delivered more for me than just a new office building. My original plan had been to construct a two-storey affair, but the Docklands Development people were desperate for me to go for three storeys, to create something with a bit of prestige that would mark the arrival of the first freehold entrepreneur builder in Docklands. The trouble was I only needed two storeys: my company was a bit wobbly; I had come to Docklands to save money, not to spend speculatively. I said as much to Reg Ward, pointing out that the extra storey would cost £300,000. He asked what the interest on that might be. I hazarded £15,000 a year. At which point he promptly offered me a consultancy for precisely that sum. The consultancy, he said, would involve me persuading others to follow us down to Docklands. I think he suspected I was a bit of a salesman.

Reg then added that the LDDC themselves needed a prestige space and that they could rent that third storey at £25,000 a year. Now I not only had an extra storey, I also had a tenant. It was all agreed in double-quick time.

I set to work to sell Docklands to others. The first call I made with Reg was to Lord Hartwell, who owned a newspaper called the *Telegraph* in Fleet Street next to the *Express* building. He had a room with a three-bar electric fire, and a shirt that was a bit frayed as posh people sometimes do, and a very posh cardigan. Broackes and the LDDC wanted him to build a print site at West Ferry in Docklands, I explained, and I was there to persuade him because I was a leading publisher who had put all my money into the area. I told him how great it was, how it was the future. He bought the idea, and later went on to get the Express group involved as a partner.

Hartwell certainly had vision, but he turned out not to be very good at financing and ran into cash-flow problems. The Canadian entrepreneur Conrad Black therefore stepped in with a £20 million loan, on the condition that if Hartwell needed further cash, Black had the right to buy the company for a fixed formula based on the £20 million he had put in. In the event Hartwell did need more, so by 1985, when the West Ferry project was well under way, Black was the new owner of the *Telegraph*. He also tried to buy the *Express* from Lord Stevens, buying shares through nominees. Stevens could always trace these nominees back to Conrad, and later told me he never understood why Conrad did not just come straight out and make a bid. He would happily have sold the *Express*, he said.

Later the *Guardian* and the *FT* came to print in Docklands, too, after an IRA bomb devastated the area close to Canary Wharf. From that time on, West Ferry Printers could boast of being the largest print works in Europe. From my office window, I could look over at this vast works, and when in 1992 we moved to a larger building across the dock, I could even look down on it. Newspapers were, in effect, a dominant industry in the new development, and their presence brought me into contact with some of the big media players. Perhaps the proximity of the *Express* had an effect on me. Perhaps I said to myself, someday. . . But that day was still a while off.

In the meantime I met a guy called G Ware Travelstead who was a rather colourful entrepreneur at Credit Suisse. Around 1984 we showed him Canary Wharf, a small piece of land with a bomb crater where the TV puppet comedy *Spitting Image* was made, and as desolate a spot as any in the area. Accompanied by Reg we travelled in cavalcades of hired cars from the Dorchester, showed what we could of the site, and made page upon page of presentations. I was once again the Leading Publisher Who Had Put All His Money In. We convinced Travelstead that he should get involved in a scheme for two massive towers that would form the centrepiece for London's 'second city', as Reg called it. Ultimately, owing to the ups and downs of the property world it was not Travelstead who actually built the towers in the end: it was Olympia and York. Nevertheless we laid the foundations. I earned my £15,000 a year.

In due course our own building was complete, and we were able to move our staff in. We had already taken them round the area, and had even organised helicopter rides so that they could see exactly what we were doing, and how we were pioneering the future. A couple of my directors, Paul Ashford and Martin Ellice, had gone so far as to buy houses on the Isle of Dogs near our building; others were more nervous. This wasn't even the East End – this was still half wasteland and half building site. On moving day I was nervous too. I had lain awake the previous night wondering whether any of my staff were actually going to turn up. But in the event they all did except one.

Because we were the first company to have its own building in Docklands, we needed a grand opening. We were still having a hard time profit-wise, so there were limits to what I could afford. I did, however, have a PR man who had been hired at the insistence of Mr Kemble of Yamaha (still responsible for half our business). He was an elderly gentleman called Alan Tulloch who had once worked for British Lion at Elstree and who claimed to have had a hand in writing the song 'Nellie the Elephant'. I told him about our new building and he asked whether I would like Princess Anne to come and open it. I said that would do nicely, without really believing he would manage it. But he did.

Mr Broackes and the great and good could not believe this stroke of good fortune. They then all ended up having to gatecrash the event because it never occurred to me to invite them: I suppose I assumed they saw Princess Anne all the time.

On the great day, we had lunch and then gave the princess a tour of a building which, of course, housed some highly respected music magazines and hobby magazines – and also *Penthouse* and *Forum*. In order not to embarrass Her Royal Highness I gave strict instructions about what could and could not be on display, and told staff that they were not to admit working on anything that might cause blushes. Her Royal Highness, however, quickly worked out what was going on and proceeded to interrogate people in depth about precisely what it was they did. The person being interrogated would then give a very vague answer, saying, for example, that they were an editor.

'Editor of what?' she would ask.

They would say, 'Well, Your Royal Highness, just sort of this and that, you know, whatever I get asked to edit.'

It went on like this for about an hour. The press corps was present, and of course there was a lot of whispering. 'Does she know?' 'Has she been told?' The atmosphere was very tense. At the end the princess gave a speech in which she acknowledged we were the worldwide leader in publishing music magazines. 'And,' she added, 'in case members of the press think I was born yesterday, I DO know they publish other things. And the best of luck to them!'

The room dissolved into laughter and cheers. We were headline news the following day with 'I Wasn't Born Yesterday'. Reg Ward booked a special poster advertising campaign: '*Penthouse* has moved to Docklands'. I cannot remember if it had a crow on it.

The princess's visit established us as the pioneer in this brave new world set in the exciting waterscape of London's old docks. And the area started to boom, initially in keeping with Reg Ward's vision. It was he, for example, who insisted that the massive cranes that used to load cargo ships remain in place – they were a 'vertical component' to the skyline at a time when the tallest building was our three storeys. The development was served by a road surfaced distinctively and attractively in red brick (unfortunately, as traffic increased, the bricks started popping out here and there, so in the end the road had to be resurfaced). Then the Docklands Light Railway was completed – not without some drama: one of the first trains fell off the end of the elevated track due to an issue with the computerised braking system. But whatever teething problems there may have been, there's no doubt that without the DLR, and the Limehouse Link road tunnel, the location would have been a non-starter. And then finally the airport arrived: first just for turboprops, then 'whisper jets', then, when local residents had got used to the idea, larger passenger jets. We'd become an international business hub.

The warehouse where I first met Reg and his team became the Docklands Arena so I suppose you could say we were a leisure and entertainment hub, too, though this was two decades before the O2. A wise old promoter mate of mine called Jarvis Astaire prophesied, after the chesty coughs with which he prefaced every remark, that 'East will go West, but West will never go East' – and so it proved to be.

Yet we quite liked being East. I think it would be fair to say I brought some of my Northern & Shell sales culture to the LDDC, while we certainly embraced the culture of the new Enterprise Zone. Everything took off too quickly for the early pioneers to form much of a community, although I do recall forming the Society of Docklands Investors Over A Million Pounds whose main function seemed to be to consume drinks and Chinese meals at the Good

Friends restaurant with David Donoghue of Limehouse Studios. But there was definitely a character to the area: smart and business-like, but also risk-taking, maverick, driven. We were outsiders and a little contemptuous of Establishment competitors in Central London or King's Reach Tower. They in turn regarded us as unpredictable and probably threatening. We certainly hoped to be.

Our building was conceived as a showpiece and it definitely looked the part, especially when it stood alone before all the tower blocks were built around it. We spared no expense internally with the exception of the lift, which was in reality just a goods elevator; it was well finished but travelled very slowly. However, I saw that as an advantage because it made our building seem taller than it really was. We had space to work, the ability to expand and we could entertain advertisers and clients in an environment that left them in no doubt that we were a company going places. The heart of the building was a prestigious boardroom with a beautiful walnut conference table based on the design of the table at the United Nations building in New York, although on a slightly more modest scale.

It was during that era, the mid-1980s, that many of the routines and practices that came to define our company culture had their origin. We were in the communication business and I always saw internal, face-to-face communication as vitally important. Accordingly the group was effectively run from that boardroom table through regular meetings which I chaired, at which all levels of management were present, from editors to accountants to distribution executives to operational guys. (We sometimes had marketing people there too but I never found anyone any good at marketing.) The idea was that everyone would hear everything, and everyone would have a voice. Our meetings were long and detailed – ten or twelve hours was not unusual – so we evolved mechanisms which we retain even now to introduce a little humour and relieve the intensity. Rumours about a butler bringing me bananas on a silver plate originate from these meetings. It was not really silver and he was not a real butler, which is probably why when we had the munchies and sent him out for bagels he once returned, after a long delay, with Bibles. It is true, however, that we had the tradition of a bell being rung to celebrate the contribution of a particularly good idea, and, sadly, a hooter reserved for an unusually bad one. The decision as to which was which was at the chairman's discretion.

There was also a rule that if anyone made a remark that appeared to incorporate a line from a song or an album title (perhaps that we were reaching a turning point, or that we were tired of waiting), proceedings would be halted until someone successfully identified where the song came from, who had written it and probably, if I felt like really probing, the record label on which it had been released. And for those present at these meetings who are still puzzled, I should explain that *The Turning Point* was an album on Polydor, while 'Tired of Waiting' was a song on the Kinks second album *Kinda Kinks* released in 1965 on Pye.

Yet, as I have suggested, authoritative as we were in matters musical, our expertise was not going to make me my first million, and nor were *Penthouse* and the various small leisure magazines we controlled. The Enterprise Zone, however, had potential. I was never a property speculator, I was an owner-occupier, and the move to Docklands would have been logical to me even without any uplift on the value of the premises. But as time went on it became increasingly clear I had made a daring but very shrewd investment.

On the insistence of the LDDC we had followed the most exacting architectural and stylistic guidelines in erecting our building. So I was outraged when a couple of years later the owner of the neighbouring site was allowed to put up a large tin shack right next door to us. Hardly in keeping with the rules. I complained bitterly to Reg

Ward. What was sauce for the goose should be sauce for the gander. Reg was a little embarrassed by this relaxing of standards, but argued that I should not be too upset as I had doubled my money. My local Docklands lawyer Peter Johnson, who was smart, said that if I had doubled my money perhaps Mr Ward would care to guarantee that value by undertaking to buy it at the higher price if no one else would. Reg immediately agreed. Now I could continue at the site as a tenant but would be able to release some capital. I could pay for the house I had borrowed against and give back money loaned by the bank, and I would have £1 million extra cash to invest in my business. I'd be a millionaire.

The deal was done. Reg was a masterful user of space. He gave planning permission on our land to put another building up with 15,000 square feet, and the LDDC rented it – they needed more room anyway. Then he allowed a building in the water on stilts – rented to Price Waterhouse because it was indeed a waterhouse.

By now it was Christmas Eve 1987. I had my cheque and with Paul Ashford and the finance director, an American called Tom Flatt (who wore a fraternity ring), and John Kelly, we had Christmas lunch in our canteen and got drunk. Then we went back to my home and got even more drunk. I had an Irish wolfhound which was large and had a rather volatile temperament, and Tom Flatt began feeding it champagne. The dog bit Janet. I had to take her to Casualty, which is not the best place on Christmas Eve, while a very drunk Flatt insisted he would drive everyone else home in his Mini. I believe the others succeeded in relieving him of his keys, and after that they walked home because it was Christmas and there were no cabs.

The following morning I woke up and I looked at my cheque, and I looked at my, well, what *Forum* magazine used to call manhood. It wasn't any bigger. I didn't feel any different.

So that's how it is to make your first million.

7
SPECIALISTS IN EVERYTHING

N ow we were installed in Docklands we had the space and facilities to grow. We were determined to take on the 'corporate
monoliths', as we were fond of calling the likes of IPC at the time.
We wanted a single product that would shake up the magazine
business the same way Virgin had shaken up the airline business.
We had an enthusiastic team and a determination to succeed. We
even had the funds to acquire or launch a new magazine, although
admittedly still only at a very modest level.

We also had a formula that worked well for specialised titles, and
that we had developed since the early days of *International Musician*
and *Recording World*. Whatever passion a particular magazine
might cater for, its basic structure always remained the same. The
front of the magazine would consist of collaborative interviews and
features involving prominent figures in a particular field (who
would talk to you because they shared the passion themselves),
while the back end of the magazine would be a service section with
'how to' features and reviews. The reader and the magazine thus
became part of the industry they were devoted to.

If, for example, the magazine were *Bicycle* you would have Lance
Armstrong on the front cover (at one time there was no shame in
that) and at the back you would share tips on road racing and

review Campagnolo groupsets. If the magazine were *Venture UK*, serving the business market, top entrepreneurs would be interviewed at the front and you would run items on debt factoring and accounts systems in the back. If it was *Fitness* magazine Victoria Principal and Joan Collins (it was, after all, the 1980s) would tell you what they did to look good in the early pages, and you would review the exercise gear in the second half.

In the mid-1980s we had four music magazines in the UK and around a dozen editions abroad. We also had magazines on business, entertainment, technology, cars, cookery, exercise, diet and sport – and of course *Penthouse* and *Forum*. Unfortunately there seems to be a rule that if 30 million people ride bicycles or play an instrument in the UK, only a few tens of thousands will be sufficiently passionate about the subject to buy a magazine. There's also a rule that even if a particular magazine doesn't sell that many copies, it requires as much attention to detail as the largest. Consequently our small management team felt a little stretched. We found it hard to match the scale of the previously mentioned corporate monoliths. We knew we would be better off with fewer, larger titles. Our attempted solution, therefore, was continually to try to turn our small enthusiasts' magazines into major players.

Fitness, for example, was a stylish and authoritative title which we bought from Sylvester Stein for £30,000. If you wanted a toned body and a flat stomach, it was really the only way to go. As always I wanted to do it big. We had a decent team of journalists on the staff, some of whom have since become well-known names (such as Lisa Armstrong, now of the *Telegraph*). I believe we even sent the editor on a two-week SAS training course to learn some hints and tips for our readers. Unfortunately, she fell in love with the officer in charge, married him, and left the industry. An occupational hazard, I suppose.

Anyway, the challenge facing us with *Fitness* came home to me one month when I was leafing through a particularly attractive issue. It cost £1.50 and contained 96 pages. An issue of *Cosmopolitan,* by contrast, which cost £1, had 324 pages, and carried an additional 84-page exercise supplement called Zest. From a customer's perspective, there was no contest.

Of course, a celebrity endorser is always helpful. My idea for *Fitness* was to bring in Debbie Moore of Pineapple Dance Studios, who had just been named Business Woman of the Year. I cold-called her, and she agreed to come on board, and proved to be very charming, very helpful and very creative. With her we made our first foray into video: a joint production with Pineapple Dance Studios showing dance and exercise workouts. We used the flamboyant Mike Barnett from Limehouse Studios, who was very enthusiastic about everything and said he was a producer, although he may possibly have been the floor manager.

The deal we did with Pineapple was this. We would provide Mike, the studio facilities, and promotion via our magazine. Debbie would recruit suitable talent, choreograph the moves and endorse the regime. What could be simpler?

Well, it soon started to get complicated, not least because there was the issue – as there always is in a promotional partnership – as to whose product would get promoted most. The suggested compromise – which we all thought seemed fair enough – was that half the girls in the video would wear Pineapple tops, and half would wear *Fitness* tops. On the day, however, the girls all emerged wearing Pineapple tops. Since the clock was ticking, we agreed to do a sequence using those. However, we said that at the first break the girls would have to switch to the *Fitness* tops. The break duly arrived, and the girls went back into the changing room. When they emerged again, they were still wearing Pineapple tops. The stylist, who had been hired by Debbie, explained that the *Fitness* tops were not trendy enough to be filmed. There was a heated debate. This was followed by the revelation that the *Fitness* tops appeared to have gone missing. Here we were at a disadvantage, because while Debbie's team, being female, enjoyed unfettered access to the girls' changing room, Paul Ashford, who was representing my interests, could not really go in and check. Fortunately, we controlled the editing so we stuck big *Fitness* logos everywhere throughout the video. I'm not sure they improved the overall visual effect.

Owing to the amount of time that had to be wasted on the issue of the tops, the schedule did not allow us to deal with the other major problem this production faced, which was that Debbie's girls, although attractive, seemed entirely lacking in any sense of rhythm and were therefore incapable of synchronising their actions. This was particularly distressing to me as a drummer. One lady did a passable imitation of Corporal Jones in *Dad's Army*, consistently executing the movements about a second after everyone else. Mike Barnett ran up and down shouting that everything was sensational.

Our *Fitness* video with Pineapple is probably now a collector's item but at the time it did little to move us into the major league. *Fitness* stubbornly refused to be anything but a specialist title. It did at least warn me off serious television production for a few years, until I was ready.

So, in spite of efforts like these, in print we were still not a big player. But we were slowly becoming a bigger player. I'm not sure how we looked to the rest of the industry. I suspect we were probably either loved or hated, but not much in between. Nevertheless we were determined to punch above our weight in the news trade, and not just in terms of selling products. It was at this time that I became very closely involved with the Old Ben charity, also known these days as the NewstrAid Benevolent Fund. It was the key charity for the news trade, and publishers had traditionally played a major part in supporting it. We, too, had always been active participants, both for altruistic reasons and because Old Ben helped bring us closer to the major names in publishing – including, in those early days, a certain Mr Robert Maxwell.

During this period I was friendly with a bit-part actor called Davy Kaye, whom I had met through the Variety Club charity. Davy's day job was working as a sort of ambassador for casinos, getting celebrities to patronise them, which would in turn encourage the ordinary punters. This he did in return for small sums of money and big meals. He'd sit there smoking the cigars they had on the tables and putting half a dozen in his pocket. At my request, and probably in return for some money and a few cigars, he agreed to take on the additional role of rallying celebrities to Old Ben – and on the annual charity walk the two of us bumped into Sir Simon Hornby, the boss of WH Smith and then president of the charity. Sir Simon was truly posh, and a real character. He invited us as his personal guests to the Old Ben dog evening at Wembley. I have to confess, I felt I'd arrived: the boss of Smith's was giving recognition to the owner of a few little magazines.

To reciprocate, and at Davy's suggestion, I took the bold step of inviting Simon for dinner, and he said he'd be delighted. And that caused a certain panic on my part. I felt I was moving into a different league – a thirtysomething magazine owner about to entertain a sixtysomething pillar of society. I knew I needed to get it right. We had for a previous occasion bought proper silver: the real gear, Queen Anne plate, although that dinner fell through so it had never been used in anger. I also called my friend John Ratcliffe of the Variety Club and begged him to attend. 'You know how to handle yourself at the table!' Thankfully, he agreed.

Fortunately, the evening was a great success. Simon's wife Sheran, like Simon himself, was very posh (she came from the Cazalet family, top drawer, second cousin to the Queen) but was very friendly, and full of admiration for Janet's dessert: 'Oh Janet, you're so clever! I can't boil an egg. We always had chefs at home. . .'

(I seem to remember that Sheran said her original chef was Michel Roux, though I might be wrong about that.) She smoked and Janet smoked and Simon and I smoked cigars, and we all got on well. At the end of the evening Simon suggested I should take on the chairmanship of Old Ben, once Bob Maxwell (the current chairman) had finished his stint. It would put me in a line of succession that stretched back through Murdoch and Rothermere and other big publishing names right back to Charles Dickens and beyond. Davy then immediately pledged to help me raise record levels of donations. So did John.

I later discovered that Vere Rothermere objected to Hornby's proposal on the grounds that I was a very small publisher (if he had any other reservations in line with the *Mail*'s historic prejudices, it is not for me to say). I understand that the debate got quite heated. But Simon stuck to his guns, saying that if his judgement was not accepted he would resign as president. So Rothermere backed down. Then Hornby said that I'd 'better go round and see Bob', and I duly set off for Worship Street. Here everything was in a state of complete confusion. This apparently was par for the course. Maxwell, who was doing eight things at once, including being on the phone to three heads of state, said it was very nice to see me, and that yes, he was going to nominate me as his successor, and it would all be great.

So in time I became chairman of Old Ben and we went on to raise more money for the charity than had ever been achieved before – or since. I believe the total was £750,000. Originally, the intention was that this sum was to be used to build a new home for the elderly, but people later decided that it would be better spent on day care. Well, I did my best, and I suppose they acted as they felt proper. They still write to me every year, asking me to send £1,000.

The meeting at Worship Street was not actually my first encounter with Maxwell. I'd initially come across him some time earlier when he'd inadvertently taught me a valuable business lesson as I was looking to purchase a specialist title, *Cook's Weekly*, which was a weekly for, well, cooks. At the time it was owned by Maxwell's group, and had a warranted weekly circulation of 40,000. That number was the basis on which we made our offer. Unfortunately, once we'd done the deal, we discovered that the circulation was actually 20,000 – in a good week.

I decided to be diplomatic. I contacted Maxwell, told him I knew he was an honourable man, but then went on to say that his executives must have made a mistake. They had warranted that the magazine was selling 40,000 copies when the true figure was half of that.

'It's quite embarrassing for me,' I added. 'I don't know what to do now. I don't want to sue you because I am not litigious – and I know you're not either. But the fact is that the magazine is not worth what we paid for it – and it's going to make us a loss.'

Maxwell's response was to send his son Kevin round. 'Dad says here's a cheque for half what you paid,' he said. 'The other half is pay for a valuable lesson – don't trust anyone.'

I smiled and accepted. I probably had little alternative, and for me there was always something of the lovable rogue about Maxwell: in one-to-one dealings it was hard to get angry with him although everyone has a different story.

By the time Maxwell came to invest me with the Old Ben chain of office that Charles Dickens had once worn, things had moved on for him, and when we spoke after the ceremony my polite enquiry as to how he was getting on was met with a frown.

'I'm very worried, Desmond. Very worried. Let me tell you something. Never listen to these fucking bankers, because I've done a really stupid thing. I bought Macmillan publishing in America, and it's going to ruin me.'

'I'm very sorry to hear that, Mr Maxwell.'

'Yes, and what's worse I bought it in dollars and I didn't hedge, so the price I owe goes up every day. My investments are all going wrong, and I will probably go bankrupt.'

Now this was a man I had never spent more than a few minutes with, yet he was telling me these details – two years before he fell off his boat. I thought at least that was very honest so at the time I liked and respected it. I nevertheless believe he took on more than one man could possibly deal with and that was part of the reason for his downfall. I met him once more when he wanted to pitch for the printing of *Penthouse*. We had a three-course lunch, starting with smoked salmon and avocado, then steak, then dessert. Maxwell piled everything together on his plate and ate the whole three courses together in about 30 seconds.

'I want to print for you,' he said between mouthfuls.

'But your management is terrible. When I have a problem at three in the morning, who am I going to phone?'

'You call me, Desmond.'

We did not print with him. And I think his answer to me on that occasion summed up his problem. There was only ever really him – he never built up a proper team around him.

In the meantime we continued to diversify; we continued to try new titles. Remembering my old days with O'Mahoney and the Beatles magazines, we brought out a range of similar fan mags. Duran Duran sold well, Boris Becker didn't.

We also pioneered CD magazines. We had once published one of our music magazines, *Electronic Soundmaker*, with a cover-mounted cassette specially produced for the title – something that was unheard-of at the time. So by the time CDs came in I already knew at least one thing about publishing with cover-mounted sound products. You did not have to pay VAT on the package because they were nominally free, making it a good way of marketing collectable tracks in a pre-Spotify era. I may have allowed myself to be a little self-indulgent with the first of these magazines, *Rock CD* or *RCD* (the initials might sound familiar), since by a strange coincidence it featured all the tunes I liked best. But we quickly followed on with *Soul CD*, *Country CD*, *Classical CD*, *Pop CD* and a few others into the bargain.

We kept on trying. We were specialists in everything. By now my original music magazine *International Musician and Recording World* was being outflanked by smaller publishers who were breaking the sector down into even smaller specialities. We, of course, were the 'complete music magazine': we would interview musicians and review instruments across the spectrum of guitars, drums, keyboards, PA equipment and so forth. But that meant if someone else published a magazine just for drummers, they could print ten drum reviews to our couple. If you were a drummer, which would you buy? We responded. We did our keyboard and computer music titles and specials on studio gear and pro audio. My beloved *IM&RW* had to become *Guitar Magazine*. It was well received but somehow it was not the same.

Each specialist magazine we ran had to have an ad manager and an editor, and because the editors were often enthusiasts rather than journalists we would have to contribute guidance on presentation, magazine production values and marketing. To make life even more complicated, each title inevitably only served one particular industry, meaning that you had to go to all its trade exhibitions if you wanted to please the advertisers. It is hard to specialise in 50 areas, particularly when your sole expertise is music. The disadvantages of trying to build specialist knowledge across such a wide range of subjects was brought home to me on one occasion when I was at Royal Ascot and made the mistake of mentioning our magazine *Stamps*, about which I only knew that the contributors were boundlessly enthusiastic but rather old and that at least one of them had died when dropping his copy into the office. 'Ah, yes, philately,' came the response from the assembled throng. Not being very well informed on the subject, I thought this was a rude word and was about to become offended. Luckily Janet put me right.

By the mid-1980s we had around 100 people working for us. We were also troubleshooting the agency with its failing client base, and *Penthouse* with its eccentric licenser. And now another venture came our way. Through Old Ben I had met the boss of Hachette's Seymour Press, Hugh Begg, a very smart and proper man, and in the course of conversation one day he said, 'You must meet my son-in-law Adam Cole – he went to Harrow and he's very keen to talk to you. He owns Electric Blue.'

'What's Electric Blue?'

'Well, it's like *Penthouse* – but it's video.'

In fact what they did was produce X-certificate videos which sold alongside more conventional films in UK shops. I set up a meeting with Adam, to which I also invited Paul Ashford, and Mike Barnett of Limehouse Studios, who we still thought might know something about video. The meeting was scheduled for 2.30. We waited till ten past three, then we gave up. Finally at four o'clock our old Harrovian turned up. I greeted him with some highly uncomplimentary language, saying he had wasted hours of our time and had made me look an idiot.

Adam Cole was very polite. He said simply, 'You're right. I'm sorry, goodbye.'

I called Hugh to complain further but was told he wasn't available because he had had a death in the family, a grandson.

With a sense of dread I asked, 'That wouldn't be Adam Cole's son would it?'

It was.

My God, what had I done? I felt terrible – never again. Now if someone comes in late, I always ask if there was a personal problem.

At the next dinner I had with Hugh we spoke about the meeting. I said I was a complete bastard, that my behaviour was inexcusable, and that I felt really ashamed of myself. Hugh said I had no way of knowing, and that I should call Adam. But I just couldn't. A couple of months later Hugh told me Adam still wanted to speak to me, and another meeting was arranged. He came, and we spoke about everything and nothing. When he said he had to go, I offered to drive him home. I would have done anything. Eventually he agreed I could drive him to the bus stop at Mile End and on the way, seemingly as an afterthought, he told me that he and a fellow named Roger Cook, before they had got into videos, had produced all Paul Raymond's adult titles. He suggested they could produce magazines of the same type for us and we could print and sell advertising.

I said, 'Fine!'

Whatever he had suggested I would have said fine.

'You'd just have to pay us a fee and pay a royalty.'

'Fine. Of course.'

I thought about what to call the company. At that time we were exploring the idea of local radio for Docklands with a fellow called Cass Edwards whom I knew through the London Federation of Boys' Clubs. We even set up a company called Power Radio Ltd, although in the end we didn't go ahead with it. But that, at least, left us with a company name. Adam came in with his partner, Roger Cook. You have to imagine Del Boy if Del Boy had gone to Harrow (Adam), along with Rodney with funny hair and with his sweater tucked into his light blue jeans because he was so thin (Roger Cook). I showed them a contract, they looked at each other knowingly and then signed without hesitation. It was only some time later, when I knew them better, that I ventured to ask why they had taken everything on trust in this way.

'Because it was meant to be,' said Roger. 'Because of Tony Power.'

Roger and Adam, it turned out, had had a third partner named Tony Power, who burned to death in mysterious circumstances, which they were both convinced had something to do with Paul Raymond. This was the same Tony Power who had gone to bid for *Penthouse* when I had, but who had failed to show because he was drunk, or drugged. I had not made the connection because I had misheard his name as Powell. But when I said Power Radio they assumed they were signing to a company dedicated to their old mate – that it was Karma, something Roger strongly believed in. I suppose the initials PR may also have meant something, too.

Certainly, the real PR was unenthusiastic about our new enterprise.

The magazines went well. They were produced by Roger Cook at his home on the Isle of Wight. The first launch was *Electric Blue* magazine, named after their brand of videos, and like the videos that magazine was very 1980s, with elaborate sets on yachts and in luxury resorts. But Roger would visit us regularly and would come up with new ideas for further titles of a slightly less glitzy nature: the 'big breast market', the 'over forties market', the 'readers' wives market'. Oh, and of course, yes, *Asian Babes*.

'Same terms?'

'Same terms.'

A colourful stable of titles quickly assembled itself, unfortunately reinforcing the stereotype of us as adult publishers. These magazines, after all, offered rather more fun for the rest of the media to write about than *Stamps, Mountain Biker* and *Cook's Weekly*.

And we also had a problem, in the form of Paul Raymond. He was convinced that he himself owned Electric Blue.

Apparently when Roger and Adam had been working on Raymond's magazines they had suggested that he should produce videos, which they as employees would make for him. Raymond had told them it would never work, so instead it was agreed that they would set up on their own to make videos, but that they would give Raymond a third of the profits in return for advertisements in his magazines.

Soon Roger and Adam were doing very well, but that seemed to irritate Raymond, who now stopped advertising their wares in his magazines. By the time Roger and Adam came to do their deal with me, therefore, no advertising had run for many years. But that didn't stop Raymond suing everyone because he could not accept that he no longer had links with Adam and Roger. I called him to try to calm things down, but he just ranted, 'I own a third!'

Adam and Roger became very nervous. 'You don't know what he might do,' they kept repeating.

I called Raymond and told him that they were scared he would kill them. 'I might' was his response.

So the compromise I suggested was that Adam and Roger should pay him a reasonable amount to get him off their backs. I may also have mentioned that if the matter of the yearly brown envelopes of cash became public it would not help his situation with the tax man.

'A quarter of a million,' he demanded.

This seemed very unreasonable to me, but Roger and Adam immediately agreed to pay. For my part in the negotiations I got Raymond to agree that I should be sent a box of cigars and that the Variety Club charity should be given a Sunshine Coach, in his name. Neither ever appeared.

One way and another, our *Electric Blue* venture proved both colourful and low risk. From time to time, I'd go and visit Roger on the Isle of Wight, where we would be constantly interrupted by people delivering pieces of artwork. I now understand that most of these people were simultaneously employed by Paul Raymond but did freelance work for Roger.

And then one day we received a telephone call from Roger in the course of which he announced, 'I'm dying, I'm dying.' He requested that, since he was not long for this world, we pay up the quarter of a million pounds we were due to hand over to him in six months' time, and he also offered to sell us his royalty rights for £1. I pointed out that that would be a bad deal for him, but he insisted, and the deal was done. He also shared with us, whether we wanted to hear them or not, intimate details of his medical condition, along with a summary of the advice given to him by the various American health gurus he was at that time employing. As far as we could tell, it was all consistent with a very bad case of constipation.

In the end Roger didn't die, he went to Marbella. It was just a shame, given how creative he was, that we weren't able to find a platform for him later on when we took over Channel 5. His unorthodox ways of working made him disliked by 'professionals', and so the man who at 24 was UK CEO of Warner Brothers and a copious producer of Dr Who stories never quite found a new niche with us. He would always say that he was happy to listen to Paul or me but would not 'take shit' from people who had not proved themselves by succeeding as he had.

In June 1987 my father passed away. His later years had not been spent alone, as I had once feared they might be, because when he learned through a *Times* obituary that the husband of an old flame had died, he re-established contact with her (funny, because he normally read only the *Daily Express*). Eventually he and Felicity married. Since she had some money of her own, he was saved from spending his final years in the council flat in Edmonton to which his gambling addiction could so easily have reduced him. His funeral was held at the United Synagogue in Bushey. Dickie Pearl was present, as was my mother, who had visited Dad in hospital to say goodbye. But it was a quiet farewell to the once expansive CJD. We'd had our ups and downs, but he was my father; I had some good memories of him, and some of his advice has stayed with me throughout my business career. It was Dad, for example, who said that you can never go wrong by turning up in a good blue suit, and that when you leave someone after a meeting, it is good to be over-heard remarking what a terribly nice fellow he is.

Two years later, on 10 June 1989, my son Robert was born. Janet was 36 and had been worried that it might be too late, that there might be health problems. We had Darren, Janet's son and my stepson, and I hadn't been sure whether Janet wanted more children – or indeed whether I did. I was, after all, very busy. But when Robert was born it was a miracle – pure happiness, pure love.

He would, in due course, do everything that I could not do: get a scholarship to Highgate School and go on to take a BA Hons at Cambridge in Computer Science. The first in the family who'd gone to university, he would be star of the Cambridge 'fives' team and a stalwart of the Jewish Society there.

I was so excited when Robert was born that the first thing I did was to call a close friend in the Orthodox community, who worked at a north London synagogue. He'd always been kind to us in the past, arranging hospitality from another family when we had nowhere to go on a Passover evening and my brother was busy enjoying himself over at the cabinetmakers. I had always had good reason to feel grateful to him, and now I was eager to share my news.

'Fantastic news!' I said. 'I've got a son   fantastic!'

'Why are you telling me?'

'Well – I'm excited!'

'Well I don't recognise him. Janet never converted. Why should I recognise him?'

'Hang on. I've known you since I was 12. You've eaten at my home. We've done functions together.'

'Well it's one thing what I do in a house in private or at a function. I can't recognise him officially. I suppose you want me to help with the circumcision. I can't do it. Sorry.'

He seemed about to put the phone down. I was devastated. I asked, 'Could you at least tell me where to go?'

'Oh there's some lunatic fringe in Israel that would probably do something for him . . .'

This time he did put the phone down.

I was in tears. I could not believe it.

But my brother, on this occasion, was a real big brother. He consulted another synagogue which proved to be very different from my old one in two ways. First it was liberal. Second its rabbi was a woman (and a short woman at that) – Rabbi Alexandra Wright. She told my brother I should call her up, and I did. 'Well, look,' she said, 'are you going to bring Robert up to be Jewish?'

'Of course. He'll know about Christianity and everything, but I'll bring him up to be Jewish.'

She said, 'That's fine.'

She put us in touch with a mohel (a medic certified to do circumcisions) and told us to bring Robert in afterwards for a blessing at the synagogue. And now I found myself in an enlightened, friendly and welcoming atmosphere, one that I think is vital to the survival of Jewish faith and Jewish identity. As I said years later at Robert's bar mitzvah, without the liberal movement the Jewish community would have lost Robert, and therefore they would have lost me. If they didn't have me perhaps Jewish charities wouldn't have done so well. Without Robert – well, apart from his contribution to the Jewish cultural life at Cambridge he went on to become a world expert on the Holocaust and carried out a whole programme of fundraising and commemorative activities, including cycling all the way to Auschwitz.

I was able to help my Jewish Orthodox friend out more recently with a personal matter and I thought he might have changed his view on Robert, but he had not. I find it difficult to accept this, just as I can't respect Jonathan Sacks, the former Chief Rabbi, for failing to attend the funeral of the inspirational Jewish community leader and educator Hugo Gryn because it was not an Orthodox service. So in 1989 I became a Liberal Jew.

As a Liberal, I don't worry about any insistence that Jewish identity has to be passed down the mother's side. In the UK there are 100,000 Jewish families, so the chances are that people will marry out. What matters, then, is how they feel about being Jewish, not how orthodox they are. And actually, what really matters is what makes you tick. My second wife Joy is not very religious, while her father is Christian and keeps giving my daughter Angel books that don't have much to do with Judaism. But if they're not exactly 'right', they're not far wrong either.

Having said that, I actually discovered from Joy's brother that her maternal grandmother came from Italy, made challah bread, used to ornament her speech with the occasional 'Oi vey', and had to be concealed in a cellar during the 1940s when the Fascists were in charge. So, it is little wonder that Joy likes the warmth of the Jewish community and the friendships there. Every Friday night Joy makes her own challah bread, we light the candles, I say a couple of blessings and we thank God in English for everything we have. When Angel goes to the synagogue and runs up to the front to hold hands with her friend, the rabbi's daughter, I am as proud of that as of anything I have ever done with magazines or newspapers or Channel 5.

8
THE FULL MONTY

By 1987 we were no longer a small company; we were, as you might say, a medium-sized company. We employed around 100 people and had a turnover of around £30 million. We had a respectable range of titles, and a range of less respectable titles. I used to walk around – and sometimes I still do – saying, 'It's not the size of a man's budget that matters, it's the scope of his ambition.' The scope of my ambition could not be faulted. But if anything I've said so far helps describe how a tiny company can become a medium-sized company, there still remains the question of how a medium-sized company becomes a big company.

I suppose the answer is you can try one of three things: going public, doing private deals, or launching a product that goes to the top of the hit parade.

We tried all three.

The first time we discussed a public offering was as early as 1985 when I met Luke Johnson of Kleinwort Benson, who had seen what we were doing with our specialist magazines and *Penthouse* and said we should float and buy EMAP. We were not sure EMAP was for sale but the model he cited was the up-and-coming Blue Arrow buying Manpower.

That brought on another Maxwell moment. For a flotation, I

needed a proper finance director. Now my friend Paul Dobson of Studiomaster had a finance director called Reg Mogg, who had originally worked for Maxwell and had now returned to him. I thought: if this guy could work for Dobson who is colourful and Maxwell who is a lunatic, I'm halfway in between so he might be right for me. A conversation took place, arrangements were made, a salary and more importantly a car were settled upon – we bought a Jaguar XJS with the number plate RAM 246. Bearing in mind we were skint during this period, this was a big item.

Mogg was scheduled to join us the following week but just before he was due I received a call from Robert Maxwell saying, 'Desmond, I'm so sorry to disappoint you, I can't let him come.'

I replied that, powerful as Bob was, he didn't own people. But he insisted he could not let Mogg go, he was sorry and he would compensate me for getting Mogg to breach his contract with us, but no. What persuasion Maxwell used I don't know but Mogg confirmed he could not join us, but he still wanted the car and the number plate. I had Bob's son Kevin on the phone again, offering £40,000 compensation but in return we would have to give them the car and the number plate. The transaction meant we made a considerable financial gain, and we remained friends with Maxwell, which at the time was probably advisable. But the loss of Reg was a setback.

We continued nevertheless to pursue the idea of going public. The matter was extensively aired with BZW and County NatWest. We talked about whether adult titles would be an issue, and whether I had the proper range of skills to be at the head of a public company, and concluded that the adult material wasn't a problem because it was carried by the mainstream news trade, and if I didn't already have enough finesse for the City I could probably acquire it.

Meetings took place, consultants were hired, and accountants went into small smoke-filled rooms for long periods. To help our profile we did a rather expensive deal with Brian Basham, then at Broad Street Public Relations. The brief was that he would keep me, and us, out of the press for a year. With hindsight I have a feeling that fee was probably one of the easiest ones Broad Street ever picked up, since, as it turned out, the financial press had no particular interest in talking about us anyway. To that extent, Brian's efforts were a huge success. We worked out a calendar for the float and arrangements reached a quite advanced stage.

What finally prevented people being able to buy shares in Northern & Shell plc in 1987 was a thing called Black Monday. At the height of Thatcher's boom, everyone was an investor, everyone was a capitalist, everyone was going public if they could. In the months preceding October 1987 the markets rose 44 per cent. You might think that would trigger some warning signals, but as always, people get carried away. On Monday 19 October it all went pear-shaped. The FTSE fell 22 per cent in a day and went on falling. My flotation was put on hold. Which is where it still is.

So much, then, for a public offering. What about private deals? During the eighties we did look at various opportunities, including one to buy Pearl & Dean's old outdoor posters business from its current owner Clive Hollick, but my life-changing deal with Hollick was still many years away.

However, we did get somewhere with premium-rate telephone lines, the 1980s version of new media. This enterprise had its origins in an attempt we made to sort out the difficulties we were having in America with our music magazines. It has to be said, things were often difficult in America with our music magazines. We had therefore decided to send an ex-music industry salesman called Alan Marcuson, who had been with me a few years, out to the USA to see if he could find a buyer. Alan was a distinctive character, very short and nearly as wide as he was tall, who drove a

Jaguar XJ12 despite not being big enough to see through the windscreen, which meant he often hit the kerb; passing cyclists went near him at their peril.

After a few nights staying in New York's best hotels, Alan met up with an entrepreneur called Carl Ruderman. For some strange reason, though, instead of talking about music magazines he ended up telling Ruderman about *Penthouse*. And while chatting about *Penthouse*, he mentioned that we'd started offering a service whereby you could ring a number to hear messages from Sam Fox and other girls. Ruderman asked – how much did we charge? Well, we didn't, it was just a bit of promotion and publicity. In fact in Britain during 1986 charging for phone lines had only just begun to be technically possible. Ruderman explained that things worked rather differently in America, where you could create an entire business based on advertising service lines and charging for them.

Initially Marcuson on my behalf – showing what I considered rather extraordinary but uncalled-for initiative – signed a joint venture deal with Ruderman's company, which was very generous of him since we had no need for either their content or their know-how. Furthermore they were known for adult lines, which was not a profile that would be appreciated by BT for the new premium-rate services; we needed to partner with BT for our lines and our charging mechanism, so we had to show them that we were planning a broad base of mainstream services. Then things took an interesting turn. At the time we had a very posh marketing director called Jamie Cawley, who was ex-Cadbury's and wanted to be a Liberal MP (another hire for our advertising agency insisted upon by Yamaha's new contingent of posh young executives). Jamie gave such a high-flown presentation about how we would handle the business, filled with all the latest jargon and visual aids, that Ruderman lost his cool and told us we just didn't get it. Service phone lines, he said, were all about 'instant gratification', not about fancy marketing concepts. He tore up the contract.

This proved doubly fortunate for us. As I've said, I never thought that Ruderman had anything to offer us. And then it turned out that his best British friend at the time was Paul Raymond. For a fundamentally dislikable person Paul Raymond had a lot of friends. One way and another, we were now left free to make our own arrangements.

We contacted BT, were duly checked out, and paid £1 million for dedicated lines and the hardware we needed (at that time premium-rate providers were not allowed to pay standard line rentals like ordinary users but had to make a capital payment). We had, however, discovered how to lease assets courtesy of Michael Goddard of Baltic Leasing. The arrangement is equivalent to having a kind of mortgage on your assets, so it frees up money. We were not only able to sell and lease back the telephone hardware but also to do a complete asset register across our whole business and sell and lease back every asset we could find, from cars to production equipment to furniture. That deal and the sale of the Docklands building gave us some disposable cash. We did not have to buy left-hand drive Ford Escorts any more.

We thought, for a while, that premium phones might be the route to achieving real growth, and true to form produced lines on everything under the sun from the weather, diet, finance, horoscopes and news, to racing and Patrick Moore talking about the night sky. We only had one major competitor, which was EMAP. And because we had the advertising agency we could book ads in the *Mail*, the *Sun* and yes, the *Daily* and *Sunday Express* and the *Daily Star*, and we got excellent response rates from them. But the way things panned out is, I am afraid, a reflection on human nature. It turned out that far more people were interested in finding out what Maria Whittaker liked in terms of lingerie, than in hearing what Patrick Moore had to say about the Orion Nebula. Not only that, Patrick Moore's fee was a great deal higher than Maria's. So while the phone lines were a great business for us as far as they went, it wasn't far enough. They were colourful, responsive and cash generative. But they were not taking us in the direction we wanted to go.

The answer, I felt, was to do another deal. In due course, I met a fellow named Stephen Kirk who seemed to be doing very similar things to me in the telephone area, and suggested we put our two businesses together, with him heading up the technical side and us doing the production of the lines, the marketing and the publicity.

He thought it was a terrible idea, and then countered with a very generous and immediate offer to acquire our whole premium-rate group. I told him he didn't have the money, he said he did, and the matter was concluded quite rapidly. The day after the acquisition, he proceeded to transform what he had just bought into something completely unrecognisable, dropping all of the services we had built up. I have noticed more than once that people tend to do this when they buy a business, throwing away exactly the things they've just spent good money on, and I have never quite understood why. Our lines, in any case, ultimately went to News International.

But Stephen was pleased with his deal. Afterwards he reminded me he hadn't argued over a penny and suggested therefore that I ought to take him and his wife out to dinner anywhere they wanted.

'Done.'

'Anywhere?'

'Yes.'

'Well, we would like the Cipriani in Venice.'

'Done.'

My lawyer and my accountant were convinced we would never see Stephen again once we got the cheque, so why bother with a lunch in Italy, but I had promised so I went. It proved a wise move. Some years later I was negotiating a pivotal deal on the transponder that got me into the television business with a man called Bruce Steinberg of UK Gold. And the reason that deal got done, he told me, was that he was a friend of Stephen Kirk who told him the story of how I stuck to my word.

Now that we'd sold the phone business, and with our music industry clients and Yamaha in decline, our advertising agency, DeMonde, had become a shadow of its former self. And I have to confess I'd fallen out of love with it: it's quite difficult to stay enthusiastic about a company that is prey to the whims of a few very large outside clients and that builds other brands rather than its own. But there was one account I was still keen to get: JVC. I had wanted it from the early eighties, since my friend Kurt Lowy, the chairman, liked our pitch for the 'as easy as JVC' campaign which accentuated how simple it was to work their machines, but was overruled by the Japanese owners who hated it because they wanted to say everything was very sophisticated and hi-tech.

Now Kurt has always stayed in my mind as an example of the strange twists of fate that sometimes underpin business success. His background was a dramatic one. He and his father had left Prague in 1939 before the outbreak of war but the rest of the family had stayed because they thought they were Czechs. The Germans, though, didn't think they were Czechs. I don't know what the Czechs thought but at that time no one was asking the Czechs what they thought. At any rate, the rest of the family was wiped out by the Nazis.

On reaching London, Kurt, like every Jewish refugee, was handed 1s 6d at Russell Square by what was the forerunner of World Jewish Relief. He and his father got on a Tube train and, noticing that one of the stops was 'Arsenal', decided that was where they would live since they liked football. They even managed to get to some games, and Kurt said, 'One day I will drive to the Arsenal in my own Rolls-Royce.' A big idea for a young boy who started out with 1s 6d. But father and son went on to open a small electrical shop in Caledonian Road, it expanded, and when in due course the father died, Kurt took over. Shortly afterwards he received a visit from a Japanese salesman for a range of gadgets from the Far East manufactured by some company called JVC. He was offered UK distributorship but said he was not interested. Then, as he showed the guy the door, he asked as an afterthought, 'What does JVC stand for?'

'The Japanese Victor Corporation.'

'I'll take the deal.'

Kurt's dad had been called Victor. Kurt went on to become sole distributor of JVC and a director of Arsenal and drove his own Rolls-Royce to the ground. And – a bit late in the day, given that we were starting to dismantle the agency – offered me the advertising account. Because I liked Kurt and I love a challenge, I couldn't resist.

By now we'd dispensed with the services of most of our agency staff, so for the presentation we did to JVC we had to rely on our magazine people: fortunately, they were just as creative and just as scruffy as the agency types who preceded them so no one could tell the difference. We got the account and the renewed agency enjoyed a mini-boom. But my underlying reservations about the agency remained, so I looked for a buyer, and within the year the agency was sold.

That deal was the right thing to do, but the fundamental challenge remained: our core business still lacked a big league title. We launched and acquired more magazines. I believe this was the era of *Disco News, Zigzag, Venture UK*. Our acquisitions had become opportunistic but none really had star quality. *Penthouse* and related titles were making less and less. They were run in-house by a chap called Derek Botham, who used to walk around calling himself the Porn King of Britain. I am glad he wanted to be that because I definitely didn't.

In 1989 people started to become concerned about global warming (ironically first highlighted by *Playboy* magazine) and Margaret Thatcher made a speech at the United Nations saying we all need to become 'green'. In fact, Thatcher championed environmental issues much earlier and much more profoundly than any other national leader, perhaps because she trained as a chemist.

This new awareness of environmental issues and the impact they would inevitably have in time on the way everyone lived suggested that there needed to be a dramatic change in the way we all led our lives. Maybe this was an opportunity for an up-and-coming publishing company and for something public-spirited that would help change the world for the better. If we all needed to adopt a brand-new lifestyle, I felt, there ought to be a place for a brand-new lifestyle magazine.

We launched *Green* magazine in 1990. In her big speech on environmental issues Margaret Thatcher had argued that we needed 'unprecedented cooperation' to deal with the problems we faced. Our first experience of this was to get a call from Lord Someone-or-other of Greenpeace threatening to sue us because we claimed (quite accurately) to be using the same paper that they did. Our second experience was the Which? organisation waving the threat of litigation at us because we had a column called Green Which? So much for cooperation. Nevertheless I got to know people like the ecologist David Bellamy, whose son was to join us, and Jonathon Porritt of Friends of the Earth, with whom I shared a nice lunch eating environmentally friendly oysters in Wiltons. We still felt we were on the side of the good guys.

Now, given the massive upsurge of commitment to new values and a new-found determination to save the planet, you might have expected a new magazine about a green lifestyle to sell a few hundred thousand copies. And indeed when we commissioned the research group that EMAP used for their consumer titles, we were told that while the new magazine might not sell half a million it would definitely sell over 220,000.

When the magazine actually came out and circulation hovered stubbornly at 60,000 I may have expressed colourful opinions about the effectiveness of research, and perhaps even about Paul Ashford, who had suggested doing it. I may also have concluded that while it is very easy for both consumers and businesses to claim they have bought into a strong principle, it is much less easy to get them to put their principles into practice.

Still, we pioneered coverage of many issues that later became familiar in the more general media. We were praised by MPs and European commissioners, and supported by environmental leaders and even business bosses like Ian MacLaurin of Tesco, who was happy to tell us how much fuel his new lorries saved. For ordinary people, however, life went on much as before, except that they were now using unleaded petrol in their cars and more efficient (but less effective) light bulbs in their homes. So far as my company was concerned, we won a few accolades, but we still did not have a new *Cosmo* or a new *Good Housekeeping*. We pioneered coverage in many areas that were later adopted by the rest of the media, but perhaps we were too innovative. In due course some of our best writers on *Green* magazine ended up on *Loaded*. I do not know what that implies.

But my experience is that if you keep a goal in your mind, if you push at every door you come to and keep pushing until one opens, if you consume pages for breakfast, pages for lunch and pages for dinner, sooner or later you get close to what you want. And for us, the constant drive to create a breakthrough magazine came right with the publication of *For Women* magazine, in 1991.

For Women was an explosive and overnight success. It was our Top 10 hit. Without its news-stand success we could never have achieved everything that followed: *OK!* magazine, Express Newspapers and the Channel 5 deal. And the people I have to thank for it are – perhaps a little surprisingly – two Labour MPs, Dawn Primarolo and Clare Short.

What happened was that they objected to our top-shelf titles. Not so much to the images, which were regulated and not very shocking to anyone, but because they were sexist and made women into 'sex objects'. Not that anything else in the print, TV and entertainment media ever made women into sex objects ... Anyway, we were very hurt by the accusation that we were sexist, and felt we needed to respond positively to the 'off the shelf campaign' that had been launched. So we decided we would show how open-minded we were by having a magazine that made handsome young men into sex objects too.

In the era of the Chippendales, the formula we arrived at was perhaps an obvious one: a combination of the upbeat, bold editorial that the best women's magazines were already carrying, and pictures reminiscent of *The Full Monty*, which they weren't; and sprinkled into the mix, a celebrity component (we found that many A-list hunks were surprisingly amenable to being featured in the new magazine's pages). Just as the media world in 2012 was suddenly wowed by *Fifty Shades of Grey*, as if there had never been an erotic book for women before, so everyone was rapturous about *For Women* magazine. It was seen as groundbreaking and liberating.

We launched, cautiously, as a *Penthouse* 'special', called *Penthouse For Women*. This way we could put a new title into the trade without a long and complex 'selling in' process. And the initial *Penthouse* connection sent a certain message about the content to its target

One of my first public appearances. I always was a handsome fellow!

My first motor (I have since upgraded).

From left to right: brother Gerry, me, my mother Millie and my sister Janet.

Strolling on holiday with my very stylish mother.

My impersonation of Sir Winston Churchill at a Butlin's talent show (which I won), in Margate. I finally gave up cigars in 2015.

With my father, Cyril. When he lost his hearing after a business trip to Africa, I would often accompany him on his sales calls.

Visiting Tower Bridge in the early 1960s. My riverside offices in Lower Thames Street, London command a similar view.

The Manor House pub in North London where, aged just 13, I worked
as a cloakroom assistant and rubbed shoulders with the bands.

A player in the London music scene.

When I left school at 15 I had no
qualifications whatsoever.

HAPPY DAYS AHEAD FOR LOCAL GROUP

THE new local progressive group, Renia, is showing a lot of determination in its efforts to turn professional and make good.

This group of four lads only got together earlier this year but in this brief period they have had at least 60 bookings.

Les Greig, the lead guitarist, is from Friern Barnet; Rick Desmond, is the drummer and hails from Hornsey; and Southgate is represented by Peter and Malcolm Sutherland who play organ and bass guitar respectively.

All the group are the same age, 21, and although they have been playing in various other groups since the age of 14, they never had much recognition.

But happier days seem to be on the way. Since they came togther as Renia they have (apart from their 60 bookings) played with a top American group, the James Gang, and have toured alongside British groups such as the Groundhogs and Stray and Medicine Head.

At the moment the group is still semi-official with three of the crew working by day and Malcolm studying at the Northern Polytechnic. All four players have their fingers crossed however, as several record companies are said to be taking an interest in the group's music.

Renia have been booked to play at the Alan Pullinger Centre, Southgate High Street, on Friday, October 15th.

The four members of the Renia progressive group, from left to right: Les Greig, lead guitar; Rick Desmond, drums; and Peter and Malcolm Sutherland on organ and bass guitar.

With one of my bands, Renia (a 'progressive group', as a local paper described us), when I was 17.

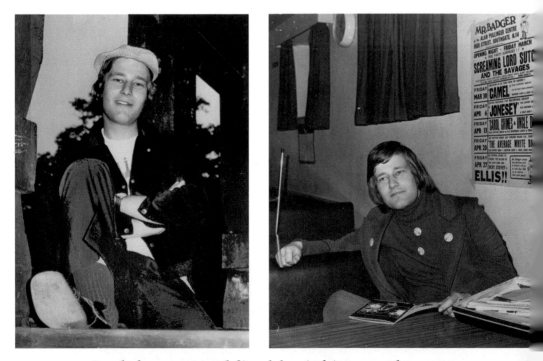

I worked as a musician (left) and then (right), in my early twenties, started booking bands like Thin Lizzy to play at the youth club, Mr Badger, in Southgate.

The founders of *International Musician and Recording World*: (from left to right) Ray Hammond, me and Malcolm Green.

A Rolls Royce with just the right numberplate outside the offices of Cover Publications Ltd (our company name at the time this was taken in 1976).

The first ever cover of *International Musician and Recording World*, from February 1975.

Prime Minister Edward Heath was an early supporter of my second music title, *Home Organist and Leisure Music*.

An early sales call. Drinking fizzy orange at 5.30 am in Sweden.

I may have given up drumming as a career, but I've never lost my love for it.

Visiting Ludwig Drums HQ in North Damen Avenue, Chicago, with Julius Graifman, 1977.

I first got involved with the Variety Club in the early 1980s.

Donating a Sunshine coach to charity. Model Sam Fox stands beneath some celebratory balloons.

With Bert Weedon, Frankie Vaughan, Joe Brown, Bernard Bresslaw, Stephen Lewis, David Kaye, Danny La Rue and Screaming Lord Sutch.

Princess Anne admires one of our more upmarket publications at the opening of Northern & Shell's first Docklands building in 1984.

With Barbara Windsor and my first wife Janet *c.* 1987, at an event to mark my appointment as chairman of the NewstrAid Benevolent Fund ...

... or Old Ben as it was popularly known.

My second, larger building, in Crossharbour, Docklands. We moved there in 1992 and launched *OK!* a year later.

My son Robert was born on 10 June 1989 ...

... and swiftly took to drumming.

readers, although it sold independently and was placed far away from the traditional men's 'top-shelf' titles.

Our first print run was 80,000 copies and they hit the news-stands on a Saturday. And they leapt off the shelves. I remember that we had taken our son Robert out for a Chinese meal that day, and on the way back called into a newsagent in Barnet to see how things were going. No only had the newsagent sold out, he chased us down the street to make us give him more stock. I phoned my distributors.

'It's a sell-out!'

'You must be very happy!'

'No – I'm furious. We didn't print enough! We need to get more out there, as soon as we can!'

There was a lot of telephoning that weekend. We reprinted 200,000 and those went, too – there was still a feeding frenzy to get hold of one. We printed a further 300,000. Those, too, were snapped up. At £2.95 each – a very acceptable price for a magazine of a hundred or so pages – we were, at last, in the money.

Just six months before we had been struggling over cash. So tight had things become that I had had to tell our PR man, Tony Brainsby, the late Rolls-Royce owning, chain-smoking, former PR guru of the Beatles and many others, that I couldn't afford his services any more. He had said if it was OK with me he would stay on without charge. It was he who handled the devastatingly successful PR for the *For Women* launch. Afterwards he came to me and asked, very nervously, whether perhaps he could now be paid for the work he did.

The reinstatement into paid employment carried with it a very substantial bonus in addition – we were motoring.

For Women, of course, wasn't all plain sailing. It faced, for example, the same regulatory constraints as the men's top-shelf magazines. I understood there was a protracted exchange between our editor Isabel Koprowski and those at John Menzies in Edinburgh whose job it was to vet photographs and whose world view was roughly that of the Scottish Presbyterian church. The particular issue that exercised them was that they felt one of the models, due to the dimensions of his private parts, must be in a state of excitement, which would contravene their guidelines. Isabel said they were wrong: this was the model's natural size, and indeed, so far as she could see, it was not unusually large. The point was debated forcefully. Authorities were referred to. To complicate matters, the argument came at a time when the editor of a national red-top newspaper that had carried out a national survey on precisely this topic had decided to knock a couple of inches off the final result to make more of his readers feel good about themselves. Compared with all these shenanigans our later experiences with the PCC were positively dull.

At the time we were being distributed by Seymour Press, with their offices above a garage in Norwood. But we were now the talk of the news trade and our business was suddenly very valuable. I took a table at a charity evening for Save the Family organised by my friend Ivor Arbiter at which Princess Diana was present, and had among my other guests Ron Wickers (the managing director of Seymour) and his wife, and also Andrew Cameron (MD of Express Newspapers, as it was then known) and his wife. Two nominees from our table were allowed to go up and spend time with Diana, and since Janet and I had already met her I gave our tickets to Ron and his wife. A disappointed Linda Cameron asked her husband why he hadn't been offered the tickets, and Cameron explained that Wickers was our distributor and therefore very important to us. Linda replied, in that case Andrew should distribute our magazines.

Andrew invited me to lunch at Ludgate House to discuss the matter. I explained I was very happy with Seymour, which was true.

'But we're the Express group – we can do a better job!'

'Well, I am very loyal but if you give me a £1 million non-re-coupable advance, plus you pay me in advance on the copies I print and I pay you on returns when it's all cut off in a few months – I might look at it.'

'Done.'

The idea was that they would fund our expansion by giving us cash flow so that we wouldn't have to talk to a bank if we wanted to do new launches. We had just wowed the industry with *For Women*, so obviously everything we did would be a success. For my part – this was the opportunity I had been waiting for – it would position me to do the big consumer title of my dreams. We would have a newspaper company helping us. If I could find the right title I might be able to launch by distributing sample copies with the *Sunday Express*, as *Elle* had been launched with the *Sunday Times*. Plus United had a tired magazine operation called Link House that could use a helping hand. We knew a lot about magazines. It would work for everyone.

A contract was drawn up. Millions of lawyers at Denton Hall went through it all for United, and we had Peter Johnson with his small practice in Docklands. Cameron invited me to lunch at the Savoy Grill and gave me a gold Cartier pen to sign the contract. He said that is how the Express treated their clients. We had recognition at last.

Simultaneously, I was negotiating new and much larger premises in Docklands overlooking West Ferry Printing. There would be room for plenty of new ventures and new titles. The Duke of Edinburgh agreed to open our building. We had space, funds, a positive reputation and a powerful ally.

What could possibly go wrong?

9
DOING OK

A visit to a print plant can be a boring affair, but there was one that changed my life.

My host on this occasion was a salesman called Patrick Walker from a printer called Watmoughs in the north of England. Because I was still planning new titles, I needed new facilities, so I'd gone to see him with my then production manager, Julie Squire. Patrick proceeded to show me that his set-up was the best in Europe, or it may have been the world.

Predictably, there was not much to be learned from looking at the presses. In my experience a printing press always looks like a printing press. Nevertheless we did the tour, had a bite to eat and Patrick talked about the various plants he had around Yorkshire, as well as a new one they were setting up in Madrid.

Leeds, Garforth, Batley – Madrid? It sounded like something you might see on a van in *Only Fools and Horses*. I asked, as you would, why Madrid.

'Well, to print *¡Hola!* of course.'

And that's when I learned all about *Hello!* and its parent company in Spain. I was struck by the contrast between the scale of the operation, with Spanish print runs sometimes approaching a million, and Walker's description of how it ran like a family smallholding, with the

85-year-old grandmother in charge and approving layouts on a kitchen table, her 60-year-old son handling administration, his 18-year-old son just joining the firm, and a host of other family members and pensioned-off Spanish aristocracy coming along for the ride. Even transport from the print works was handled by a brother-in-law: if he had a spare lorry they printed extra copies; if he didn't, they didn't. All very quaint and colourful and Spanish. Except that my host said that *Hello!*, their UK title, was suddenly doing very well over here.

'How well?'

'We're printing 800,000 to sell 600,000.'

'*What!?*'

The rise of the magazine had been very rapid and there was also no UK competitor. The style and use of images owed a little to the old English periodical *Picture Post*, but what set *Hello!* apart on the news-stand was its large format, which meant the magazine was very restricted in terms of who could print it. That, and, of course, the fact that it relied very heavily indeed on celebrities. Its skill lay in building relationships of trust with those it featured, in much the same way that our specialist magazines operated with our cover stars, the top names who worked with us on the basis of a shared passion so that rather than adopting the often antagonistic, probing methods of the British press, we went for a form of journalism that was collaborative – and informative. The one thing that gave away *Hello!*'s continental roots was its bias towards European aristocracy. A British publisher would have been more interested in local celebrities.

Hmmm.

A night or so later, I went to dinner with my neighbour Peter Woolf, who owned a fashion house called S R Gent; Peter's wife Susan had a range which supplied the retailer Episode. During the meal, Peter correctly observed that as a result of my new distribution arrangement I would have some cash available for fresh ventures and asked what I was doing next.

'Well, I'm thinking of starting a new magazine to go up against *Hello!*'.

'That sounds great,' said Susan at once. 'By the way, I'm about to leave Episode — we're starting our own chain called Susan Woolf.'

'So you'll need to advertise and have a catalogue?' I replied, thinking about my old music business days when this sort of deal was my bread and butter.

'Well, if you brought your magazine out in March, we could run 16 pages of advertising in it. If we did that, I suppose it would be quite cheap for you to print off those same pages separately to act as our catalogue?'

'What about £20,000?' I suggested. In 1992, that wasn't a bad price.

'We'll do it — but it has to be in March.'

This was in late November — and I had a strong suspicion that she didn't think I'd be able to launch in time. The next morning I called Paul Ashford and Martin Ellice in and shared the idea. I also explained that I had followed the usual Desmond practice, and got the advertising in first. I expected them to say, as often happened, that I was mad and that it would never work. Instead they looked thoughtful. What this possible venture had going for it, they agreed with me, was that it would not involve us having to go head-on with the big battalions of IPC, still the Goliath of UK women's magazine publishing. Moreover, we already had some expertise in the celebrity arena that would come in useful.

Martin thought that BPCC, the ex-Maxwell print plant, could print it gravure. As for a name, well, maybe *Hi* or something like that? Probably too downmarket? Then Paul said, 'I think we should call it *OK!*' — he had read somewhere that it was one of the most commonly recognised words in the world.

Miraculously it turned out that no one had registered OK for magazine use. We were on.

I went round to see Terry Mansfield of Natmags, Nicholas

Coleridge of Condé Nast and Christopher Ward of Redwood, thinking someone would do a deal to sell ads for us for 20 per cent commission. No takers. Meanwhile Paul looked for editors. We spoke to a number of highly placed and fragrant ladies who, it transpired, did not necessarily want to work for a company in Docklands known for publishing *Penthouse*. But these were the kind of problems we were used to.

What we hadn't counted upon was United getting nervous. At the time, we had only fairly recently signed our rather advantageous deal with them, whereby we were not required to reconcile our account immediately, but after five or six months when any magazines that had been put out but remained unsold had been returned and when we therefore knew precisely how many had actually been sold. Obviously, this arrangement helped our cash flow considerably, and United were clearly worried that a major new launch would stretch our credit with them even further. Then again, the initial idea had been that they would fund our expansion.

United's chief executive, Graham Wilson, came to visit me at our offices for lunch and said they were concerned about the terms they had signed with us.

'If Smith's or Menzies go broke we can't get our returns money.'

'If Smith's or Menzies go broke,' I pointed out, 'every publisher in Britain is ruined, especially Express Newspapers, because they distribute everything. But since they get paid by the retailers they can't go broke unless all the retailers simultaneously go broke as well. I wouldn't worry about it.'

But Wilson did worry. He could hardly eat his main course. Fortunately, my chef had made a big trifle for pudding, and he had three or four helpings. I also gave him a cigar. He seemed a bit happier after that.

Not long after that meeting, Lord Stevens invited me round to his house in Chelsea. I admired his shoes, which were very shiny.

'Do you realise you could bankrupt United?' he said. 'In your contract there is no limit to the number of copies you can put out.'

'It's not my intention to bankrupt anyone. Would you like to put a limit on it?'

'Yes please.'

What I did not appreciate was that if we changed our arrangement with United Distribution, that would void the clause which meant it was guaranteed by United Newspapers, so it would be without value. Fortunately, our Docklands lawyer Peter Johnson had worked this out and stipulated that a parent guarantee could only be valid if it had the same date as the original agreement; it could not have a later date.

So we made the alteration, but made sure it was done in a way that the guarantee would not cease to be binding. Then I invited Lord Stevens round to my house to celebrate. By now, I knew how to feed the great and the good. However, I was very aware that my knowledge of wine was a bit shaky. Fortunately, though, I happened to have a bottle that my friend Roger Cook had given me for Christmas, and I knew it would be good quality. Certainly, it would do for my guest. What I did not know was that it was worth £5,000 at 1992 prices. Actually, Roger didn't know anything about wine either because he didn't drink: he just used to go to a wine merchant in Chelsea and ask for the most expensive bottle they had. Stevens was in raptures, and took the bottle and the cork home with him as a souvenir.

We didn't talk about the new deal that evening. The next day, however, I was staggered to receive a letter of termination. The grounds for this were highly technical. Apparently, according to the terms of the contract, if one of the signatories received a court judgement against it, the entire agreement would be null and void. It turned out that United Newspapers had indeed had such a judgement against it. The judgement had been obtained by one of its own subsidiaries.

We contacted city solicitors SJ Berwin and called legal counsel and started proceedings. I also called Brian Basham, the PR guru who had helped BA against Branson, whom I had got to know when we were looking at ideas for a flotation a few years previously. Peter Johnson briefed him about use by United of 'a device and a sham'. Basham called the *Financial Times* and we made the front page, after which the share price of United Newspapers began to drop dramatically.

I was at SJ Berwin going through the legal implications of it all when the phone rang. It was Janet, who said she had received a call from Maritza, Lord Stevens's wife, saying it was very silly how we boys were fighting when really we liked each other so much, and why didn't I come round to see David tomorrow and work it all out over a nice box of cigars.

I agreed. The next day I took my team and Jonathan Metliss, my lawyer from Berwin's, to see Stevens. I let him know I was a bit hurt that he had come round and eaten at my house on the evening prior to dropping a bombshell that would clearly have the effect of destroying my business. After all, I was in the middle of launching *OK!*, my first major consumer magazine, already had a number of other titles, and suddenly we had no distribution.

'Look – it's ridiculous,' he said. 'I'm sorry. I apologise. My people are idiots. You've got us by the balls with this contract and we need to get out. I've worked out a way of sorting it out, though. We will buy your magazines. That way we'll pay you the 20 million that you owe us, and you can pay back the debt with that money.'

'But I don't owe you 20 million.'

'You have our 20 million of cash.'

'Only until the returns money comes through.'

'Look – we'll give you a cheque for 20 million for the magazines. You give us a cheque for 20 million now and when the 20 million returns money comes due, you don't have to repay it. So you end up 20 million ahead.'

'But that's not the way I operate. I didn't want to make a quick buck. I'm gearing up for new titles – I've just bought a new building.'

'How about if we take two floors in your new building and move our magazine operation Link House in there? You can still be involved with your magazines, and we will make you a consultant for Link House for, say, £15,000 a year.'

'Well – 15,000, it's not very meaningful, is it? I mean, you've already seen the wine I drink. That would hardly pay for more than a couple of bottles.'

'What would be meaningful?'

'Half a million a year.'

'Half a million over three years – and you wouldn't have to work for it.'

At this point Jonathan Metliss interrupted, saying he had terrible toothache and would have to leave the meeting. I was sorry about that because I was sure Stevens was about to offer something even better. Anyway, a new agreement now had to be prepared, and we started to work through the details – my small team pitched against United's huge army with its 20 top lawyers and accountants. Among the things we discussed were the adult magazines, which I rather wanted to dispose of; in the end United decided that they would not fit their business. Cases of white wine began to appear, which, since we left them untouched, helped to even up our debating fire power with United. We worked through the night. At six in the morning we reached what we thought was an agreement.

Then, the following day, we had another meeting. In the course of it, United's Graham Wilson announced that they had gone through all the figures again and discovered that our magazines were not worth £20 million; they were worth £11.5 million. That's when I lost it. I went berserk. I had to leave the room and take a walk over Blackfriars Bridge. My position was simple: 'F*** off. This is a point of honour. You've geared me up, broken the contract, you said twenty, and the price is twenty.'

My advisers all said I should take the £11.5m. I flatly refused, though I was eventually persuaded to return to the room. Stevens said that the best thing to do would be to let the accountants on each side try to work out why the disagreement as to value had come about. This was agreed. There was much studying of spreadsheets, and then my financial director, Barry Foxon, an enormous man who was nicknamed 'The Fridge', ambled over to Stevens and said in his Ray Winstone accent, 'Look, My Lord, you've double-counted the printing bills. That's what's put the profit down.'

So the deal was on again – provided it could be completed by midnight (the next day was Budget day and that, apparently, had some significance for United as a public company). Wilson continued to raise objections that I felt were not of primary importance. He pointed out, for example, that the figures for 'work in progress' in the paperwork we were examining kept changing. I explained that this was because work in progress means work that is, er, in progress, so it changes.

Then it got nit-picking: they said that the office equipment summary listed 48 desks and 48 chairs, but that they had only been able to count 47 chairs. The temptation to present them with the missing chair in a manner that would leave a lasting impression was strong, but I am pleased to say I resisted it.

So the deal was signed. In the end we were presumed to owe United £16.5 million on our current magazines, subject to any returns. (In point of fact, it ultimately turned out that that figure should have been around the £21 million, which was to our advantage.) We were to pay them this £16.5 million immediately, and in return they would pay us £16.5 million for the titles we were selling them. That presented me with a small problem: I did not have the full amount to hand in cash. However, I went to NatWest in Piccadilly and asked for a banker's draft for the difference between the money I had and the money I needed, on loan for 24 hours. It was not an everyday sum I was asking for; it was several million.

The manager was called. His view was this: 'If you have a customer, you either trust him, or you don't. If you trust him, he's going to give the money back tomorrow. If you don't trust him you shouldn't be doing business with him in the first place.' They wrote the draft, I paid United, and I returned the money the next day. I have remembered that business philosophy ever since.

Meanwhile, I had a major consumer magazine to launch.

The circumstances I found myself in weren't exactly the ones I would have wanted for my assault on the big-league women's publishers. I no longer had my raft of leisure titles. What I did have was a range of top-shelf ones which did not sell in significant numbers (the world-famous *Asian Babes* would notch up a circulation figure of 3,000 on a good month), and a new, four-fifths empty building (United did not follow through on their proposal to move Link House in). I was therefore left in the distressing position of having to be a spectator as the magazines I had launched, nurtured and loved were neglected under my very eyes, while the staff looked at me reproachfully as if there was something I could do. I rang Lord Stevens and told him I had to help – I was, after all, a consultant. His response was to tell me I was not needed and to pay me off the balance of my fee. It was the first time I had been fired since Sean O'Mahoney got rid of me.

I had given Paul Ashford, Martin Ellice and Barry Foxon, the great double-counting detective, 1 per cent of the proceeds of the settlement. Rather to my surprise Barry announced that now he was rich he would go and lie on a beach somewhere. I asked the other two if I had done something to irritate him, but they explained that Barry simply considered himself to have become a gentleman of leisure, and that my notion of being rich and other people's were not the same. I suppose the thought may have crossed our minds that perhaps we had made it, that perhaps we could now relax, whatever that meant. But I looked around us and I said I thought we had a choice – either rely on the few pounds the adult magazines still made, and stroll in to work in jeans and open-necked shirts when we felt like it, or stick to our plan and try to make something of the *OK!* project.

We all agreed we could make a go of it, so we rolled up our sleeves and got to work.

The early days of *OK!* were pretty unglitzy. There wasn't much in the way of going to parties and meeting celebrities. Instead there was a lot of setting up of invoicing and administration for the new magazine distribution company we needed now that United were no longer partners. We decided we could only afford to make *OK!* a monthly publication to begin with, even though our rivals *Hello!* were weekly. Then we got to work putting a team together. A very practical editor from *Woman's Realm* called Annie Wallace joined us – she did not always say the right thing to advertisers but she could pull material together and get it onto the page. She brought in a favourite freelancer called Richard Barber, ex-editor of *TV Times*, who was well aware of the fact that if you wrote something about Princess Di, readers would want to read it.

Still, we got the team in place, we negotiated the advertising, we began securing exclusives, we made the rounds of the stars, the agents and the publicists, we created dummy issues, we threw away dummy issues, we created more dummy issues, and finally we had a magazine, on schedule and (more or less) on budget. We took a deep breath and printed 400,000 copies of our first issue, featuring Princess Diana on the cover.

A week after the launch we were ecstatic: WH Smith gave us an estimated sales figure of 350,000 for that first issue. This was easy! We immediately made plans to go weekly, and began to commission material and arrange print deals. I felt immensely proud of what we had done and although I had a policy of not giving interviews –

because I didn't like the way journalists always brought the conversation round to *Penthouse* – I agreed with my PR Tony Brainsby that I would speak to Ruth Picardie (now, sadly, the late Ruth Picardie) of the *Independent*. The interview, it was decided, would appear on the Saturday of the week that Prince Philip visited *OK!* for the grand opening of our new building (of course, we had actually been there a little while). It would give the new magazine a nice bit of extra publicity – and me, well, I had arrived – so why not.

Paul Ashford sat in on the interview with me, and together we answered a good number of questions about the magazine, the market and the business. Ruth took notes, and then, when we thought she was about finished, she added casually, 'How is your dog?'

My dog was a large Irish wolfhound called Henry, who had been a gift from my music business friend Paul Dobson of Studiomaster. He was a bit temperamental and inbred – the wolfhound, that is, not Paul – but as far as I knew he was otherwise fine. I said as much.

'Oh. We heard he'd had his head cut off by the Mafia.'

'I see. You've been talking to a fellow named Philip Bailey, haven't you?'

'Well, actually, yes.'

What had happened went back a couple of years, and while not directly relevant to the growth of my publishing empire, it did create a story that would haunt me for a good while. Back in those days, I employed Philip Bailey to run our advertising agency and when it was sold I tried to find him other work in our publishing division. On one occasion he happened to be in New York (something to do with getting a licensee there for *Electric Blue*) when there was an incident.

I do not know, and probably now never will know, exactly what happened. But I do know that early in the week he was there I received a call saying he had lost his briefcase. I did not regard this as significant. If anything I was puzzled – I have personally never lost my briefcase but if I did I do not think I would feel the need to tell my boss. Then, on the following Saturday, I was about to go with my friend Ivor Arbiter to watch Hendon Football Club, which he owned, when I had a call from an ex-*Penthouse* circulation man called Irwin Billman.

'Bailey's been beaten up. He's been pistol-whipped, he's been cattle-prodded – they picked him up at his hotel and threw him out on the freeway . . .'

'Is he with you?'

'No – he called me.'

I called John Evans from *Penthouse*, who said it sounded odd but, OK, what did I want him to do? I repeated what Billman had told me. I said I thought Bailey was flying back that afternoon – in any event could John get to him and see that he was safe? John took things a step further and called Bob Guccione's security people, who were of the highest calibre, because Bob was constantly expecting to be shot. I think they took Bailey to Bob's house. According to John, Bailey was convinced he could see snipers on the top of buildings.

I said to John, 'You have to report this to the police.'

'He doesn't want to report it.'

'Well you have to.'

I managed to get hold of Bailey. He said he was in agony and that he'd taken a beating for me, and what was more 'they' were coming on the next plane to get me. I could not quite work out why anyone would want to do that, but then nothing about the situation made much sense. Nevertheless, I felt I had to tell Janet what was going on and she was understandably a bit worried. 'What if there's something in it?' she said.

Further cross-examination of Bailey revealed that he thought his trouble might have something to do with gangsters who were connected with an advertising agency we happened to have dealings with. I called Ivor Arbiter who said it sounded a bit far-fetched. He did, however, consult Robert Maxwell's old security man, an ex-chief superintendent of police, who pointed out that if gangsters were unhappy with you, it was unlikely that they would beat up a colleague in New York and then send a warning that they were on their way. If people like that wanted to come and get you, they came and got you. That was reassurance of a sort, I suppose.

Bailey duly arrived back in the country, very shaken. We let him and his wife stay in our house, where he peered through the curtains convinced that he could see gun barrels gleaming in the bushes on the Heath behind.

Janet, meanwhile, had somehow managed to acquire some heavies to keep an eye on us via a cab driver she often used, who was fond of telling her about his links with the Kray twins. The heavies were keen to give good value. My journey to work now involved convoys, decoy cars, and two or three diversions from the usual route.

Ultimately, nothing happened, but Bailey wanted out and we came to a financial settlement with him. A year or so later, I learned that he had formed a company with my ex-confidant and lawyer Peter Levinger, and Andrew Cameron, the ex-managing director of the Express group and our closest contact there, and that they'd gone off to Bob Guccione to pitch for the *Penthouse* licence. There was a legal spat, after which I gave no further thought to the matter – until Picardie raised it in my interview.

She seemed to accept what I could tell her, although she followed up her enquiry about my dog with one about my car (apparently it had been blown up) and a very bizarre one about my relationship with Maxwell (apparently I was his puppet and had secretly hidden him following his 'faked' suicide). I answered as best I could and she nodded her head in all the right places, and even went out of her way to be friendly to my old mum later in the week when they travelled together on the Docklands Light Railway to see Prince Philip open the Northern & Shell Tower. I just had to hope that she'd give me a fair write-up.

The opening was a huge success. Prince Philip was very genial, waving cordially to the four women who had turned up to protest because we published *Penthouse* and who remained unimpressed when we handed them copies of *For Women*. 'You dirty duke/you make us puke!' they kept chanting. But Prince Philip merely grinned. Once inside, he talked to me about beer and nice places to eat, and went round to see the magazines being put together, complete with pictures of him and his celebrated daughter-in-law. Like Princess Anne at our last grand opening ceremony, he was attentive, good-humoured and companionable, and also like Princess Anne, he made us headline news.

I told all my friends to go out and buy the *Independent* that Saturday. It was a mistake. The interview with me was faithfully reproduced as the first part of the article. But the second half, which appeared under the general heading of something like 'weird rumours', and which was therefore legally unassailable, read like a script for *The Sopranos*. I felt sick. I decided not to give further interviews after that.

And there was more bad news on the way. After a few months, when all the returns on that first issue of *OK!* had been taken into account, we discovered what the real figure for the sales of the first issue had been. It wasn't 350,000 as Smith's had estimated. It was 120,000. That might be a respectable figure for some magazines, but for a major consumer monthly we needed to be selling at least double that.

On the other hand, I reflected, had Smith's given us the true figure at the outset, we would have had to close the magazine within a week. As things stood – we were in. We had nowhere to go but onwards.

10
BEADLE'S
ABOUT

The launch of *OK!* may ultimately have proved to have been less sensational in commercial terms than I had originally hoped and thought. But there was no faulting the glitz that surrounded it. We staged a whole series of parties in venues that ranged from Drones in Kensington to Madame Tussaud's to the Orient Express. My good friends Joan Collins and Barbara Windsor were wonderfully supportive. At Madame Tussaud's we also had the benefit of the company of Princess Diana and Michael Jackson, as well as Marilyn Monroe and Elvis. None of them said much, but they posed for pictures with our other guests, which is the important thing.

The point of all this was, of course, to convince people that we were indeed the iconic title we would eventually become. In fact, in the months after the first issue, we were too busy to share the party mood. As our guests assembled for a good time we already knew the reality of the initial sales figures, so we knew we were in for a long slog. I remember being at the Orient Express event we arranged for our advertisers and watching gloomily as everyone swilled champagne and scooped up caviar paid for by money it had taken me half a lifetime to earn, and which – who knew? – I might be in the process of squandering. It was only Barbara who seemed to guess what I was thinking. She put her arm round me reassuringly and said, 'Richard, it's going to be all right.'

Even so, I was only occasionally dispirited. *OK!* was a challenge, but I knew it was the right sort of challenge for us. I ignored all those, including my own financial director, who said that it was an ego trip and that I should concentrate on my core business. And even as we ate through the first few million of the United settlement, and sat around the table each evening going through the numbers, I knew we had a business model that could work – something that was worth aiming for. I knew precisely what our target was: a sale of 250,000 copies and £160,000 of advertising revenue a month – that would represent, at last, the big time.

In the meantime, since we had been forced to set up our own distribution company, it struck me that it might be a good idea to have more products to distribute. So we got into computers with an early adopter, Richard Hease, and launched *Computer News Weekly* (or, as it turned out, weakly). Richard talked about databases all the time which is perhaps why I have never liked them since. We also started to lay the groundwork for *Attitude*, a gay lifestyle magazine that was to run groundbreaking interviews with everyone from Madonna to Kylie Minogue to Tony Blair (twice – during the time when he was a serving prime minister). It went on to win countless awards and set records in just about every department except, possibly, circulation.

We also got into TV.

It started, like so many things in my life, with a charity donation. The lawyer Brook Land had suggested that I might like to meet Gerald Ronson, and to support his charity CST (a self-help and educational organisation for the Jewish community). I had never previously met Gerald, who belonged to a slightly earlier generation, but to me he had always been Mr Big, despite his difficulty over the Guinness matter (where, as an outsider, I suspected, he was made the scapegoat). I went ahead with the meeting and made a £1,000 donation to Gerald's charity.

Shortly afterwards, a man named Stephen Kaye rang.

'Gerald's asked me to call you. He says if you play with us, you have to give a proper donation.'

'Well, I'm terribly sorry: I thought I had. I gave a thousand.'

'No. A proper donation is ten thousand.'

So I gave ten thousand. Gerald then took me out for lunch, and began our conversation by saying I was a fat git – or it might have been a skinny git. Whichever it was he said I should go to his gym and get myself in shape. This gym was located on the ground floor of his building, and it turned out that alongside Gerald and me would be Lord Wolfson, Lord Young, and a few other lords of various kinds, and that all of us would be taught to lift weights by a tough guy called Vincento to whom Gerald (who is in fact a softie) gave the job of personal trainer because Vincento had been nice to him when they had served time together in prison.

It was Gerald who first mentioned television to me. He'd come to see me in Docklands for some reason or other, had eaten a lot of nuts, followed by lunch, followed by cigars, and had then offered the following observation: 'You know, everyone says you're very clever, but I think you're an idiot.'

'Why's that?'

'You do all these adult magazines, but you've missed out big time on adult TV. Do you realise you could have had it?'

'How do you mean?'

'They came to see this guy who said he was your MD – they offered your company a 30 per cent share in the Adult Channel but you weren't interested.'

'Well, I never heard this mentioned.'

It appeared that 'they' – and by 'they' I think he meant a chap named Chris Yates who had launched the Adult Channel a couple of years earlier – were disappointed by the lack of interest expressed on my behalf and had gone instead to Stephen Kaye, who was not a media man but had a business based on bulk buying and selling, whom they approached perhaps because they thought he had the necessary ready cash. Kaye sold out a few years later and made a tidy profit.

I was annoyed and frustrated by this bit of news. A few million a year would compensate for adult magazines whose circulations were declining drastically. In particular, such a sum would take care of the problems that *Penthouse* was posing. By now, as I have already mentioned, this particular old warhorse had become a nightmare of litigation as Guccione got rid of his old retainers and began listening to a bunch of lawyers and accountants who had no feel for the licensing business and were being spun a line by our (and United's) ex-employees. A cash-generative business like the Adult Channel, I felt, would have underpinned *OK!* until it came good.

But then I thought that even if I had missed the opportunity to buy into adult television, I could still launch my own enterprise. We did some research. We even took a trip to some very dingy premises in north-west London to watch a yob spraying some uncomfortable-looking girls with a hose for what we understood to be the final of the all-England wet T-shirt competition. I came to the conclusion that, by comparison with this, even the production values of the *Fitness*/Pineapple Dance Studios exercise videos looked pretty sharp. Camerawork, studios, editing, I decided, wouldn't be a problem for us. It even turned out that the versatile John Kelly had aspirations to do moving pictures. Creating programmes, in other words, wasn't a challenge.

What was tricky was the technical side. To create a specialist channel right at the beginning of the cable and satellite TV era meant being available on satellite. To be on satellite you needed space on a transponder. And at the time the only people who appeared to have transponder space at their disposal were Murdoch's Sky, who also had a stranglehold on subscription and payment systems. Accordingly, we arranged a meeting with two very friendly people from Sky called David Chance and Sam Chisholm, respectively a smooth Oxbridge character and his gruff New Zealand boss who wore £1,000 shoes and looked like he could pick a fight in an empty room. They said they would get us space on a transponder. Sam even made a dramatic phone call in front of us, in the course of which, when he discovered that the uplink he wanted had been promised to an Asian channel, he yelled, 'Throw 'em off, then!'

But nothing happened. Nobody got thrown off. No transponder space ever appeared. The Sky route clearly wasn't going to deliver anything in a hurry.

Around this time I met Jeremy Beadle, who was then at the height of his fame with his TV shows 'Beadle's About' and 'You've Been Framed'. He was, you might say, the Simon Cowell of his day.

It wasn't even at a charity do! It was at Willoughby Hill School in Hampstead where Robert went and where Jeremy also sent his children. He came rushing up to me one day, saying, 'Hello, my name's Jeremy Beadle,' which, if you hadn't spent the last ten years on Mars, you probably didn't need to be told.

'You've got *OK!*, haven't you?' he said. 'I've never heard of Northern & Shell, but I'm really into publishing. I used to edit *Time Out* for Tony Elliott – his kids come here too. Look – I want to come over and see you. I want to spend a day at your offices – not just with you – I want to wander round and meet everyone and see everything.'

And he did – throwing out schemes and ideas left, right and centre and wowing my staff because he was, well, he was Simon Cowell. Then he said, 'Right. What are we going to do next?' (From the first, whenever he talked about my company it was always 'we', never 'you'.)

'Gerald thinks I should be in adult TV,' I said, and I told him about Stephen Kaye, the Adult Channel, and Sam Chisholm and his unsuccessful attempts to throw people off satellites.

'Then we'll arrange for you to come to my next charity do and

I'll make sure you sit at a table with the right people. They'll help you get into it.'

And so he did. But on the day, things didn't look too promising. I spoke to former LWT chief Greg Dyke, but he said he had sold his shares and now just went to art auctions. I talked to John Hegarty, the agency guy, but he couldn't help, and it turned out that Norman Walker, the boss of Hasbro, was not into TV. He did, however, want someone to do monthly magazines on Action Man and Sindy, so at least something came of this particular conversation.

At our table there was also an American woman in her fifties called Barbara Thomas who looked like an actress out of *Dynasty* – impeccably dressed and with very elaborate hair. But although my wife Janet spoke a little to her husband, I didn't get a chance to talk to her, and to be honest I thought she looked a bit forbidding. Afterwards, when Jeremy asked me how I had got on I told him about the blanks I had drawn, the good news about Action Man and Sindy, and the fact that I hadn't spoken to Barbara and suspected that, in any case, we wouldn't have got on.

Jeremy disagreed. He said he had helped her when she first came to England and I should definitely invite her round for dinner. I didn't do anything. But then, two weeks later, I happened to be at Claridges when a woman suddenly waved to me from the back of the restaurant and rushed over to my table, almost knocking me over with her handbag as she did so. It was Barbara. 'Jeremy said I should have spent time with you at the dinner,' she said. 'I'm so sorry – I hear you need some help.'

'Well I've got a little TV station, but I don't know where to start . . .'

She said she would come to my offices. I said I would send the Rolls for her: she was definitely that sort of person. So we got together and chatted for a while. Eventually she said, 'Well, I don't like people who swear and I don't like people who smoke and I certainly don't like adult stuff but I can't help liking you, so I am going to help.'

She named her fee. It was a lot, but as Mr Ashford said at the time, a very high annual fee is only high if you expect the arrangement to last a year, and if it does, it must be working, in which case the fee ceases to be a problem.

The first thing that Barbara worked on for us was the advertising side of *OK!*. Quite simply, we desperately needed more business coming our way, and Barbara became our headhunter. First she lined up the publisher of *Vogue* to talk to us, then the publisher of *Marie Claire*, and so on down the list she had drawn up. All agreed to come because she asked them to – and if some of them found it difficult to cope when they realised they would be meeting me, too, at least they still turned up.

Our final meeting was with the person from *Tatler*. All seemed to be going well, when, rather to my surprise, Barbara suddenly announced that she'd have to leave early because she had a previous engagement. And she did. I have to confess that my surprise was mixed with a degree of resentment: the negotiation about the fee was still fresh in my mind.

When I came in next morning, our receptionist said that Barbara Thomas had been trying to get hold of me. I rang her back, intending to give her a piece of my mind about abandoning me in the middle of a meeting. But she wasn't listening. 'I'm in Scotland for my board meeting,' she interrupted. 'It starts in a minute – so I've gotta be quick.'

'How can you be in Scotland? You left early last night for a dinner in London.'

'Look,' she said, ignoring me again. 'I know this guy called Bruce Steinberg. Call him up. Here's his number. He's got one of these transponders you were talking about. But whatever you do don't smoke and don't swear 'cos he won't like it.'

And that was how I heard about Mr Steinberg. He lived in Hampstead and liked playing blues harmonica. Barbara had met his wife Ashley Dartnell at some evening event or other and had explained in the course of conversation that she worked for a very difficult guy who wanted a transponder (Barbara, of course, did not know what a transponder was). Ashley had said: 'My husband might have one. He runs UK Gold. He's over there.'

I arranged a meeting the same day. Bruce, it turned out, did indeed have a transponder. In fact he was just about to sublet it to – the Adult Channel. But fortunately, as I mentioned earlier, we had a business contact in common. 'You're a friend of Stephen Kirk's, aren't you? He bought your phone business. You took him to Venice and you picked up the bill. I think I can work with you.'

The Adult Channel offer for the transponder space was £600,000 a year over 3.5 years. There are times when you know to negotiate and times when you know not to.

I said, 'Put a one in front.'

'Done.'

One point six million pounds of annual commitment later, we had broken through into adult TV. We were the Fantasy Channel. To fill it, the conventional route was to buy up films made by various American companies for the big hotel chains to play on their systems, but these were standard issue Bob Guccione-type productions and the companies very unreasonably demanded to be paid up front. Luckily Roger Cook, still on the Isle of Wight, had a lot of videos he could let us have access to as a result of producing *Electric Blue* for decades. We also had a British team who played everything for laughs and did end-of-pier Benny Hill-type stuff. We had just moved buildings, so that our old premises could house the production element, and I had the bizarre experience of seeing my beautiful panelled office of many years transformed into an editing suite. Barbara Thomas proved immensely helpful and in fact became a 10 per cent shareholder in the venture, but after one of the early viewings of the material she decided to renounce her shareholding. I believe what did it was an item about the adventures of Shagnasty and Muttley.

Of course, as with all our specialist products we were not averse to moving into the mainstream if the opportunity came up. *OK!* would in time become the home of celebrity exclusives. For its part, very early on the Fantasy Channel had its own celebrity exclusive. In 1995 the actor Hugh Grant picked up a prostitute in a white BMW convertible in Los Angeles, and what followed seems to have given him such enjoyment that his feet kept inadvertently kicking out and activating the brake pedal. The resultant flashing of the rear lights attracted local cops, and gave rise to a world-class celebrity scandal. My faithful LA lawyer Dennis Ardi picked up the girl involved, Divine Brown, after the court hearing and after a brief bidding war, she agreed to tell her story exclusively on the Fantasy Channel. Her performance was a bit tame because having become a big star she suddenly got very prudish and didn't want to say anything 'tacky' (to be honest she was not the most articulate person in the world and actually had difficulty saying anything at all). But it all helped us get on the map.

There was, in any case, a demand for the channel's brand of 'soft' adult material, regulated by Ofcom. Progress was, however, hampered because the gatekeepers were Sky and the only way they would allow people to subscribe was if they requested, filled in and posted back a document comparable in length and complexity to a tax return. Then Sky revealed why they had been so unhelpful over the transponder matter: they suddenly announced that they had gone into partnership with Hugh Hefner and were planning to launch a UK Playboy channel. So, as with magazines, we now had overproduced Americana versus the British 'girl-next-door' approach. I was beginning to believe it was my mission in life to prove, contrary to popular opinion, what hard work it is to make money out of adult material. Or out of anything else, for that matter.

. . .

Meanwhile, we had still not given up trying to replace the magazines we had lost with United with a new range that could take advantage of our distribution company. This led to the one time in my business career when I can say I was well and truly conned. True, the conman in question also managed to ruin himself in the process. But it wasn't much consolation.

I first met David Elias for breakfast in the Savoy. We had been introduced to one another by Brian Basham who had been so helpful to us over the United affair. He was a small, wiry fellow who had a kind of schoolboy air like the hero of the Jennings books – you had the feeling he was about to ask to borrow your pencil sharpener. I suppose that should have been a warning – as should his mention of the fact that his chairman was Ernest Saunders (though, to be fair, Saunders was known to be a clever marketing man). Elias explained that he had a fuel credit card operation which he bought from Gerald Ronson. Such cards were given out by companies for their drivers to pay for fuel rather than using cash and claiming it back; the companies would pay Elias, Elias would pay the garages. Elias was the first person of my acquaintance to talk freely about billions – which since it was only breakfast time I found a bit hard to stomach.

The essence of Elias's business proposal was this. His fuel cards, he explained, were taken by 12,000 garages and he had the option to settle his accounts with them either in cash or in goods which they could then sell. At that time garages wanted magazines because the news-trade wholesalers would not supply them. So why not, he suggested, produce a range of – say – twenty magazines covering the most popular topics and put, say, five of each on a special stand in each of the 12,000 retailers. When you did the sums it made a very sizeable business.

Now, I'm not naturally trusting. Years before I had encountered a well-known operator in the finance business, and had witnessed at first hand how easy it is to create a convincing false impression: he would fill an office with actors and its car park with expensive vehicles. So when I visited Elias's premises near Bath I looked in all the drawers of the desks to see if everything was for real. The one thing I didn't see was the agreement Elias had with the garages but this was not a concern because as our business was conceived as a 50–50 joint venture he stood to lose just as much as us if the agreement wasn't what he claimed. That logic was good so far as it went. But the lesson I was to learn was that you need not only to check whether people are deceitful, you also need to check whether they are idiots.

It turned out the agreement Elias had signed did not oblige garages to accept magazines. Never mind. We would sell them in. Elias then showed me a picture of an enormous yacht staffed more or less exclusively by girls in silk stockings. The implication, clearly, was that he owned it. There was a big show coming up, he explained, he could get to the retailers there and invite them down to the yacht to do deals. Maybe there would not be quite so many participants in the scheme, but there would still be a healthy number.

As it turned out, there was not. And by then we had started producing magazines. And filling warehouses with them. We used every contact, every source and every facility. We produced a record amount of titles in a record period of time. But there were no customers.

We lost money. Worse, we lost a year. Worse still, our reputation was on the line. I really do not like looking like an idiot. I called Basham, but Basham pointed out that he was a PR man, not an entrepreneur. I called Jacob Rothschild, who had been an investor in Elias's business to the tune of £20 million, but he was quite offhand with me. He said he was semi-retired and what he really cared about was the Royal Horticultural Society. He did not know what his people put money into.

We had no choice but to sue David Elias. We won the case, and bankrupted him, but there was little pleasure in it. He went to Singapore and it was later announced that he had died there. Given how untrustworthy he was, though, it's possible that this is not true either.

The garage magazine range ceased production, and we settled down to just *OK!*, *Attitude* magazine, our newly launched Liverpool and Arsenal magazines, *Action Man*, *Sindy*, *Power Rangers* and of course the adult titles, which at least could advertise the new TV channel. I knew, though, that the key to success still had to be *OK!*. It had to succeed.

Then I was thrown a challenge. It was a call from our picture editor, who had got word of a big exclusive in America. Pamela Anderson had had a new baby and if the price was right, a UK magazine could get the deal for world rights. With *OK!* it was always largely about the money, but never exclusively so. You had to pay your dues, you had to have established a reputation that was trusted, the celebrity had to know not just that you would pay them, but that you would use the very best photographers, stylists and writers so that their life event would be presented to the world exactly as they would wish themselves to be seen. This was especially so with the big American stars – and Pamela at that time was the biggest. In other words, you had to demonstrate that you considered yourself privileged to be allowed in. As a matter of fact, in due course I discovered that Pamela was great company: very down-to-earth, and extremely knowledgeable about drummers and drums, which I consider to be most important in a celebrity. But that was later.

Anyway, from a money point of view it was put up or shut up time: we had to find £250,000. Since magazines, whether in the UK or the USA, simply did not pay at that kind of level, everyone thought – not for the first time – that I was nuts to consider the deal. But my view was that this gamble could be our 'three-legged stool' (as Hartley Peavey from the music industry days would have said): it would give the magazine great content, it would attract the advertisers (especially the ones with baby stuff), and it would promote our product because of the coverage from the rest of the media. Of course, a quarter of a million quid was a quarter of a million quid. On the other hand, that was only money. Not for the first time, faced with the choice of the *Yachsen* or the *Gelt* (loosely translated from Yiddish, the status or the money), I opted to go for the *Yachsen*. The *Gelt*, I hoped, would follow.

That Pamela Anderson baby edition sold 65 per cent more than the previous edition. So now, at last, we had a formula that worked – we just needed enough life events with famous enough stars, and enough cash flow to fund the process. During the summer and autumn months of 1995 *OK!* graduated from being 'the poor man's *Hello!*' and became what it was supposed to be, and newsagents and advertisers started demanding it. We had an ABC of around 220,000 (ABC circulation figures are the news trade's accepted independent audit of copies sold), we had advertisers who liked us, we had celebrities who liked us. The title showed a profit for the first time. We had a semblance of stability, even though *Hello!* was still the dominant force: it is tough to be first for celebrity news if you come out once a month and the opposition comes out once a week.

On the minus side, we had eaten through nearly all of our seed money. Under such circumstances you would have to be mad to take another major business gamble. Like breaking with all known women's periodical publishing tradition and turning a monthly magazine into a weekly.

Wouldn't you?

11
DON'T STOP TILL YOU GET ENOUGH

I once had a finance director who said 'tut, tut, tut' a lot, and was very thin because he rode a bicycle 100 miles every day. He kept saying to me, 'Why do you want to do this *OK!* magazine weekly? Stick to the core business. You've got it to break-even now, as a monthly. That's enough.'

He was not the sort of person I liked to spend my spare time with, which was a shame in one way because if he had come along to the park with me and Robert on a Sunday afternoon he'd have understood my frustration. Everyone around us was happy and having fun, but I was thoroughly miserable. I felt like I was stuck on the roundabout while *Hello!* was on the swings. They were soaring up and up, selling 600,000 copies a week and making £8 million a year, while we were going round in circles as a monthly. How would we ever be 'first for celebrity news' (which was later to become our slogan), when we were always lagging weeks behind.

So I made the decision to go weekly – fuck it.

That really upset my finance director. In fact it upset everyone. I remember getting a note from John Morgan, who was the top tax guru at Price Waterhouse, urging me to stop and warning me that if I went ahead with my plan I'd go bankrupt. His attitude was that I'd made my £20 million so why was I risking it.

I tried to explain to them that it just had to be done.

So we became a weekly and we sold 80,000 copies of the first few issues. I told myself that was a success because as a monthly we'd sold 220,000 a month and this was 320,000 a month. But there was an attendant problem: we were now losing £200,000 a week on *OK!*, as opposed to breaking even as a monthly. Advertisers like Estée Lauder were supporting us, and we just about had Lancôme and L'Oréal too, but the prices they were paying weren't great. What's more, because we were buying exclusives, in some months the loss (or, with hindsight, the investment!) sometimes went well over the million mark. That was in addition to the £500,000 a month we were losing on the Fantasy Channel.

Yet still, in terms of turnover, we were an expanding business, and an ambitious one.

Around this time I met Ian Irvine, who used to be the boss of IPC and who suddenly had the thought that I could combine our energy and determination with some of their big but sluggish brands. Why shouldn't I buy IPC, he suggested? I knew they were making £30 million a year but I also knew that the company was being run with all the dynamism of a vicarage wine and cheese party. I was convinced that it could easily make twice that amount.

I took Ian out for various lunches and in the end he said, 'OK, you can buy it for £300 million.' I didn't quite have that so I got in touch with my friend the lawyer Brook Land, again, and the PR man Brian Basham – same old people – plus John Morgan of Price Waterhouse. The three of them said I needed to see a guy called Keith Harris, who could help me get financial backing for the IPC purchase. Not the Keith Harris with his hand up a duck called Orville, but the ex-HSBC banker who worked for a company called Apax. Along I therefore went to see Keith at Apax Ventures, in Portland Place. Just as I am always more impressed with the bloke who wears a suit, tie and smart, polished shoes than the one who slouches around in jeans, so I like an office set-up to look right too. Apax looked all wrong. There was a big gold plate on the door which seemed a bit showy to me and the owner, apparently, lived in West London and was 'fond of the arts'. Not my kind of operation at all.

Once I got inside, however, I realised that the bloke I wanted – Keith – worked up in the attic, squashed in with a load of other blokes. *That's* the sort of place where real work gets done.

He said, 'Right, we'll get you the money. How much have you got?'

'I've got about £10 million, and I'll throw the business in, too.' How casually we say these things when we're desperate.

The first potential investors Keith took me to see were the rock group U2. Keith was friendly with their manager, Paul McGuinness, but he made it very clear that while they weren't sure what they were looking for, they certainly weren't looking for us. Next Keith flew off to Korea, to try and find a backer there, but again without success. Then he went to a private equity company called Wasserstein Perella, and got me a meeting with a corporate American bloke with a cauliflower ear. I explained what we wanted to do, but I obviously did it with too much passion. The feedback from Brian Basham, who was trying to help, was that I was 'too angry'.

Then one Friday afternoon I got a call from a fellow called Julian Treger, who was an investment adviser. When I confirmed that I was trying to buy IPC he told me that he had someone who would like to back me: an entrepreneur who, it seemed, was currently 'in the hemisphere'.

The hemisphere – it was the first time I'd heard that word in business. I asked him who the person was and he said that it was 'the greatest figure in the media'.

'Rupert Murdoch?' I asked.

'No.'

I had no idea who he was talking about.

He asked me if I was interested in selling all my business, or half my business, and putting it into IPC, or would I buy IPC and work it out from there.

I hadn't really thought about it. Nor did I know whether, as he put it, I'd also be prepared to 'throw my building in too'. After all I'd only just bought it. It was an £18 million building that I'd picked up for £2.1 million from the receiver.

We finished the conversation and I was left none the wiser. But the following Monday at five o'clock he was back on the line to tell me that this mystery bloke 'in the hemisphere' would definitely like to meet me. He suggested Wednesday, which I thought was odd since he must have known it was Jewish New Year.

'OK,' he said, 'how about Thursday?'

Now I've only ever worked on the second day of the Jewish New Year once, and that was when I was doing *International Musician* in America with my manager there, Julius Graifman. On that occasion things turned out so disastrously we decided we'd been cursed. First, we caught a plane which, because you are not supposed to travel on a Jewish holiday, we both thought was going to get struck by lightning. Then, at our first meeting of the day, the guy from International Music Corporation showed us the number of responses he'd had as a result of advertising in *Guitar Player*, which was a gazillion, followed by the response level from our very own *International Musician* – which was about two – and almost threw us out of his office. The next meeting was a no-show. And when we turned up for our third meeting, the receiver was there.

Julius and I decided that, whatever happened, we'd never work over Jewish New Year again. I explained this to Treger, who I believe was Jewish too so he ought to have understood.

'Well that's a shame,' Treger said, 'because he will be gone on

Friday. If you can't make Wednesday or Thursday it'll have to be tomorrow — in Paris.'

Our mystery man, it appeared, had only moved hemispheres for a few days. It was now 6pm on a Monday and I could not call the people I'd usually ask for advice on such a matter (this was in the days before mobile phones). So I confirmed I'd meet Treger at 7.30 the next morning and fly out to France.

We reached the entrance of the Ritz in Paris to find a contingent of heavies standing on the steps. We were then taken to a vast suite where, even though it was a hot day, a fire was blazing. And there I saw a huge bloke in a light blue shirt sitting at a computer, something which in those days you didn't see top executives use, peering at stocks and shares. He looked a real thug. Two minders were perched on the couch; I took my place between them.

The man in the light blue shirt stood up: 'How do you do, Mr Desmond? My name's Kerry Packer.'

Kerry Packer . . . I searched back in my memory for what I knew about this bloke, that he was Rupert Murdoch's big rival for print and TV in Australia, that he had reacted to not having TV sports rights by putting together his own world-class cricket squad, that he was reputed to be, well, a little aggressive.

He told me that he was very impressed with what I'd been doing, and proceeded to take me through my entire life and history from *International Musician* to *Green* magazine, *Action Man*, *Sindy*, and the first and second buildings in Docklands. He even knew where I lived. In fact, he knew everything, every detail. I thought: this guy is really sinister. Then he informed me that my net assets were £10 million and that he wanted half, including my house. We would buy IPC together, he said, become partners and split everything down the middle. But I would have to ring him every night before I went home and every morning before I got up, so that he'd always know what was going on.

Just as I was beginning to think that 'sinister' was too kind a description for this fellow he confided the final part of his plan. Once we'd bought IPC he'd *ruin* me.

'I *definitely* have more money than you,' he said. 'I'll just keep upping the stakes until eventually you'll end up with *nothing* and *I'll spit you out!*'

Oh dear, I thought, this bloke is insane.

From the Manor House onwards, I'd met a few villains in my time, but they'd never really bothered me. This character, though, was in a dangerous league all of his own. He moved towards me. I was very aware of his minders on either side of me. He said, 'Now, Mr Desmond, let me make it very clear to you. I don't want you talking to your friend at Price Waterhouse. I don't want you talking to Rothschild's, your friend there. Next week you'll have the contract and you won't argue about it, you'll sign on the dotted line. And if any of this gets out . . .' he leaned further towards me and drew his finger across my neck for emphasis, '*I will slit your throat from ear to ear.*'

I believe I may have said, 'OK.'

'Now,' he added pleasantly, 'would you like some lunch?'

'Very nice of you, Mr Packer.'

He told me that he wouldn't be eating because he had to have injections. I discovered later that he'd clinically 'died' in a riding accident and was being kept alive by medication. It just added to his grim image as far as I was concerned.

I have never been more relieved to be safely seated on a plane home than I was after Packer finally let me go. Treger's only remark on the way back was that I had seemed a bit quiet. That was an understatement. I decided, there and then, that I would write Mr Packer a polite letter saying thank you for the kind offer but I'm not really interested. Frankly I considered myself lucky that I still had some fingers to write with.

For weeks afterwards, I had nightmares about Packer. Sean O'Mahoney, my old boss at *Beat Instrumental*, had liked painting everything a lurid lime green, which I had hated, and in my dreams I would turn up at the office to find it painted that hideous colour. I'd ask our receptionist who was responsible for this and she'd tell me that Mr Packer liked it lime green. I'd ring Packer to complain. 'What?' he'd sneer, 'you don't *like* the lime green? I'll slit your throat if you don't *like* the lime green . . .'

There's no doubt that owning IPC might well have solved a lot of problems for me. On the other hand, working with Packer was obviously way too high a price to pay. Yet, strangely enough, the whole Packer incident gave me enormous encouragement right at the time I needed it most. Here was the greatest man in world media (well, maybe the second greatest), endorsing everything I was doing just when others were expressing their doubts about *OK!* going weekly, and saying that he was determined to buy into it – even if he planned to chew me up and spit me out in the long run.

And I needed that encouragement. The cycling finance director had left, but when it came to his replacement, the song, as Led Zeppelin would say, remained the same. We'd eaten through the whole £20 million, he said, and *OK!* was still killing us. The staff were on the point of revolt. He insisted that the only things that made sense were the adult magazines and the Fantasy Channel. I didn't agree with that at all because the adult magazines were so small and their circulation was declining every month.

To make matters worse, NatWest, which had recently loaned us £500,000, started to get cold feet. They were not happy with the way things were going and insisted on sending Arthur Andersen in to do a special audit of the company – at a cost to *us* of £20,000.

We were told: if Andersen's don't like it, we're pulling the plug on your half-million.

Things were looking really bleak. I decided to call a staff meeting, at 8.30am, which was early for us in those days, at which I asked everyone if they wanted to continue with *OK!* Whatever decision they made, I said, I'd go along with.

I said, 'Look, this is the situation: we have severe financial problems. That's why you can't have your new computers, your new car, your pay rise. My choices are these. I can close down *OK!* now. I can do a partnership deal with an Australian I've just met, but let me just tell you what happened in the meeting . . . Or we can battle on. But if we do decide to keep *OK!* going, we must battle on because this piece of rubbish, *Hello!*, is selling all these copies and they're so *pompous* and so *condescending*, and the whole thing was started in the time of General Franco and his fascists! They are *everything* I hate so if we're going to carry on, we've got to win!'

It wasn't quite as good as the eve-of-battle address in *Henry V*, or Queen Elizabeth I's speech last time we had trouble with the Spaniards, but it worked just as well. Everyone, including the finance guy, agreed to carry on. I worked out some deferred-bonus schemes to help motivate the staff, and even issued a bond to staff at one point, but I knew that what everyone really needed was a bit of luck.

At 5 o'clock one afternoon, the phone rang. David Chance from Sky was on the line. 'Look,' he said, 'I've spoken to Sam Chisholm, he's spoken to Rupert, and although we don't think it'll work . . . we're prepared to give you the instant turn-on you requested for your adult subscription service on a trial basis for six months.'

Oh my word. Phone in, get turned on. No more weeks of waiting, no more long forms. Cash flow.

'But,' Chance continued, 'if we get grief we're turning you off, straight away. Oh, and if it works we may copy what you're doing . . .'

The fact that subscription to the channel was now easy and instant rather than tortuously difficult and involving up to a month of delay meant a massive upturn in that business, which translated into a million pounds of cash a month, with half a million going out. So I had £500,000 a month I could invest in *OK!*. We could really get going. I knew, also, what we needed to do. The Pamela Anderson exclusive had been the template. We needed to aim high, spend big, get major media attention that would promote the sales and attract the advertisers. A year or two earlier I had tried to explain to the then editor of *OK!* that whilst I didn't want to spend money on couriers and taxis and photocopiers I was quite happy to spend money on things that would sell more copies of the title. Spend it on the content had always been my mantra, and nothing had changed.

So when it was mentioned at a board meeting that Michael Jackson had just become a father, I only had one thought: *let's get it.* I called up Dennis Ardi, my lawyer in America. Dennis had long been involved in the music business, in particular at Casablanca records, the big disco label that owned Donna Summer. He had also had some dealings with Michael Jackson when Michael had bought Northern Songs, the Beatles' publishing company. Ardi was a very urbane and calm operator, who drove a black Ferrari (which he later crashed into a tree).

Jackson turned down our first offer of $1 million, so I decided to go for the knockout bid. I wired Dennis $2 million, told him to tell Jackson it was there and waiting, then give him a contract to sign.

Dennis Ardi called me back. 'You've done it. But he wants another one hundred grand.'

I dispatched the then deputy editor of *OK!*, Martin Townsend, who had had some dealings with Jackson's people in London, to Los Angeles to secure the exclusive. I was, shall we say, very focused around this time, so I told him, 'Don't bother coming back if you don't get it.'

The plan was that Jackson himself would arrange to have the photos taken and then hand them over to *OK!*, along with an exclusive interview that Jackson's team would conduct based on questions we submitted. Initially the pictures were going to be taken, and handed over, in Los Angeles, but then, 24 hours after he arrived in LA, a message came through from Jackson's office that it would all take place in New York.

We had a lot riding on this shoot, so the wait was nerve-racking. Townsend flew to New York and, once there, was told to await instructions. Initially we were told that the photographs would be deposited in a safe deposit box at the UN building, and we'd be called to come and pick them up. The whole episode was becoming like the plot from Alfred Hitchcock's movie, *North by Northwest*, which involved the same building and just as much dashing around for Cary Grant.

To add to the tension, we were also up against a deadline. If we didn't have the pictures in London within 48 hours we'd have to wait for another issue, which would play havoc with advertising and printing. What's more, if we ended up leaving it another week, the news of the baby's arrival might grow stale or a paparazzo might manage to get a photo ahead of us. I told Townsend to stay up all night, if necessary, because the Jackson people – who were all calm, soft-spoken women, and who seemed to work 24 hours a day themselves – might call at any time.

Eventually, two days into the trip, one of the women from Jackson's team called Townsend just before midnight and told him that the photographs would be delivered to his room at 4am. Taking a chance that the delivery would take place, we booked him on the first flight out of New York on Concorde at a cost of $3,000. He could be back in London with the pictures in three hours.

At 4am precisely, Townsend heard footsteps coming down the corridor outside his room. When he opened the door a towering black gentleman, 6ft 6in plus, stood there. He was dressed entirely in black, a beautifully cut suit and long coat. He did not introduce himself.

'Have you got any proof of your ID?' he said.

Townsend showed him his passport. The man then produced, from behind his back, a large, flat Kodak box. 'Check the pictures, call whoever you like,' he said. 'If you like them, we have a deal.'

Townsend called me at home, and went through the images one by one.

'Are *you* happy with them?' I asked.

'Yes,' he said, 'they're fantastic.'

'Then tell the guy we have a deal.'

The tall gentleman nodded. 'What time is your flight in the morning?' he asked.

Townsend told him.

'Well, there will be a limousine waiting for you outside the hotel. It will take you to the airport where the final picture will be handed over.'

'Where do I go, at the airport, to get this picture?' Townsend asked.

'You don't go anywhere. We will find you,' said the man. He shook Townsend's hand and stalked back up the corridor.

The gentleman was as good as his word. Next morning, at the airport, as Townsend stepped out of the back of the limousine and walked up to the entrance of the departures building, a small, elderly gentleman appeared to his right. He didn't ask Townsend his name, nor did he ask for ID, he simply handed him a single, 35mm transparency. All the rest of the pictures had been in large, print format – hence the Kodak box – but this little slide in an old-school cardboard frame, like your dad used to load into a projector, was the key shot. It showed Jackson, the baby and the mother of the child, Debbie Rowe, together. It was the only photograph where all three were in the shot – and would eventually become our cover picture.

When Townsend and the photographs arrived back at the office in Docklands, it became clear that we had enough shots to get two issues of the magazine out of our exclusive. Even so, it would be the most expensive feature we had secured up to that date, and I was really nervous about sales. Was Michael Jackson as popular as he had been back in the late 1980s when his *Thriller* album sold 40 million copies around the world? Or would readers find the concept of a newborn baby suddenly turning up in his arms, not to mention a 'wife' they had barely heard of, just too weird.

I decided to take a gamble. The usual procedure with exclusive stories on *OK!* was to guard our exclusivity jealously, even to the extent of sending out 'hands off' legal letters to the newspapers, warning them not to try to steal our stories. But on this occasion I decided to give the front cover of the Michael Jackson issue to the *Sun*, on the strict understanding that if they wanted to show Michael Jackson's new baby they had to use the whole front cover, including our *OK!* logo. I knew we might lose some sales doing this – after all, some people would be satisfied just seeing the one picture – but I balanced this against the fact that it was a free advert for the issue, and that it would alert the world that *OK!* had arrived and was dealing in massive exclusive stories.

I was also keen to fulfil a little ambition of mine: I had always wanted to get *OK!* on ITV's *News at Ten*. To try and ensure this, we arranged a 'launch' for the issue in Piccadilly Circus in London with copies of the magazine being delivered (naturally, by armoured car) to a news-stand on the corner opposite the statue of Eros. I figured that there was not a more public place in the whole of London, and duly invited all the biggest news operators, including *News at Ten*, to cover the great event.

It all worked like magic. We got our TV news slot, and within hours of the magazine reaching the newsagents on 4 April 1997 it became clear that we had more than doubled the usual *OK!* sale.

For the first time since *OK!* had become a weekly publication, I really felt we had arrived.

But how could we capitalise on our success?

The answer came, just days after the second Jackson issue appeared, when Sylvester Stallone's representatives contacted the *OK!* editorial office. They had liked the way we had handled the Michael Jackson story: would we be interested in exclusive rights to cover Stallone's forthcoming wedding to model and actress Jennifer Flavin at Blenheim Palace.

This ticked all the boxes for us: a huge Hollywood star tying the knot with a slightly less well-known, but very beautiful fiancée. And all at Churchill's old home in Britain! We were off again, with another potentially big-selling issue.

The Stallone wedding, being on British soil, presented a new problem to us: how could we prevent other publications, including *Hello!* but also aggressive news-gatherers like the *Sun* and the *Daily Mirror*, from trying to 'gatecrash' our exclusive by taking pictures of Mr and Mrs Rocky on the day? Our usual legal letters wouldn't be enough.

I therefore had to do some serious thinking about security. Most stars had their own security people, to keep away photographers and unwanted fan attention, on a day-to-day basis, but they were not necessarily going to be savvy enough to keep determined British paparazzi from their prey. Often these people would hide out in bushes or attempt to sneak into the wedding itself as guests. I decided that we must have our own security man, with a team trained to protect our interests, and so we contacted a chap called Kevin O'Brien who had a reputation in celebrity circles as efficient and discreet. On the face of it, Kevin did not look like what most people would think of as a 'bouncer'. Soft-spoken, scrupulously polite and with a kindly face and snowy white hair, he looked more like your favourite uncle. But underneath that affable exterior, unlikely to frighten or give offence to any celebrity or their friends or wedding guests, he was a hard-as-nails, no-nonsense ex-soldier. He quickly put together a team of security men very much in his image: tough when they needed to be but unthreatening enough to speak to a celebrity's maiden aunt at a wedding without giving her a heart seizure.

To try to placate the daily newspapers, I decided that, rather as with the Michael Jackson exclusive, we would release one picture to all news outlets. Not a 'crown jewel' picture – like one of the bride in her wedding dress – but a picture taken on the day. It might just keep some publications from making life difficult for Kevin and his team.

As it turned out, the Stallone nuptials proved to be another triumph for us, selling 300,000 copies yet again. We had established the first, simple formula for *OK!*. Success equalled weddings and babies.

In 1997 there was also one person who could sell magazines whatever she chose to do: Princess Diana.

Hello! magazine, being much longer established than us, claimed to have 'owned' the Princess of Wales for years. She had featured on the cover of more editions of *Hello!* than any other 'star'. Although, as a member of the royal family, she was not allowed to make money from exclusive stories, *Hello!* had worked with various charities and organisations with which she was associated to secure an enviable number of exclusives or near-exclusives with the world's most famous woman. But, during the early part of 1997, rumours began to circulate that Diana and *Hello!* might have had a bit of a falling-out. The details of the row were obscure but it seemed to involve a shoot with a ballet company.

One day our editorial office received a call from a Mr James

Campbell, who told us that while not claiming directly to 'represent' the princess, he was in a position to broker some exclusives involving Diana and various charities. He would not confirm that the princess had turned her back on *Hello!* but said she was 'keen to explore some different outlets' in which to publicise some of her charity events. I was delighted with this because I have always, throughout my career, supported a whole range of charities and would much rather buy the sort of celebrity exclusives from which the poor, disadvantaged or disabled would benefit than simply hand an already well-paid star a big cheque.

Campbell operated from a small but very smart office in Villiers Street, near the Embankment in London. A small, impeccably dressed man who gave off a military air, he was exactly the sort of bloke, I thought, who would appeal to Diana: debonair, discreet but commercially-minded. Our arrangement with him was very simple: we paid a sum of money to a charity that Diana supported and he arranged some degree of exclusive access to the princess. Not an interview, nor a complete photo shoot, but sufficient pictures and direct quotes from her to give us a cover story that would sell. Coming in the wake of our success with Jackson and Stallone this seemed like the final piece of the jigsaw: a real working relationship with the most glamorous member of the royal family.

The first exclusive story we published, under this new arrangement, was an auction of the princess's dresses. Word came back to us from James Campbell that Diana was delighted with the way that we had covered the event. She would now like to invite us, he said, to send a writer and photographer to a charity lunch she was giving to raise money for an orphanage in the Caribbean. From being the outsiders, looking for crumbs while *Hello!* gobbled up all the best Diana stories, we were now, literally, at the top table.

And then, of course, tragedy struck. At 6am on Sunday 31 August 1997, I was woken at home in Hampstead by a phone call from

Sharon Ring, the then editor of *OK!*. 'Richard, Princess Diana has been in a car crash with Dodi Al Fayed. He has been killed and she's in a really bad way.'

I couldn't quite believe what I was hearing. I turned on Sky TV. Within minutes it was clear that the crash, which had taken place in the Pont de l'Alma tunnel in Paris, had claimed the princess's life too.

I quickly assembled all of our editorial team at our offices in Docklands and I called Martin Ellice, my managing director in charge of production: 'Martin, we are going to need a lot of paper.' The rush was on to be the first colour magazine on the news-stand with the news and tributes, and I was determined that magazine would be *OK!*.

We worked all day Sunday, through the night and well into Monday morning to produce both the regular issue of *OK!* with news of the death and all the latest pictures, plus a 100-page special issue, 'perfect-bound' (that is, with a proper, book-style spine), covering Diana's life and times. As I had expected, there was already enormous pressure from publications all over the world to grab enough paper supplies to feed the frenzy to produce tribute magazines and souvenirs. Even by the early hours of Monday we weren't sure if we would be able to get enough stock but Martin Ellice rang everyone he knew and we got there. The first Diana issue of *OK!* appeared in the week of 5 September 1997, alongside the 100-page tribute magazine. We managed to get the first 60,000 copies of the magazine out before anyone else could publish and they sold out in about two seconds. Diana's funeral, to be held at Westminster Abbey on Saturday 6 September, would give us a cover for the next issue of the main edition of *OK!*. In the meantime I decided to keep on producing further 'tribute' issues, each with updated words and pictures as more details of the crash emerged and crowds descended on Kensington Palace, Diana's home, to lay flowers and messages of sympathy at the gates. The cover of each one was given a different colour: the first tribute issue had a black cover, then there was a white one and finally purple. In total we sold about a million copies of these.

I was proud of what we achieved with these magazines, and still think they were the finest tributes to Diana that appeared. They also proved to me that we really did understand the media: when there was a hot story we knew we had to go, go, go. When it came to the crunch, we could outdo daily newspapers on their own ground.

And in the next few years there would be a lot of hot exclusives, including, perhaps, the hottest one of all.

12
WHAT I REALLY, REALLY WANT!'

In January 1998, a spread of pictures in the *Sun* announced the engagement of Manchester United footballer David Beckham to 'Posh Spice' Victoria Adams. Now, at the time, the Spice Girls were no longer quite at the height of their fame, and David Beckham was a respected footballer but not a household name. (In fact, he was to blot his copybook a few months later when he gratuitously kicked an opposing player at a World Cup game and so – in some people's eyes anyway – lost the match for England.) But despite all this I thought the couple had the potential to be media stars. There was a vacuum at the top of the world of celebrities now there was no longer Diana with her irresistible style and her dangerous liaisons. To me, Victoria and David seemed the glamorous golden couple who would go down so well with readers of *OK!*.

We got in touch with David and Victoria's PR man, Alan Edwards, and I was delighted to discover that he was steeped in music. I've always felt most at home with people who like rock 'n' roll, and Alan had an impressive pedigree in that department: he'd started his career with the legendary PR man Keith Altham, who had looked after the Who in the wildest days of Keith Moon's antics. Alan had gone on to try his own hand at rock management, and had then founded his own PR and management company, Outside, which was to become the trendiest in London.

Alan knew who we were, too, because in the *International Musician* days he used to go drinking with one of the reporters. And in our first phone conversation with him, I couldn't resist the musical note: Martin Townsend had initiated the call, but I grabbed the phone and started singing, 'I tell you what I want, what I really, really want . . . I want Victoria to come in so I can have a chat with her.'

Alan started laughing – I knew I was going to get on with him – and he said, 'Well, that shouldn't be a problem. She's called Posh, but she's actually an East End girl, so she's straightforward to deal with. They live in Goff's Oak, which is sort of an extension of the East End, and Beckham comes from Leytonstone.'

He told me that the *Sun* might well offer up to a million for the wedding. I told him to forget about that: I would *definitely* offer a million. Alan seemed a bit stunned. I don't think anyone had offered him that much cash for a couple of photo shoots before.

Within a few days the deal had been agreed in principle and we started drawing up an agreement. Part of that arrangement was that we should keep the million-pound figure confidential.

Later that week he brought David and Victoria down to Docklands. I didn't quite know which way Beckham was going in his football career, nor Victoria with the Spice Girls. I didn't even know if they'd be more or less popular by the time they got married. But they were very charming, and as they sat there in my office, I suddenly had a thought.

'You know,' I said, 'Diana's gone: we need a new King and Queen of Britain . . .'

They looked at me blankly.

'What I am going to do,' I said, 'is make you the new King and Queen.'

David literally fell off the couch laughing, but Victoria nodded. She obviously loved the idea. She fixed me with a look and said, 'How, Mr Desmond, are you going to do that?'

'It's simple,' I told her, 'we are going to put you on the cover of *OK!* – which everyone knows is the world's greatest celebrity magazine – as often as we can!'

Victoria soon became very friendly and, over the next few years, would visit the office quite a bit, sometimes with her mum or sister and later, after Brooklyn was born, with the baby. My PA, Allison, would say to me, 'Are you *sure* you want these people taking the whole day up? The baby running round the office, the mum, the sister . . .' But I had rarely been more sure about anything in my life: this couple were going to be show-business royalty.

At this point, early in 1998, the Beckhams' wedding was still over a year away. But it didn't stop the national press taking an interest in it – or, for that matter, in us. After all, for the past 12 months, our stories and exclusives, not to mention our huge sales figures, had become a story in themselves. With *OK!* now outselling *Hello!* on a regular basis, the circulation battle between us and our Spanish rivals was spawning news features and even TV documentaries. So when one of the Sunday tabloids managed to get hold of a copy of the Beckham contract, and publicised the million-pound fee, the battle between the two celebrity magazines was back in the headlines again.

A survey was carried out which asked the question: 'If *OK!* and *Hello!* were male film stars, which stars would they be?'

We were delighted with the result. According to magazine readers, *Hello!* would be George Hamilton IV, old, permatanned and yesterday's man, whereas *OK!* was George Clooney, Hollywood's latest matinee idol. We felt that perception was pretty much on the money.

Part of the problem at *Hello!* was that, whatever the UK end of the operation wanted to do, ultimately they had to answer to the decisions of publisher Eduardo Sánchez Junco and his family in Madrid, who owned the magazine: as I've already said, I was sure that the Spanish version of the magazine was laid out by Eduardo's mother on the kitchen table. So the UK edition of *Hello!* was invariably full of ageing European aristocrats (the Monaco royal family were a favourite) and Spanish stars like Julio Iglesias who were getting past their sell-by date. What's more, there seemed to be an opinion at *Hello!* that the world of TV, and in particular the world of the soap-opera stars, was somehow a bit demeaning to the readers. With the likes of *EastEnders* and *Coronation Street* regularly racking up ratings of 12 to 15 million viewers per episode, this was a big mistake.

OK! took advantage. No Hollywood star, no matter how big, was as popular in the UK as the leading actors in these soaps. So *Hello!* were welcome to Julia Roberts and Winona Ryder. They were even welcome to Liz Hurley (we moved mountains to secure the first exclusive cover shots when she became the face of Estée Lauder, only to find that the issue flopped). British readers preferred *EastEnders* stars Patsy Palmer (Bianca) and Martine McCutcheon (Tiffany).

When, therefore, Patsy Palmer announced her engagement to film director Nick Love, a handsome young geezer with a gold tooth who would go on to make stylish films about gangsters and football thugs, we quickly signed up the exclusive rights to cover their wedding. A year before, the fictional marriage of Bianca and Ricky Butcher (played by Sid Owen) had drawn an audience of 22 million to *EastEnders*. So Patsy's real wedding, we reckoned, should be spectacular.

I had met Patsy on a few occasions and really liked her. She was a down-to-earth girl from a close family in the real East End neighbourhood of Bethnal Green, with a beautiful smile and a lovely, carefree personality. I decided to attend the wedding myself, along-side the *OK!* editor, who by now was Martin Townsend.

The wedding was to take place in the Spanish golfing resort of La Manga and I borrowed a private plane owned by the pop star Chris de Burgh to fly us out there. Patsy asked if I wouldn't mind transporting her wedding dress, because it was very fragile and she didn't want it going in the hold on a scheduled flight. I agreed, of course, but didn't realise, until the day of the flight, that the cardboard box holding the dress was absolutely enormous. Chris's plane was small but perfectly formed (a bit like him!). Trying to fit me, the editor and the dress into it ended up looking like a scene from a Marx Brothers' movie.

La Manga was as dreary as I thought it was going to be. I hate golf, the resort seems quite remote from the sea, and there's nothing much to see from your hotel window except miles and miles of golf course. To me, it seemed like a slightly odd-looking version of one of the north-west London suburbs I'd grown up in: Stanmore on the moon.

As for the wedding itself, this was the first I have ever attended where I found myself indulging in hand-to-hand combat. Patsy and Nick had decided to get married in a tiny chapel, then have a big reception at their hotel. The problem was that although the chapel only had one small entrance, trying to prevent rival photographers from getting a picture of the bride, even when she's only got to step from a car into a doorway, was a nightmare (a recurrent problem over the years). We had Kevin O'Brien and his security boys out there, obviously, and they could do a good job of making sure the photographers kept at a distance, but I felt we needed something more. These snappers push, they shove and they have every angle covered.

Patsy was very good and agreed to keep her dress concealed by a shawl as she arrived, but I was still concerned someone was going to get a picture. Then I had an idea. Just across the road from the chapel was one of those funny little Spanish supermarkets that sell everything. Outside they had a big display of beach umbrellas. I bought one, Martin bought another. And, as Patsy arrived, we stood guard either side of the chapel door. A gaggle of photographers were a few yards away, kept in place by some of Kevin's blokes. As Patsy's car drew up, the editor and I put up our umbrellas and used them to shield Patsy and her dress from the lenses. This drove the snappers mad and they started trying to elbow through Kevin's guards. It only took a few seconds for her to get into the chapel, but in the melee that followed her arrival, my umbrella was almost destroyed. It worked, though. Not a single decent picture appeared in a rival magazine or paper. Funnily enough, for years afterwards, I noticed that expensively hired and suited security men carried big umbrellas to celebrity weddings. Another Desmond innovation.

Back in London, the features we'd lined up that would culminate in the Beckham wedding were not going as smoothly as we'd hoped. Alan himself was very supportive, but elements in his team were negative and seemed to be winding things up with Victoria and the Spice Girls' office. The net result was that whatever we suggested, they didn't want to do. I needed to talk to Victoria.

'Look,' I said. 'We are going to be doing this wedding with you, but forget for the moment the money we are giving you, because money's only money. The point is this: I employ 100 people which is 100 families – 300 to 400 people – plus the other people involved in our business. So there are a lot of people here whose futures depend on this all working. I'm going to be printing, probably, a million copies of *OK!*. If it's not right, we're finished.'

She said, 'What do you mean?'

'Well the magazine goes out on sale or return. The retailer only remembers the returns. So if we mess it up, it's going to be a disaster for everyone involved who has worked so hard, including you. So, Victoria, you have to behave and please *not be a moody cow.*'

We walked to the lift, went down to the car park, and she got in her black Mercedes with tinted windows. Just as it started to move away, the window came down and Victoria's face appeared.

'I am not,' she said, 'a moody cow.'

Her company was called Moody Productions so whenever I paid a cheque to her, subsequently, I made it out to Moody Cow Productions instead.

I may have sounded light-hearted, but I was nervous. What I told Victoria was the truth. If we messed up, that would be a catastrophe. And there were plenty who would have loved us to take a fall. This was, after all, the period when the *Sunday Times*, in the course of a full-page article on *Hello!* magazine, took a big sideswipe at me, stating that 'insiders' viewed me as a pornographer from the East End who shouted and swore and locked people in cupboards. (For the record: I did not have a person-sized cupboard.)

While preparations for the big day were being put in place, we tried to sort out how we would produce our wedding issue. We had planned to print with BPCC, the main British gravure printer, but they had just hiked up their prices. The only other gravure printer we knew was an eccentric fellow in Blois, in France, who walked around wearing badges that signified he was a knight of the realm, or whatever the French equivalent was. He told us that he could cope with the job, but then said that the way he would handle it would be to print some copies in Blois, some in Paris, some in Lille, some here, some there. All in all it was a bit difficult to see how it would all come together – particularly when general industrial action broke out in France and French lorries decided to blockade the ports.

And then there was the other big question: exactly how many copies of the wedding issue did we think we could sell? We sat round the boardroom table on a Friday morning discussing it. Some people said half a million, others thought 750,000 or 900,000.

When I told them I thought we'd sell 2 million, everyone thought I'd completely lost it. But I had the vibe: I knew that if people thought we were mad and were attacking us to this extent, then we must have something. In the end – because of course I am always very democratic – I settled at 1.75 million, an ambitious number given that our usual weekly sales were 250,000–300,000. But I'm not going to pretend that I wasn't apprehensive. The week before the wedding I remember being at Hurtwood Park, where we used to sponsor celebrity polo matches, and feeling more nervous than I had ever felt. The skin was peeling off my feet. I was itching all over. I thought I was going to have a heart attack and die.

Still, 1.75 million it was.

At last, off we went to the wedding itself, which was held at Luttrellstown Castle, just outside Dublin. There were the Sky and BBC helicopters thundering overhead. There were our security people thrashing through the bushes all around the grounds looking for hidden photographers. There were all the players from Manchester United, and some of the England team, too. It was beautiful madness. By this point, I was beyond nervous. Now the skin was coming off my hands as well. I hardly had any skin left. But I also thought, 'I've done it. I've fucking done it.'

On the day before the wedding I met up with David and Victoria in one of the castle rooms and presented them with my gift: one of those lovely toasters with a wheat sheaf drawn on the side. Well, that's what everyone gets for a wedding present, isn't it? Victoria seemed a bit bemused, but David roared with laughter.

I asked them why they had chosen this castle, which, even in

July, seemed pretty cold to me. They told me it was because it was a fairy-tale wedding. Yes, I understood why they wanted a wedding in a castle, I said, but why this one? Were they Irish? No. So why come here? Well, that's where the castle was. But surely there are castles in England, I protested? More laughter. I never did get to the bottom of why we had all ended up at Luttrellstown.

I can't remember much of the wedding because I was so uptight, but I do remember a load of doves being 'released' from a cage and being a bit reluctant to fly. Oh, and Ryan Giggs in a top hat playing the piano.

When it came to the photo shoot Brian Aris, the photographer the Beckhams always chose, set up a makeshift studio in the only building he could find: a dusty old barn adjacent to the castle. On the eve of the wedding his assistants had spent hours sweeping it clean of straw and old cobwebs. Here, throughout the wedding day those same assistants processed and developed hundreds of the (pre-digital!) pictures as they were taken, because the couple needed to approve the ones we could use in the magazine before they set off for their honeymoon.

In the small hours, when the wedding was finally winding down, David and Victoria nipped out of the castle, in slippers and towelling dressing gowns, and came down to the barn to go through the shots. Victoria was as painstaking as ever despite the lateness of the hour, dropping any pictures she didn't like straight in the bin. Meanwhile one of the assistants amused David with tales of how he stalked round the countryside pushing over sleeping cows. Strange people, photo assistants.

By about 3am it was done, and Manchester United footballer Dwight Yorke, whom I would get to know even better in the coming years as the father of Katie Price's son, Harvey, invited me to go clubbing in Dublin. David Beckham wagged his finger at me. 'Do NOT go out with him, Richard,' he warned.

I went back to my hotel but I couldn't sleep. On Monday we all flew back, holding the approved photographs tight. We spent hours working on the cover. It turned out brilliantly: the template for every *OK!* wedding cover since.

By Thursday the first copies of the wedding issue were trickling on to the street. On breakfast TV, presenters were filmed flicking through the magazine and holding up various pages to the camera. It was lovely to see TV playing catch-up with the printed word. Also on television that morning was footage of the scenes at a newsagent's at King's Cross station where people were fighting for copies – they were actually trading punches to get their hands on the Beckhams' nuptials! Not even the Harry Potter books would provoke that kind of hysteria. By Friday, similar incidents were being recorded all over the country.

But we still didn't really have the big picture: we didn't know how many copies we were actually going to sell, particularly as the bulk of the magazines were not due to hit the streets until Saturday. That night I could not sleep and at 7am I drove to King's Cross station for my first news-stand call. As I arrived I met David Arculus, the boss of EMAP publications, who was on his way back to Peterborough.

He asked me what I was doing there so early. 'Checking the news-stand,' I said. 'We've got the Beckham wedding issue out this week.' Didn't all magazine owners check the news-stands? (Actually I know the answer to that.)

All that weekend newsagents kept replenishing and replenishing their stock but still the customers came in and snapped them up. I went to my mum's for an hour, then to Waitrose in Barnet, where, surrounded by sell-outs on every side, they hadn't shifted any at all because they hadn't bothered to bring the magazines out of the stockroom. There were robust exchanges between me and the shop's management. All the months of work we had put in, the sleepless nights, the attention to detail and someone leaves the final product in a stockroom.

Well, I suppose if you want a thing doing – do it yourself. I found the stockroom, located the missing magazines and heaved some of them off the shelf, at which point the entire pile collapsed on top of me, cutting my head open. The job finally done, I sought refuge for some reason in the shop next door, which was a phone shop. I was still shaking with anger and also bleeding profusely. The girl at the counter there was very nice. She told me to calm down and offered me a cup of tea.

On Monday we got the first proper sales figures and yes, it looked as if we'd sold the whole lot. I said: 'Right, let's do Issue 2: the second part of the wedding.' The line on the cover that Paul Ashford used was 'The Wild Party', not inaccurate, and a phrase we employed quite a lot on post-wedding issues in subsequent years when featuring the story of the reception. This time we put out 2.25 million copies.

I don't think I quite realised at the time the chaos I was causing at the printers in France, but I'm not sure that if I'd known I'd have cared. We sold 2 million of Issue 2. So, of course, we had to do an Issue 3! We had had a stroke of luck at the wedding when Brian Aris persuaded Victoria and David to pose with their baby son, Brooklyn. Initially they had not wanted him to be on a magazine cover but Alan Edwards managed to persuade them. In any case, I think the pictures were so stunning that they couldn't resist.

One way and another, we sold 6 million Beckham-related magazines at £2 a time. And for the period July to December 1999 we posted, for the very first time, an ABC circulation figure in excess of *Hello!*'s. We had finally beaten the Spanish! We were ecstatic! We were over the moon! We even celebrated by halting the board meeting and having an apple. It was a resounding triumph after all the years of scratching and scraping and pursuing what, at times, had seemed like an impossible dream.

At the height of it all, Piers Morgan, who was then the editor of the *Daily Mirror*, came round, with a cheque for £250,000, to try and buy second rights to the pictures.

I said, 'Give me the cheque.'

He handed it to me. I looked at it, smiled, and tore it up. It was the right thing to do. Then he insulted Martin Townsend by saying, 'Oh, I could be a great editor too, if I had unlimited budget.' He couldn't have been more wrong: a big budget helped, but our success was also about hard work and relationships and schmoozing the stars and their agents.

The wedding was over but our friendship with David and Victoria was just beginning. Almost every Friday, it seemed, Martin and I would drive up to Victoria's parents' detached house in Goff's Oak, with its tartan carpets, its suit of armour and its swimming pool in the back garden, and would plot and plan the next features we'd do. They were great people, the Adamses, but if David wasn't around, they didn't seem to eat very much, so we got into the habit of having a few sandwiches at my house before we went. Once there, Victoria and I would chat about this and that, and she'd ask me to recount my various memories from across the years.

Once, at about midnight, Victoria said: 'Oh, I fancy cassis and champagne.' So David and I went out to Tesco in Cheshunt, and I let him take the wheel of my Bentley. He was a very good driver, a very calm driver.

'Richard, do you know what cassis is?' he asked.

I said, 'David, I haven't got a fucking clue: anyway, she's *your* wife.'

We had to ask people what cassis was. Apparently, it's red stuff to put in your champagne.

David and I made several trips together, during which I would

check the news-stands and hide *Hello!* if I found any copies of it.
(This was standard behaviour among the *OK!* staff: once in Scotland,
one of my board directors, Stan Myerson, even dismantled a special
Hello! display stand with a screwdriver and replaced the *Hello!* cover
with an *OK!* one as the staff of the shop looked on, a little bemused.)
David was happy to help me tuck *Hello!* away under stacks of
Woman's Own and *Practical Fishkeeper*, though I don't think he
would have gone to the extremes that Stan did in Scotland. There
was a good vibe between us.

It would have been nice to have worked with the Beckhams on
a whole range of business ideas. For instance I discussed with
David the possibility of setting up football schools, something that
I knew had always been close to his heart, and suggested using
Hendon FC in north London, which was owned by a friend of
mine, as a location for the first of them.

We also discussed launching a brand Beckham. Victoria wanted
to call it VDB – Victoria and David Beckham – and we duly started designing some logos.

But none of these conversations really went anywhere because
the couple, newly crowned by *OK!* as the King and Queen of
Britain, were still feeling their way in the world of superstardom.
Moreover, it proved nearly impossible to agree with Victoria who
would get what percentage. In any case, Beckham was still under
the glowering gaze of Alex Ferguson at Manchester United, and
what the couple were keenest of all to do was to have more children.

Meanwhile, there were other stars. We had a new mantra for the
magazine: 'no wedding, baby or engagement will escape us', and we
meant to be as good as our word.

Now it wasn't pages for breakfast, dinner and tea, it was celebrities.

13
THE FLAKES
OF WRATH

When you have established a massive advantage in the market, you have of course a new challenge: how to hold on to it. There was still lots to do. Nothing in the celebrity world was ever going to be straightforward, and there was a story behind every story we carried in the magazine. Early in 1999, for example, we signed a deal with Jill Dando for the exclusive rights to her wedding to royal gynaecologist Alan Farthing. But there was to be no happy ending to this particular show-business fairy tale. Tragically, just a few months afterwards, Jill was shot dead on her doorstep in London's Fulham.

The identity of Jill's murderer remains unknown but it has always seemed strange to me that during the last meeting we had with her, she insisted that we show her photographs of all the security men we would be employing on the big day. Was it simply that she was concerned about the prospect of her relatives being confronted by broken-nosed, cauliflower-eared heavies, and so wanted to check that they all looked reasonably civilised? Or was it that she was being stalked and wanted to make sure the culprit wasn't going to sneak in on her wedding day? The mystery was one that would preoccupy the British press well into the time we had newspapers of our own.

Meanwhile, the celebrity whirl continued and, throughout 1999 and into 2000, *OK!* was scooping all the biggest stories. We found our way into the then-trendy world of the 'It' girls, too, via Tania Bryer. Tania was a former weathergirl, an ex-girlfriend of Jamie Packer, and had been introduced to us by David Chance at Sky. She took a special interest in the upmarket fashion and lifestyle sectors of the magazine, which is why I agreed, years later and despite reservations about TV appearances, to let her interview me on CNBC.

We were also getting good at creating new 'life events' for our celebrities. Here we again had Jeremy Beadle to thank. As our fortunes began to improve he came up with the brilliant wheeze of hosting birthday parties for stars, the idea being that if we paid for them to have a big bash, they'd bring all their famous pals along and we would then have a fantastic feature for the magazine.

These parties were the envy of *Hello!* who were reduced, at one point, to throwing celebrations featuring celebrity lookalikes. At one of their events they had hired a Rod Stewart impersonator, so we carried pictures as well and took full advantage of the first name of their editor, Maggie Koumi, captioning the picture of the lookalike: 'Wake up Maggie, that isn't Rod Stewart!'

On another occasion they hired a bus for some special event. Unfortunately it displayed an 'OUT OF SERVICE' sign on the front – not really the image the magazine was trying to project. *Hello!* just never seemed to have much luck with parties.

Our Beadle bashes, however, went from strength to strength. The first one we did was for Jeremy himself, whose illustrious guest list included the rarely-seen P J Proby and Screaming Lord Sutch, alongside various television stars. Naturally Stan brought along a few advertisers to join in the fun – pages pay wages! For other occasions, we hired the Orangery in London's Holland Park, a beautiful, light, airy building that sits at the end of a long drive and is therefore conveniently screened from prying eyes. With the help of the managers, Nick and Johnny Gold, we would dress the place up and throw parties for Joan Collins, Patsy Palmer, Martine McCutcheon and many others.

With all these parties for TV stars, and another big TV wedding exclusive that we published that summer – the marriage of Nicholas 'Only Fools & Horses' Lyndhurst – it was no surprise that the TV companies themselves started to become interested in working with us. Beadle was involved here too. He was friends with a lady called Dianne Nelmes, who worked for ITV as the head of daytime (whatever that means). She wanted to make *OK!* into a series, with at-home features, interviews and parties, all the same stuff we were doing in the magazine but in television form. We knew that in Australia celebrity magazine TV had increased circulation of the print versions by up to 37 per cent, which was certainly interesting, but nevertheless I had my doubts about it.

So I got the team together and asked them what they thought. One or two were convinced that a TV version of *OK!* would double our circulation. I expressed my doubts. 'I think it could kill sales. If we're giving it all away on TV, why are they going to buy the magazine?'

Nevertheless, I let Dianne put together a production team, headed up by a bloke called Nick Bullen, who was so proud of his ginger hair that he later called his own production company Spun Gold. He demanded a lavish budget, some of which went on the meat and potatoes of production, and more on a vast variety of ancillary items such as dresses. We were never quite sure what these were for or who ended up with them, but many celebrities, like many TV people, are fond of freebies, and when we expressed our concern, Dianne would brush imaginary dust specks from her shoulders and say, 'Don't worry – it'll be fine.'

And for ITV, it *was* fine. A very glossy six-part weekly series launched in the late summer of 1999, hosted by Fiona Phillips. It boasted an amazing roster of stars: Victoria Beckham, Joan Collins, Twiggy, Nigel Havers, Paula Yates. It even boasted an at-home with Sharon Stone who kindly showed us around her mansion (one of the microphones, unfortunately, scratched her ceiling – she invoiced us for that). And it got a 37 per cent market share – on a par with the World Cup and *Britain's Got Talent*, and blasting the BBC's rival offering at the time (a gardening show whose principal attraction was Charlie Dimmock's large chest) out of the water. But there were two problems. The first was that it cost us a million pounds a week for the celebrities. The second – just as I had predicted – was that sales of the weekly magazine wavered. The show was so good that many people no longer felt the need to get their weekly celebrity news in a magazine. It was a taste, perhaps, of what would later happen to all print products as the internet found its way into every home.

One day Michael Green came into the office. He was then running ITV with his PR man David Cameron, *the* David Cameron in fact, and had come round to announce that he wanted to do another series with us. I, however, was reluctant. I accepted that a TV presence helped boost the brand, but it wasn't helping us with weekly sales. In fact, I rather hoped that Michael would be clever and say 'I'll buy *OK!*' – it would certainly have transformed ITV's fortunes at the time, and I would definitely have sold for the right price. As it turned out, though, he wasn't interested in buying the magazine: all he seemed to want to do was to take a look at the *OK!* offices in action. At the time, I think I was a bit disappointed. In retrospect, though, I think I was very lucky. Because *OK!* was just about to enter the new millennium with a bang.

For the past couple of years we'd been building strong relationships with three of the most famous female TV presenters in the country: Ulrika Jonsson, Anthea Turner – and Paula Yates. I'm not sure how Paula first entered our lives. I do know, however, that we'd secured the first interview with her, after Michael Hutchence's death, back at the beginning of 1998. Over the next two years she and her assistant would come to the office at least once a month. She'd drive her car almost through the front of the building, intimidate our receptionist, Julie, who was anything but fond of her, and then proceed to irritate her by moving things around on her desk.

At one point we really wanted Paula to do a personal story about her family with us, but she was reluctant. One of our managing directors, Martin Ellice, therefore thought he'd try something to twist her arm. He had heard that she really liked cash – as in the actual banknotes – so he sent a couple of our finance people off to the bank to get a whole suitcase-full of the stuff, just like in the movies. Then he called her in to see if all those lovely readies would tempt her. They didn't. I was a bit puzzled so I rang her up.

'Paula, we really want this story, why wouldn't you take the money?'

She roared with laughter. 'Richard, I really don't want to do this story. And it's all very well opening a bag of banknotes in front of me. But when your MD started stroking them and saying, "Think of all the lovely dresses you could buy", I couldn't keep a straight face!'

I suppose it proves money can't get you everything.

We got to know Ulrika Jonsson through her agent, Melanie Cantor, who always seemed to be inviting me out to breakfast. We did some great features with Ulrika in the magazine, including one very moving set of pictures with her daughter, Bo, who had been born with a heart defect but had her life saved by some amazing doctors.

I also did Ulrika a great favour, as it turned out, by inviting her to my 50th birthday party at the Roundhouse in London. Her star was slightly on the wane at that point so she needed a little bit of publicity. I had some great people sitting on my table including Lulu, Louis Walsh and a certain high-profile figure from the football world. But Ulrika appeared only to have eyes for Labour spin doctor Alastair Campbell and sidled over to try and get acquainted.

Now I'd always thought Alastair did a good job looking after Tony Blair's PR, but he did an even better one for Ulrika that night. Alastair, of course, was (and is) very happily attached to his lovely partner Fiona, so he gently suggested that Ulrika – who had had a few drinks by this time – might prefer to chat up the football bloke on my table: Mr Sven Goran Eriksson.

The rest, as they say, is history.

As for Anthea Turner, she would turn out to be the most high profile of the lot, thanks to *OK!* (though she may not have appreciated the fact). Her boyfriend, Grant Bovey, had left his wife for her, and we decided to put the two of them on our front cover. This wasn't a terribly popular choice with certain *OK!* readers. In fact I remember my dentist's wife, Sharon, saying, 'Oh no, we don't like that Grant and Anthea.' He had walked out on his kids, though presumably kept in touch with them, but in any event had caused a family split.

When Grant asked us for a substantial sum to cover his wedding to Anthea, I was therefore a bit doubtful. It was a lot of money for a couple who were not greatly loved, and who were even positively loathed by some. And then I had an idea. One day I happened to be practising one of my favourite business techniques, MBWA – 'management by walking around' – when I overheard some of my people discussing the practicalities of mounting a sample of a new white chocolate Cadbury's Flake on the cover of *OK!*. I asked when they were planning to do this, and it transpired that it would be for the issue in which we might – or might not – be featuring Anthea and Grant's wedding. Was there an opportunity here, I wondered. How would Cadbury's like it if I could persuade Anthea to try one of the new bars – which was called a Snowflake – at her wedding?

No, better than that. How would Cadbury's like it if I invited all the guests to eat one? They would get lots of publicity and my worries about the appeal of a wedding issue featuring Anthea and Grant would be eased by offering our readers free chocolate on the front literally as a 'sweetener'. What could possibly go wrong?

Needless to say, Cadbury's loved the idea. All I now had to do was to convince Grant and Anthea. I had them coming over to my house the following week for dinner, so I thought I'd try a practice run: instead of passing round the usual Ferrero Rocher at the end of the meal, I gave them a Snowflake each. Then I asked them whether, if we covered the wedding, we could also hand out free chocolate. It turned out to be easier than I thought. 'Actually I used to do a bit of work for Cadbury's, so that's fine,' said Anthea.

It was a funny old wedding, to be honest. Anthea and Grant lived in a big house in the middle of nowhere, which proved quite hard to find. Then, at the reception, Grant decided to employ the services of four best men – one for each decade of his life – along with various other speakers, and some of them indulged in quite a lot of banter at his expense. I felt quite sorry for him.

The caterers had kept all the Snowflakes nice and cool in the freezer and just as the guests finished their desserts, we handed them round. It was amazing how many people were keen to be photographed with them. One – the late and much lamented Alvin Stardust – said he'd worked for Cadbury's in the past and hoped he might be signed up again! It was, all things considered, a strange, slightly hysterical day. As I left I saw Grant, somewhat the worse for wear, speeding around the garden on a quad bike.

The next day was Bank Holiday Monday and we got together early in the office to go through the wedding photographs. The contract we had with Anthea and Grant stated that we had to hand out one photograph of the event to the national newspapers. This was something we'd successfully done before, of course, but it always slightly stuck in my throat. Who wants to pay an A-list sum for an exclusive when you also have to give a picture away for free?

Our editor carefully chose one that didn't give away too much of the ceremony or the bride's outfit. But it was still a rather good photograph. 'No, no, no,' I said. 'Send out one that shows them eating a Cadbury's Snowflake. No one will ever publish that.'

I couldn't have been more wrong.

The next morning, splashed across the front page of the *Sun*, was the Flake picture, with the headline 'SICKENING'.

Inside, the editorial tore into Anthea and Grant and accused them of exploiting their wedding for money. Other newspapers followed up the story. The phones at *OK!* were ringing off their hooks. It was something we had never anticipated, certainly something we had never intended, and we could understand the couple's upset and embarrassment. There was a part of me, though, that felt that what had happened had happened, and I came to the conclusion that Anthea and Grant's best strategy would be to treat the whole matter with good humour (why shouldn't they do anything they liked on their wedding day?) and also take full advantage of the opportunities with Cadbury's. But that's not how they felt. Anthea was really upset, especially when the tabloid press then accused her of hypocrisy. 'Flakegate' was born.

The 'scandal' rumbled on for about a month, not helped by Anthea's interventions and sustained by the then editor of the *Sun*, David Yelland. But all's well that ends well. I don't like upsetting people, and I was sorry that Anthea's feelings had been hurt. A few years later I happened to bump into Anthea and Grant at a Bank of Scotland cocktail party, we had a very friendly conversation, and we parted on good terms.

. . .

All through 2000, as big exclusives with Ulrika, Paula, Anthea (not to mention Scary Spice, Madonna and Guy Ritchie and a host of others) built *OK!* into the world's most powerful celebrity magazine, another big event was looming: the marriage of Welsh actress and *Darling Buds of May* star Catherine Zeta Jones to Hollywood superstar Michael Douglas.

We had been in competition with *Hello!* for various features across the years – almost always coming out on top – but never was the battle as fierce as the one we fought with them for what was popularly regarded as the Wedding of the Decade. Fortunately, we started with a certain advantage: we got on well with Douglas's agent – a highly experienced and urbane gentleman called Allen Burry, who had once represented Frank Sinatra. *Hello!*, by contrast, impressed him less, with their constant begging emails and attempts to blacken our name. In short, Allen trusted us.

As for Catherine and Michael, they wanted to 'test' this trust before they signed on the dotted line. Catherine therefore opened the doors of her beautiful home in Pacific Palisades, California, for a photo shoot with Michael and their baby, Dylan, together with the rest of the Douglas and Zeta Jones families – including Michael's film-legend father Kirk. The couple chose the photographer, selected the pictures and gave them to *OK!* for one use only, and for one-off syndication deals around the world. All that went off smoothly. They therefore signed the deal for coverage of the wedding.

I would love to say I both attended and enjoyed that wedding, which took place at the famous Plaza hotel in New York, overlooking Central Park. The guests included Jack Nicholson and Christopher Reeve, performances by Gladys Knight & the Pips and Catherine's old friend Bonnie Tyler, and an impromptu singalong at the end of the night led by Catherine's former boyfriend Mick Hucknall, with Quincy Jones, no less, on piano.

But I have to confess that my thoughts were elsewhere. I knew I'd achieved everything for *OK!* that I'd ever hoped to achieve. We had seen off our Spanish rivals. We dominated the market. We'd broken all records for weekly magazines, and the news trade were telling us we had saved their businesses in a difficult decade. But now that *OK!* was an asset whose value was beginning to be recognised by the financial community as well, I had itchy feet. I wanted to make new investments, to take up the next challenge, to become a bigger force in 'the medium'.

There was a chap who could help with this. His name was Clive Hollick. The only problem was that he wouldn't take my calls.

14
EXPRESS DELIVERY

From the first, my life has always seemed to have had a curious connection with the *Daily Express* and Express Newspapers. As I've already mentioned my dad worked for them at one point and so did my mum. A few decades later, when my own business was well under way, I discussed the possibility of joining forces with Link House, who like us published a range of specialist magazines. The initiatives I became involved with in Docklands saw the Express's printing works brought together with those of the Telegraph group at West Ferry. My breakthrough distribution deal was with United Newspapers (who became United News and Media in 1995, and then United Business Media), owner of Express Newspapers – and the lawsuit that I then fought with them ended in a settlement that funded the launch of *OK!* magazine. I even put in a bid for the *Star* in the mid-1990s, and my managing director in charge of advertisement sales, Stan Myerson, was a former Express senior executive. For me, then, there was a sense of destiny in my dealings with the group. So when I saw that *OK!* magazine, along with our other titles and TV interests, were beginning to attract attention and to be externally valued in the hundreds of millions, I knew what my next target had to be. I just needed to have a chat with the key man.

Lord Hollick, who took over as chief executive of United News and Media in the late 1990s, was known to me. But my one previous encounter with him hadn't been a particularly happy one. Back in the late 1980s we had planned to expand our advertising agency side through the acquisition of a poster site company he controlled, Mills and Allen (formerly Pearl & Dean Outdoor Advertising – a name with, of course, strong sentimental associations for me). His people supplied us with a list of the sites that would be included in the deal, and we then drove around at weekends to do a quick tally. Rather to our surprise, we discovered that not all the sites we were about to acquire seemed to be there. Since this all happened just after the big storm of autumn 1987, it's possible that they might just have blown away, but I couldn't be sure. I was given to understand it was a feature of that industry as a whole that numbers of sites were somewhat notional, but it wasn't the most promising of introductions to the future head of United News and Media.

Fast forward a couple of decades, and my understanding was that Lord Hollick wanted to be rid of the Express. The papers represented only about 3 per cent of his business, and he seemed to be less interested in running them than in using the political clout they offered to get government support for his planned acquisition of all the independent TV channels, which he hoped to amalgamate into one company under Michael Green. One of those broadcasters was Channel 5. In the event nothing came of the scheme – even though the Tory *Daily Express* defected to Labour under the editorship of Rosie Boycott – but I still felt that Hollick had good reason for losing interest in newspapers.

I tested the water, asking Michael Grade, with whom I was then friendly, to speak to Lord Hollick on my behalf. He did but the answer was no. Keith Harris, my friend from Apax who was by now running his own financial services company, Seymour Pierce, asked the same question, but again, no. In 1999 Express Newspapers was firmly not for sale.

Finally Lady Barbara Judge tried. I received a letter direct from Lord Hollick. 'Look – the papers are not for sale, would you please stop sending your "emissaries". You are off my radar.'

In spite of this I did not give up. I had a meeting with Omar Bayoumi from Commerzbank who told me my group was eminently floatable and that maybe we could raise £400 million and bring Express Newspapers into a new company in which I would be a minority shareholder. It was an interesting idea. I was then told by Neil Bennett, at the time a journalist at the *Telegraph*, that the key man to see from Commerzbank was the boss, Mehmet Dalman. Dalman had apparently come over to England without even having an office to work from and had hired people from a telephone box. But from those unlikely beginnings he had become an important player. I called in August but Dalman could not fit me in until five o'clock on a Friday afternoon in November. I took this to mean he was not very interested. Of course, at the time we were not borrowing money so our contacts with banks were quite restricted.

Then, out of the blue, I happened to receive a circular from Merrill Lynch's Neil Blackley, the guru of media analysts, which stated that the Express group was suffering from a lack of direction, that its management was poor, that it might even go out of business, and that in a sale it would be lucky to fetch much more than £75 million to £100 million. Following hot on the heels of that circular was massive press speculation that the group would indeed be sold. The smart money was on the Hinduja brothers, whose diverse family portfolio included import/export and defence companies which had once got Peter Mandelson into trouble when the brothers persuaded him to intervene for them on a citizenship application.

Such a pity I could not persuade Hollick to take me seriously, I thought.

Thanks to my friend Jeremy Beadle, though, my path almost immediately crossed with His Lordship's yet again, and this time in slightly more favourable circumstances. Jeremy had been busy setting up a number of meetings for me to explore various business options. One happened to be at Alan Sugar's house. I then gave Alan a return invitation, and when he asked if I'd invite Barbara Windsor, too (I'd mentioned that I'd recently sat with her at a charity dinner), I agreed. I rang Barbara and to my delight she said, 'Of course, darling.' (I had forgotten – but she had not – that I helped her when she hit a difficult period as a result of one of the unfortunate choices of husband she sometimes made.)

Now Barbara's presence saved the day. My dinner for Sugar proved a bit sticky at first: he was difficult, which he is prone to be. In fairness he had just had his car nearly turned over by fans who thought Spurs was a football club when Alan, who was then chairman, thought it needed to be run like a business and who adjusted his expenditure on new players accordingly. But Barbara, who had come with her then partner Robert, took one look at Sugar and then flung herself on him, saying, 'Oh, it's Sid! It's Sid James, he's back!'

Now if you look at Sid James and you look at Alan, you can see what she meant. She gave Alan a big cuddle and he cheered up. He liked being Sid James. So we ended up having a great evening at the end of which Alan invited us to watch a Spurs v Arsenal game from the directors' box. Barbara wasn't able to come, but I went with my son Robert, one of his friends, and my publicist, Arsenal fan Alan Edwards. Sugar laid everything on for us but unfortunately was not in the best of moods..

Anyway, there was another guest in the box: Clive Hollick.

He was sitting with Danny Fiszman who owned part of Arsenal with David Dein until the latter sold his shares to a Russian. I had tended to judge Fiszman by Dein – a person who once turned down my request for help when I licensed the Arsenal magazine from him and needed some assistance on cash flow and cooperation from the players. But Danny Fiszman was well disposed. Moreover I had an ally in his camp. On a visit to a local newsagent in Hampstead some time before I had been told that one of their customers had switched from having *Hello!* magazine sent to her house to having *OK!* delivered. I had asked for the name, and had been told that it was a Mrs Fiszman. I had guessed it must be the wife of the Arsenal director, and when the news agent confirmed that it was, I had sent her a note thanking her for choosing *OK!* and saying she would not regret it. This, it now emerged, was something she had not forgotten.

Alan Edwards looked at me, then at Fiszman and at Hollick, and started pushing me towards them. I hung back. For me it was like fancying a girl and not wanting to ask in case she said no. But in the end I went.

Fiszman greeted me and asked if I knew Clive Hollick.

I said, 'Well, I know who His Lordship is, of course.'

Fiszman told me to pull up a chair and have a drink. He had originally been a diamond dealer and I remember his eyes were blue and sparkling. He said, without any kind of prompting, 'You know, Clive, you've got a big problem with your papers, you're always moaning about it – you should sell them to Richard.'

'Why would I do that?'

'He would make a success of them. He does *OK!* – it's a huge magazine but he knows every person who buys that magazine – he writes to them personally.'

'How could he do that? It's not possible.'

'I'm telling you, he does. My wife changed from *Hello!* to *OK!* and she got a letter the next day.'

Hollick asked how I did it. I said I had a good team and that I was very committed. He was still cold. Then I asked about Arsenal and it emerged that he was a real fan. I asked if he would like me to send him a copy of the Arsenal magazine which I published every month.

'Thank you very much,' he said.

'Actually we also have a few mugs, T-shirts, merchandise, that sort of thing. Would you like . . . ?'

'Thank you very much.'

I was on his radar.

As soon as I got back to the office I sent him a note saying, 'Dear Lord Hollick, it was a pleasure to meet you. I enclose the magazine.' I received quite a cordial reply, 'Dear Mr Desmond, thank you very much for the magazine.'

I sent him a mug and got another 'Thank you Mr Desmond.' Then I dispatched a T-shirt – the same response. At this point, my secretary Allison asked why, if I was so keen on the Express, I didn't just write to Hollick about it. After all, she said, I'd been exchanging quite friendly messages for a while now. When she put it like that, it seemed an obvious thing to do. So I asked Paul Ashford to come up and we composed a short letter, saying that while I didn't wish to irritate him I couldn't help noticing the press speculation about a possible sale to the Hindujas, and that I could do a quick and quiet deal if His Lordship wished.

Shortly afterwards I received a call in the car just as we were about to go through the tunnel at Limehouse. I had to pull over and stop the Rolls. It was a director of United called Bernard Gray. He told me that he had learned from Hollick that I was interested in the Express, and asked if I was prepared to do a quick, quiet deal. Could we meet on Wednesday? Well, it was Jewish New Year on the Wednesday and Thursday, and as I've mentioned elsewhere I had good reasons for not wanting to transact business then. But I did agree to meet up on the Friday at Kleinwort Benson's, with a Mr double-barrel Jeremy St John Miller who was very polite and very posh.

I explained that my understanding was that I would be buying the titles for £100 million and that there would be a separate print contract.

'Oh, no,' he said. 'You would own the print plants: they're included.'

That was an unexpected bonus. Of course, I knew about the main print plant. After all I had brokered the deal that got it built and could see it from my office window. It was very large and built on prime land. I learned there was another plant of similar size in Broughton, near Preston in Lancashire. Broughton was wholly owned, while the West Ferry plant was a 50–50 joint venture with the Telegraph – but then nothing is perfect. In a subsequent meeting I had with Lord Hollick (in fact, the only meeting I had with him) it was explained that there was a formula on change of control that allowed us to be bought out of West Ferry for £68 million – not a bad discount on the £100 million we were paying for the whole thing. I was grateful for the heads-up, though it didn't help me with a fairly basic problem I faced at that point: I didn't quite have the required money.

I did know that Hollick wanted us to act speedily and that if word got out we would lose the deal. I therefore called my NatWest bank manager and outlined the opportunity. I would put in £30 million, I said, which was all I had in the world, plus my company. I needed another £70 million but could demonstrate asset value as collateral. NatWest, however, seemed reluctant, perhaps because they were owned by RBS who were simultaneously acting for the Telegraph, who were also trying to buy the Express, so there was the possibility of conflict. My understanding since is that Hollick told the Telegraph and the Mail they could have the Express for £120 million, but must put £60 million in without due diligence and complete in 30 days' time or lose the £60 million. Presumably the robust terms were because they were competitors.

For us, whatever the issues involved in raising the requisite funds, the deal itself was a no-brainer. I had a pretty shrewd idea what the business was worth. True, I had to take a guess at what their advertising revenue might be, but then I had Stan on board and he had worked at Express Newspapers for years. We didn't know what their editorial spend was, either, but then that was rather less important than what we would spend in this area, and here Paul Ashford was in a good position to arrive at a pretty accurate estimate. As for assets: if the worst came to the worst, we could sell those, and let the Hindujas have the *Express* titles for £50 million and David Sullivan the *Daily Star*, with which he had some historical involvement, for £25 million. Not that we dreamed of doing such a thing but it was nice to have a safety net and to know that if we had to we could walk away with a tidy profit, without even having to calculate what we might realise if we sold the print works. If I had been a banker I would not have hesitated. But then I am not a banker.

NatWest now sent some people down from Leeds who ate sandwiches and wanted to know who would be the art director, because they said that was very important.

Kleinwort's, who were acting on behalf of United, were a bit shrewder and said, 'Are you good for £100 million?'

'My dear chaps,' I said. 'I'm in the porn business. You know how much money is made in porn. Billions!'

They agreed, yes, they knew that. Everyone knows that. Then, because I was friendly with their vice-chairman Bay Green – though I had only met him a couple of times – I added, 'If you want to be sure, just phone Bay Green.'

They were very impressed that I knew their vice-chairman. But I have to assume that they rang to check, because just a few minutes later, when I had got back to my own office, I received a phone call from the great man himself. I could hear him chortling. 'Ha ha – I had Jeremy St John Miller on the phone just now – asking if you were good for a hundred million. I told him you were good for a *billion*. How's that?'

Kleinwort's never checked whether I was really good for the money. That was just as well, because I wasn't.

Meanwhile we were getting nowhere fast with NatWest (they did eventually say they might possibly help us if we subjected ourselves to three months' due diligence). I did notice, however, when I consulted my diary, that I was due to have my long-ago-arranged appointment with Mehmet Dalman of Commerzbank – the man who recruited staff from telephone boxes.

I have to confess I had no great expectations of this meeting, but I went along nevertheless. I decided to be direct. 'Before we start, can I ask you a question? Are you a bank?'

'Yes we are the fourth largest bank in the world and number two in Germany.'

'Do you write cheques out?'

'Of course.'

'Well, can I tell you a story, then, Mr Dalman? After you've heard what I have to say, you'll either tell me to get lost or you'll do it.'

And I then told him everything – my family history with the Express group, the growth of my companies, my abortive attempts to negotiate with Hollick, and now the possibility of a final breakthrough.

He listened carefully. When I had finished, he said there was no point in talking to his team in England, we had to go and meet the boss, Mr Patik. What was I doing on Monday?

'What would you like me to do?'

'I would like you to come to Germany.'

He explained that they would need a full presentation with slides and figures.

Well, I knew I could do the figures, but I also knew that I would have to ask Stan Myerson to come along and do the slides. And I was further aware that, from his point of view, the timing wasn't great. It was his (third) wedding on the Sunday (my board all attended and I played the drums), and Stan had been planning to get away on honeymoon on Monday. He agreed, however, that the Express was more important, and I am sure his bride did too. So off we went on a 7.30am flight from London City on the Monday.

Once we arrived, Omar and his team ushered us into a room in one of Commerzbank's high-rise office buildings and left us to hone our presentation for Dr Patik, which was scheduled for 5pm. I decided that Rob Sanderson, our financial director, should do the formal presentation. I, for my part, would look this Mr Patik in the eye and say I was putting in everything I had, plus my company as collateral. He would either trust me or we would say goodbye.

After watching my people putting together documents and slides for a while, I suggested we go for lunch. We ended up in a Chinese restaurant. To say I was stressed would be an understatement. I was so on edge that I was physically sick – top end, then bottom end – and repeatedly so. It didn't help that the toilet, which I was obliged to patronise heavily, was in the process of being refurbished and so was full of workmen.

Then back to the offices. I have to confess that, despite the business I've spent my life in, I am in fact uncomfortable with large piles of paperwork. And this presentation involved record-breaking quantities. It was an anxious afternoon. We tweaked, and we re-tweaked. Then, eventually, we were summoned to the 49th floor. Rob and Stan showed our figures and stated our case. I made my presentation, as I had said I would. This was personal, I was a successful publisher, I was staking everything.

'OK,' he eventually said. 'I do it on one condition. You don't do what the *Sun* does and put anti-German stories on the front page. We don't like that.'

I said it wouldn't be a problem.

We were then put in another office for a further hour and a half – all of us, that is, except Rob, who was escorted off to go through figures with their credit committee team (apparently an unusual thing to have to do). I am sure we were taped. We said very nice things about Commerzbank. Indeed we had no reason not to.

After that the evening became something of a blur. Mehmet wanted to take us for a marvellous dinner. He even suggested at one point that perhaps we could take his private plane to Paris and have breakfast there. We were tired and just wanted to go home, but in the circumstances we could hardly be seen to be unsociable, though I think I did have a slightly tetchy exchange with him about the urgency with which everything would need to be settled. 'I have to have the money!' I shouted at one point in the evening's proceedings. Finally, after the revels were over, we escaped – despite what I still believe was an attempt to misdirect our cab so we would miss our Lufthansa flight and be obliged to carry on enjoying ourselves.

Stan and Rob fell asleep on the plane – I didn't.

We arrived back in London assuming that we had the money. But it wasn't quite that simple. All of a sudden Mehmet announced he needed a guarantee for a further £10 million. It was crunch time. Would I need to sell the house? The rest of my pension? Would Robert still be able to go to Highgate School? I discussed the options endlessly with Janet.

In the event, though, Keith Harris of Seymour Pierce came to the rescue with a guarantee that amounted to half his own net worth. It was a deal struck on the basis of a handshake and a request, 'Please give it back to me.' I have to say I found it really difficult to borrow from a mate. But he got his money back in two months.

Even when that was out of the way, there were other mini-crises: the Germans wanted the loan to be just for 364 days; we had to conclude very quickly; there were other interested parties. It was a cliffhanger.

But on 22 November 2000, accompanied by my editorial director Paul Ashford, I walked up the steps of Ludgate House in Blackfriars as the new proprietor of Express Newspapers. We had been so quick and quiet that the whole thing had taken everyone by surprise. We, for our part, were exhausted from the roller-coaster ride of the deal. And just to add to the excitement of the day we discovered that *Hello!* had stolen into the venue where Michael Douglas and Catherine Zeta Jones were getting married, taken some pictures and then run them, landing us in a lawsuit that was to drag on seven years and cost them £11 million. Yet despite the exhaustion and the stress, I knew we'd achieved something major.

We faced a crowd of journalists, our own and other people's, a barrage of cameras and a hubbub of inane questions.

'Will you have Page Three in the *Express?*'

Almost immediately, I had a call from Prime Minister Tony Blair inviting me to go over to celebrate. I thought it more important, though, to meet the new people and to get to grips immediately with the business. I also wanted to be in the print plant that night to see my first issue come out. One of our publicity team who had close links with the *Daily Mail* had slipped the idea into my mind that for some reason it might not. I said I'd go to Number 10 the following evening.

The day went by in a blur, and at the end of it we had a cordial meal with all the senior *Express* and *Star* people on the Chinese barge restaurant opposite the print works at West Ferry. We posed for innumerable pictures, and, with indescribable exhilaration, I saw my own daily newspaper powering off my own printing presses.

The following day I had two interesting encounters. The first was with a chap calling himself Murdoch MacLennan, who somehow slipped past my secretary, who was still trying to come to grips with the change of office and the arrival of lots of strange new faces. MacLennan spoke very quietly in a Scottish accent. I could scarcely hear him.

'Jonathan sends his very best and congratulates you on buying the Express. I'm here to make you £100 million.'

'That's very nice. Jonathan who?'

'Jonathan Harmsworth.'

It was a somewhat bizarre interview and I decided to play my cards close to my chest. I said, 'Who's he?'

'He's the controlling shareholder of the Daily Mail group.'

'Well, good for him, very pleased for him, but if he wants to speak with me why isn't he here himself?'

'Well I am the managing director, and I can assure you I have full authority to offer £200 million for the *Daily* and *Sunday Express*, and you can keep the *Daily Star*.'

Despite the manner in which it was made it was, no doubt, a credible offer – and MacLennan didn't ask me to keep it confidential. But I had not gone to all the trouble of acquiring the paper just to make a quick buck the next day. Anyway I had another meeting to go to. I had, after all, agreed to see the PM.

In the chaos of moving offices my car had somehow got mislaid so I decided I'd have to take a cab. There happened to be one waiting outside the office, so I asked the driver who he was waiting for. Apparently it was a Mr Johnson who was going to Chelsea. I said I was Mr Johnson but that I now wanted to go to Downing Street. When it came to paying at the other end, I noticed that the meter reading was quite high – over £20. When I queried this, the cabbie said not to worry: some rich bloke had just bought the Express, so it would all go on the paper's account. I asked the cabbie if he knew what that rich bloke looked like. He said he did, and I asked him to look in his rear-view mirror. That conversation saved us around a quarter of a million a year on cab standing time alone from that moment.

When I arrived at 10 Downing Street, Blair proved to be very relaxed, very hospitable and very charming. I had always previously thought of myself as a Conservative, although I hadn't been happy with the way the Tories had handled things at the time of Fortress Wapping. So every Saturday I'd listen to my mum telling me how marvellous the Tories were and how you mustn't have a Labour government, and then I'd give 50 quid or 1,000 quid or 5,000 quid to the local party in Barnet because John Marshall the MP had a dinner once a year which was quite helpful for business connections.

Now I was chatting to a Labour prime minister about his Sedgefield constituency, about Burmans Music shop in nearby Newcastle, and about the Animals and various other groups. Fortunately, my son had got me into Nickleback so I could be a bit more Cool Britannia than if I had just mentioned Georgie Fame and Zoot Money. Clive Hollick, who had also come along, looked ever less at ease with himself and seemed to sink lower and lower into the settee as the conversation progressed. Perhaps he was more of a string quartet type of guy, or perhaps, since he was no longer a press baron, he sensed that his presence was superfluous.

Eventually Blair moved on to other matters. 'One thing I want to ask you, Richard, is – can you tell me something? *Forty Plus*. Is it women aged forty plus, or is it, like, forty plus in measurement?'

I looked him straight in the eye and said seriously, 'It's both, Tony, it's both.'

He asked me a few more questions about that aspect of my business, and I told him the whole story: the winning of the *Penthouse* licence, Bob Guccione, Smith's and Menzies' answer to 'self-regulation', the way we became involved with Electric Blue, and Roger Cook and his business on the Isle of Wight. He listened intently. Interestingly, though, he did not seem to remember much about that part of our conversation when he was later questioned on the subject by Jeremy Paxman on BBC2's *Newsnight*.

Finally, he wished me the best of luck, and then, as he opened the door to let me out, he paused. 'By the way, who are you going to back?' he asked.

'What do you mean?'

'Well are you going to back me? Are you going to back Hague? Who?'

'Well I haven't thought about it, mate. You're all fucking mad. I mean, who would do this job for a hundred grand a year and a free rundown house? I'm frankly not interested in politics.'

'You will be . . .'

15
AN OWNER OF INKWELLS

The following day I looked at the *Daily Mail*, whose proprietor had been so prompt with his congratulations about my deal, and I needed to sit down.

The *Daily Express*, it seemed, had been bought by a 'pornographer' of the very worst kind. No mention of retailers such as Smith's and Menzies here, no mention of Ofcom licences. The *Mail* were outraged. They appeared to have forgotten their own colourful past with *Titbits* and the dubious classified ads they were currently running in *Loot*. I don't believe they actually accused me of murder, but that was about the only thing they didn't imply about me. It would become part of a sustained campaign on their part, both through their paper and by mailshots targeted at *Daily Express* readers and home-delivery customers. The *Telegraph*, the *Guardian* and other papers swiftly joined in, to a greater or lesser extent. I thought I had done a deal to save a 100-year-old newspaper from ruin and try to give it a new lease of life by applying a bit of business and publishing common sense to it. I did not realise I had gatecrashed an elite British club and was a threat to all kinds of comfortable arrangements and presumptions which added up to a very nice lifestyle for a small number of well-placed individuals.

I tried to play things cool. Indeed I had little alternative because newspaper legislation dictated that a buyer from outside the industry had to submit themselves to a three-month probation period during which the deal could be annulled at any point if they were judged not to be 'fit and proper' owners. David Sullivan had failed the 'fit and proper' test. Then again, David Sullivan had once been in prison for living off immoral earnings, spending 71 days inside before being released on appeal. I hadn't ever been convicted of anything, but it was abundantly clear that numerous people for numerous reasons would like to see my deal collapse.

The most brutal piece to appear featured in the *Sunday Times* over the Christmas holidays. Among other things, it repeated the more bizarre parts of the Ruth Picardie interview in the *Independent* nearly a decade before, which meant that you came away from the article and the headline having only really registered the words DESMOND . . . EXPRESS . . . MAFIA LINKS. At no point did it – or, for that matter, any other newspaper – allege that I had actually done anything wrong, but it did imply I had connections with people who did, and that in some way the new *Express* owner had received unwelcome attention from the world's most notorious family business. Because everything was done by insinuation, legally there was nothing I could do. Not very nice at all. But, of course, a fit and proper person does not retaliate, even if he has a few newspapers of his own and can think of some choice observations about the guys sniping at him.

Internally, things were scarcely better. The leader column of the *Daily Express*, its editorial heart, appeared a couple of days after we took over with the first letter of each sentence cleverly engineered so it spelt out the words FUCK OFF DESMOND. I have since forgiven that, and the journalist responsible, Stephen Pollard, still regularly writes for us. He is a good bloke but was, I think, young and misguided when he attacked the new owner in that way.

As for the editor, Rosie Boycott, I had met her previously and thought she was a reasonable person. However, within three months she had managed to age my editorial director Paul Ashford – who generally can deal with anyone – by ten years, with a little help from her friends. The problem was that, as instructed by His Lordship, we had been 'quick and quiet', leaving Rosie and others to bet that the Hinduja brothers would be taking the paper over. Now she had to deal with me, and perhaps felt that this new chap from Docklands might be too 'hands on' for her taste. It was a view shared by others of the *Express* team. The managing director Andy Jonesco, for example, who used to walk round with a clipboard, realised I needed an office on the first day and quickly volunteered to share his when I was there. How often did I think I would be coming in? About once a month?

'Well I'm here now, and I'll be gone when I'm dead.'

I used that office for a little while until Andy moved elsewhere, and I found the drawers to be full of cakes and champagne bottles. I believe Paul did worse because he got the sports editor's old office which he said contained more booze than many off-licences. The trouble was, for pornographers, we were a bit puritanical.

It seems to us from that point that Rosie had begun to play a game designed either to prove who was the editorial boss or ensure a pay-off; I was never sure which. Round one went like this. My friend from Estée Lauder came in, met everyone, and said that Estée Lauder would be happy to advertise with us. The next day the editorial that ran was all about how Estée Lauder's cosmetics killed rabbits or rainforests or something. Highly principled. Then Dixons chairman Stanley Kalms, whom I knew well, offered to place £11 million of advertising a year with us. The next day the *Daily Express* carried a feature criticising Dixons. That was the end of that advertising contract, and we lost the £11 million of potential revenue. Now, I had always supported editorial freedom ever since the days of the Marshall amp which electrocuted people. This, however, appeared to be editorial freedom taken a very long way indeed. Nevertheless I kept calm.

The same sort of thing happened with our celebrity friends. When, for example, David and Victoria Beckham called by, what should have been a celebratory occasion was soured by an argument where journalists on the *Star* rejected Victoria's plea to understand that she and David were only human and to go easy on the more hurtful and judgemental pieces concerning them. Fair comment is perhaps fair comment, but equally one ought to be polite to one's guests.

I still did nothing. I had to be 'fit and proper'. But as it was clear that Boycott wanted to go, we needed to come to an agreement over a settlement. At the end of it all, I assume she got what she wanted, but I can't help feeling it might have been easier for all concerned if she'd just asked for it in the first place.

That left me with a new editor to find, and I was quite pleased when I was approached by no less a person than Andy Coulson, then deputy editor on the *News of the World*, who seemed to me very presentable and maybe a good prospect. Paul, however, said he was familiar with Mr Coulson from attempting to collaborate on celebrity exclusives and did not particularly trust him. It proved to be a lucky escape for us.

As is the case with all acquisitions our first priority was to impose our culture as quickly as we could and eliminate the more disconcerting aspects of the culture that we found. And there was plenty to disconcert us. For example, shortly after our arrival we came across a room full of scruffy people. We asked them what they did, but they said they couldn't tell us. After a little more patient questioning, I managed to unearth the fact that they were the special investigations department. I asked what they were investigating and they said, 'We can't tell you.'

Rob Sanderson, my finance director, spotted that a lot of cash linked with special investigations seemed to be leaving the business. When he asked what it was for, they said – yes, you've guessed – they couldn't tell him.

We got rid of that special investigations department. They were very surprised. They asked us why we were doing it. We said, 'We can't tell you.'

Then there was MegaStar. This was the *Star*'s very innovative and well-resourced website, which unfortunately was gobbling £10 million a year with little to show for it. We knew we couldn't afford to wait a decade or so for things to come right, so we parted with it. We also spotted that cash was leaving the business to prop up various bizarre sponsorship deals, one of which involved rides on Blackpool Pleasure Beach and another of which was tied up with a pub which the *Daily Star* paid half a million a year to be called the Star. Not to mention all the awaydays and conferences in castles in Ireland.

Each change meant a debate – and, as we were being fit and proper, each debate tended to be long-drawn-out. Under such circumstances you begin to question your own judgement. I was grateful to Peter Hill, a northerner who was editor of the *Daily Star* and later of the *Express*, coming up to me at the end of each exhausting day and reassuring me, 'I promise you it's not you – it's them.' Even he, however, thought the *Daily Express* was 'like roast beef – it will go on forever'. No amount of showing people just how grim the company accounts were seemed to convince them that in an era when newspaper reading was in decline, costs had to be kept in line with revenue.

Slowly, however, we managed to change things, and change them for the better. At the time the old Fleet Street culture still persisted – even if the actual street had given way to banks and establishments that sold cups of latte at very high prices – and it was a very boozy culture. One of my top journalists had a reputation for getting so drunk he needed to be 'folded up like a pushchair and put in a taxi home'. Another shot at a columnist with a crossbow, but fortunately had consumed so much alcohol that he missed. Both, though, mellowed when they worked for me and did a good job. I put that down to my beneficial influence.

I even began to have fun being an owner of inkwells, to use the colourful industry term for a newspaper proprietor. I cross-promoted my magazines, running a special edition of *OK!* in the *Sunday Express*: a massive sales benefit to the newspaper but not so great for newsstand magazine sales. I advertised extensively, using a little cartoon character, voiced by my young son Robert, to say the pay-off line 'Express Delivery'. I did not get involved with the editorial side, but I put a lot of work into positioning the paper in the market. I felt the previous owner had got that completely wrong because he paid insufficient attention to his readers compared with his own political agenda.

Gradually the people at the paper began to realise that I was not some maverick obsessed with top-shelf titles but a publisher determined to save newspapers that had been budgeted to make a loss of £21 million in the course of 2001 and that experts like Neil Blackley said were finished. As it happens, it would not be long before I actually sold my adult titles. Richard Branson sought me out and told me quite passionately I must not dispose of the Fantasy Channel in the same way. I do not know whether he was fond of watching it, but I believe his point was that if you start allowing yourself to be bullied, it will end in censorship of newspaper pages and song lyrics. Anyway, my reason for getting rid of the adult titles was purely commercial: quite simply, they were no longer viable.

When Tony Blair had said I would become interested in politics, he was absolutely right. I soon realised that newspapers are all about politics – and I couldn't separate the two. I even donated £100,000 to the Labour party, which got me into lots of hot water. I am not sure why it was viewed as a crime to make a donation to the Labour party – it seems to me that it was more a matter of opinion.

The donation affair began shortly after my initial meeting with Blair. I was invited to dinner by (Lord) Waheed Alli, whom I knew from Docklands (I initially believed he was a TV expert so I tried to get him to tackle the job of getting the floor of my studio straight, and then he tried to make me his partner in a gay radio station), and Baroness Margaret McDonagh, the lovely and highly efficient architect of New Labour's Millbank operation. Waheed said Tony really liked me. Would I make a contribution to the party?

What they didn't realise was that I had put everything I'd ever had – some £37 million – into the Express, along with £97 million that I had borrowed, my house and half my pension pot. Our loan from Commerzbank was only for 364 days and even on that they were trying to get other banks to share in their exposure. I had signed about a thousand documents relating to the conditions of my loan and I would love to say I fully read and understood each one, but I felt over-extended and was understandably nervous. My confidence was not helped by the fact that everyone was writing about how we were going to make a mess of the business.

'I will give you £100,000 worth of advertising – six pages.'

They loved the idea. We all went back to saying what a nice fellow Tony was, and the dinner ended. A week later Alastair Campbell, Blair's celebrated spin doctor and my ex-writer on *Forum* magazine, came round and said he needed to speak to me. 'What Waheed didn't realise was we can't take it in kind,' he said. 'You've got to give £100,000 in cash.'

'To be honest, I've signed all these documents: I don't want to breach covenants. I'm sure in a year's time £100,000 won't seem like a lot, but right now I can't do it.'

'Well, why don't you give us a hundred thousand now and invoice us a hundred for the advertising, which we will pay?'

So I gave them the cash and invoiced them for the advertising separately. Actually the advertising came to £105,000 so I made a profit of £5,000 on the deal. I remember Gordon Brown saying some time later, 'Was it true you made a profit on that advertising?' I replied, 'Yes, I did actually, I got more back.' He said, 'Tut, tut, tut.'

In brief, I felt that Blair was a man I could do business with. When a reporter from the *Evening Standard* asked me about him after our first meeting I said exactly that. Tony was a nice bloke; I could talk to him about musical instruments; he had a good team around him. If what he was made him a socialist, then I supposed I must be one, too. 'Yes,' I said, 'I support Blair.'

Tony then followed through by asking us to bring in a dozen people to Downing Street for an informal lunch each month – usually the editors in the key areas of social policy, health, finance and so on. He had a knack of making everyone feel special. He was always focused.

At the lunch just before the election of 2001 we were all standing around before the meal when he asked – as he had at our first-ever meeting – 'So who are you supporting?'

He knew how to close a deal, which I respect. I replied we would be supporting Labour. He said that was fine, and went to sit down at the table. I wonder whether we would have got our lunch if I'd said I'd be backing the other geezer. Perhaps we'd have had to eat standing up.

As a salesman, then, Tony Blair was among the best I ever met. He has a kind of charisma which Clinton also possesses – neither of them is particularly tall, physically imposing or even good-looking, but both can light up a room when they are in it. The only thing with Blair is that when he leaves the room, you feel like you'd never seen him. That said, I always felt at ease with him. He actually visited my home a couple of times and played guitar with me, although I have to reveal he is not all that good. He would, I think, have liked to recognise my achievement on Express Newspapers with an honour and he and Cherie at one point asked my first wife Janet how she would like being Lady Desmond, but Janet said we didn't hold with all that kind of thing. Tony and I exchanged looks.

By contrast, the Tories sometimes seemed to lack even the basics. Blair's rival at this time was William Hague, but while he was imposing face to face, and taller than you might have expected, he did not know how to close. I first met him six months before the newspaper acquisition and asked whether he would like to do a feature in *OK!* magazine. I did it more for him than for me, since *OK!* readers are not political. But I guessed that at least he would have a nice house. He said I would have to ask his wife Ffion. Ffion liked the idea and we agreed we would fix it up. I turned away to speak to Richard Branson who was at the same event, and after a few minutes Hague tapped me on the shoulder and said, 'I'll be in touch at nine o'clock tomorrow morning.'

But he wasn't.

That next evening, oddly enough, I gave a speech at Eton — it's funny the things you do. I had no idea what to say so I just told my life story like it was, and they seemed to like it. I told them they had a disadvantage in life going to Eton, meaning, in effect, that they were sheltered from the real world. I then told them what had happened with Hague the day before, and asked them when they thought he would call me. They all gave different dates. He never did, though.

Then some months after the *Express* acquisition I was preparing to go with David and Victoria Beckham to Mel B's (Scary Spice's) birthday party at her house which she thought was in Hampstead but was actually in Marlow, on the river, and the telephone rang.

'It's Sebastian here. How are you?'

'Sebastian who?'

'Sebastian Coe.'

'Sorry, I still don't know who you are, sir. Oh, hang on, *Seb* Coe! What can I do for you? I'm just about to go out.'

'I act for William Hague and he would really like to meet with you.'

'I am sure he'd like to meet with me, but he's a bit late, mate. It's now been two weeks and two days since we bought the *Express*, and he and I have a bit of history. Ask him about the time I met him and he didn't follow through. Ask him why he never got back in touch.'

Coe called back the following Tuesday – Hague would really like to come and see me, he said, but he was also a bit apprehensive about the prospect. Now that I was under the spotlight, I was getting lots of unwelcome attention and headlines from journalists – even mine – who thought I was a Mafia hitman and KGB operative all rolled into one. They certainly couldn't accept that I was just a bloke who ran *OK!* magazine and who had the money and the balls to buy the *Express*. Anyway, it had all made Hague a bit nervous.

I had an idea. I had promised my son Robert that I would take him to the WWF wrestling in Sheffield where Mr Hague had his constituency. I had to keep my promise: Robert did not care about Express Newspapers or Conservative politicians; he cared about Giant Haystacks or whoever it then was. But it would suit me down to the ground if Hague and I could have the meeting during that trip. Why not meet up early on Sunday morning? No one would see us, we could have a cup of tea and get to know each other.

'Mr Hague doesn't work on Sundays.'

We left it a few months and then Hague came to the office with Coe. I wanted to speak candidly and asked Coe to wait outside for a moment. I told William how badly I thought he had behaved over the feature in *OK!* I didn't care personally, but a would-be PM ought to take his relationships with the media more seriously. Blair, I pointed out, had been straight on the phone to me even though he was prime minister.

My experience with politicians, then, was mixed, but I discovered that there was one media owner to whom they all paid homage. Some time after my first meeting with Hague – and after he had lost the election and resigned as leader – I saw him at a private dinner hosted by Michael Ashcroft, then the Conservative party treasurer, and soon we found ourselves laughing about how everyone works for Rupert Murdoch even when they think they don't.

Jeff Randall, the business pundit, said, 'Well I don't work for Murdoch. I write for the *Telegraph*.'

I pointed out that he did a programme on Sky and he said, 'Oh, yeah, I suppose so.'

Amanda Platell, Hague's press secretary, had worked for Murdoch during her time on the late but rarely lamented *Today* newspaper.

Hague himself looked at his wife and said, 'Well, *we* certainly don't work for Murdoch.'

Ffion corrected him, 'Actually, my book will be with HarperCollins – so I do too.'

Strangely enough, I couldn't help liking Murdoch, despite the viciousness of the attacks made on me by his *Sunday Times*. I think it was because Murdoch is a man without a mask. What you see is what you get; he is, in that respect, very honest. He is also a worthy opponent. We had some good skirmishes. Early on in my ownership of the *Daily Star*, the *Sun*'s edgier, more feisty rival, we learned that there was a worldwide News Corp board meeting to be held at their building at (formerly Fortress) Wapping. Opposite that building

Prince Philip opens the new Northern & Shell building in Crossharbour, Docklands in 1993.

With David and Victoria Beckham on their wedding day, 4 July 1999.

The rise and rise of OK!

Princess Diana was a great fan of OK! Now OK! readers love reading about her sons and grandchildren.

With my mother, celebrating as OK! becomes a weekly magazine in 1996.

Proud owner of the *Express*, which
I bought in November 2000.

Relaxing with a good newspaper at our former
Blackfriars office.

With *Big Brother* star Jade Goody
in May 2007.

With another tabloid favourite: Katie Price

My mother makes a speech at an *OK!*
event on her 90th birthday, 11 May 2006.

With Air Commodore Malcolm White
in June 2012, after *Daily Express*
readers and I helped raise money
to fund the Bomber Command
Memorial in London's Green Park.

A meeting with the Queen in December 2008
during her visit to Ravenswood Village, run by
one of my favourite charities, Norwood.

With Hollywood royalty: Jessica
Simpson and P. Diddy at the
September 2005 launch of the
American edition of *OK!*

The Crusaders in concert, with (left to right) Simon Townshend, Lulu, me, Robert Plant, Greg Lake and Roger Daltrey at Billingsgate in 2006, performing on behalf of the Evelina Children's Hospital.

Robert, me and Greg at another Crusaders charity concert in 2004.

Me and my beloved Ludwig drum kit.

At the *Ocean's 13* party in Cannes in 2007: (left to right)
Matt Damon, George Clooney, me, producer Jerry Weintraub,
Don Cheadle and Brad Pitt.

The Richard Desmond Children's Centre
at Moorfields Eye Hospital, which was
opened by the Queen on 23 February 2007.

Proud owner of Channel 5, July 2010.

With Joy, David Cameron and Simon Cowell in November 2014.

A revived *Dallas* became a stalwart of
Channel 5 programming.

Making a speech to the Royal Television
Society in September 2013 ...

... and another to promote my
Health Lottery in June 2014.

This statue, called 'Tikvah' (Hebrew for 'hope'), holds a particular significance for Joy and me.

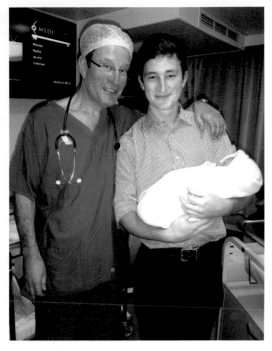

With Robert and Angel, hours after her birth on 9 March 2011.

An emotional family visit to Auschwitz, May 2012.

With Joy, baby Valentine, Angel, a stuffed toy and a
real-life dog – Star – in January 2015.

there was a giant poster site and throughout the period of the meeting we succeeded in booking it for a blockbuster *Daily Star* advertisement to entertain Mr Murdoch and his generals. For its part, News Corp was perfectly able to look after itself. When we launched *OK!* in the USA, for example, we used to be attacked on a regular basis by Keith Kelly in Murdoch's *New York Post*.

Hostilities reached a high point when I attended a Sky do at London's Oxo tower and my driver David suggested we park my Rolls-Royce so that it blocked the main entrance, obliging Murdoch to pull up further down the street and walk.

Rupert sought me out at the reception later. He said, 'Ah, Mr Desmond. I keyed your car . . .'

His son James could not understand why they would all just laugh when I had a go at them. Even though he was educated at Harvard or wherever, James is quite literal-minded: he doesn't always get when it's rock and roll.

Even the socialist Gordon Brown, I think, paid homage to Murdoch in the days when the backing of News Corp was thought to help swing elections. Sadly, Brown didn't pay me quite such close attention. I tried my best, even offering him diet and fitness advice when I discovered that he was living on Coca Cola and biscuits. When he moved into an office surrounded by plasma screens I gave him budgeting advice about the cost of all the gear, and when he came in to our offices I offered him our tax adviser's services over the matter of pensions, since he and Ed Balls seemed to be getting in a muddle. But I don't think Mr Brown wanted my advice. We had a long and painful argument during which I (the guy who wasn't interested in politics) pushed for a strategy that I thought would create more wealth and well-being, while Brown stuck to a strategy that I thought would create more state dependants, and therefore more Labour voters. Brown's kind of socialism wasn't Blair's kind of socialism, and I suppose the two of us had different priorities.

That you could be involved in the debate in this way was, of course, one of the rewards of owning inkwells. There were many others. Being in a newspaper office when major events occurred was certainly one – I'll never forget, for example, the atmosphere of the *Express* offices when 9/11 hit. I was also fascinated to see which long-running stories particularly appealed to our readers. I soon noticed that they were passionate about anything in general that smacked of mystery, and anything in particular to do with the circumstances of Princess Diana's death. I knew Mohamed Al Fayed and was fascinated by his conspiracy theories about the Establishment although I was very aware that his grief coloured his views. That said, the newspapers needed no encouragement from him or me to unravel over months and years the detective story surrounding the final days of Britain's most iconic royal.

But while people liked such stories, the coverage in itself rarely moved our circulation figures by more than a couple of percentage points, if at all. True, when we signed with John Leslie after he was exonerated from a sex charge in connection with Ulrika Jonsson, that certainly helped sales in immediate terms. For most readers, though, buying a newspaper is a routine, part of their everyday life: they're not necessarily swayed by that day's front page. The name of the game, therefore, is to reward them and maintain their loyalty rather than endlessly and fruitlessly seek to build circulation. The days are long past when any newspaper could significantly build numbers by any means other than giveaway promotions (which lose money and cannot be sustained) and price cuts (which lose even more money and cannot be sustained). Running the *Express*, then, was not so much about reporting breaking news (our readers already had that from TV), but reinforcing opinions and keeping them focused – affirmation rather than information.

In other words, the challenges I faced with my newspapers were very much the challenges I had faced with magazines, and the similarities between the two were far greater than the differences. A good piece of writing is a good piece of writing and a good cover picture is a good cover picture. Whether you did a negative review on a guitar for *International Musician* and had to go and look the manufacturer in the eye, or had a journalist captured by the Taliban and accused of spying on them and had to go and reason with them, it was a similar game. Paul Ashford did both and said some of the guys in the music industry were worse. During the Taliban incident, after we'd established that we could not get out of it just by offering money, the British consulate explained that the biggest problem with those guys was they never answered their mobile phones. It was not so much that our diplomats wouldn't talk to terrorists, then, it was that they couldn't.

In immediate terms, I had a financial mountain to climb. I had staked everything, I had borrowed extensively, and I was under great pressure to get the books to balance and to start paying off our loans. At the same time, I had to make sure that any economies I made wouldn't have an adverse effect on the papers. In other words, while I had to make cuts where I could, I also had to spend on content, particularly at the woefully neglected *Star*, which had suffered from low picture budgets and no Saturday magazine. We actually hired an eminent paparazzo called Jason Fraser for £1 million a year, thinking that with him we could dominate the picture market in papers as we did in magazines with *OK!*. Jason kept calling me guv'nor and saying how loyal he was. In practice, though, things didn't work out too well because as soon as we took him on, he decided to 'hang up his camera' and concentrate on page design, suggesting we buy in any pictures we needed. Since that's exactly what we'd been doing up until then, I didn't feel we were making much progress.

Fortunately we had some luck. On our first day as owners we had absolutely no cash in the bank, but before close of business there was a £20 million payment from our wholesalers for the preceding month's sales. Since the staff had just been paid and weren't due for their next pay cheque until the middle of the following month, that gave us a breathing space.

Then I stopped the old practice of paying suppliers early, and put them on a standard 30 days credit period. There was a paper-buying company set up as a joint venture with the Telegraph, and that too paid early: by arranging to delay 30 days I could release £10 million in additional cash flow. In a funny way I was also helped by the 2001 crash: because I'd had to liquidate all my investments to buy the Express I didn't lose anything, as so many others did. Later on even Jeffrey Archer pitched in to help me. It turned out that in his celebrated lawsuit with the *Daily Star* over sex with a prostitute he had lied in court and the *Star* was reimbursed £500,000 damages it had paid in 1987, together with £1.3m in legal costs and interest. Archer went to jail and, worse, his membership of Marylebone Cricket Club was suspended for seven years. I financially looked after the widow of the editor, Lloyd Turner, who had been pilloried in court during the Archer trial and had never really recovered. The rest went towards getting us back into the black and also launching the *Daily Star Sunday*.

In fact our financial position improved to the point where we were able to offer to pay down our debts to Commerzbank. They, like all banks, responded by saying that since we were in a position to return money they didn't really want it. I have a theory that Commerzbank's original concerns about our loan and their desire to lay it off by syndication owed something to negative opinions circulated amongst banks by the later disgraced Lord Black, proprietor of the *Telegraph* and our partner in West Ferry Printing, who stood to gain if our finances became so tight that we had to agree a quick cash deal and offload our half of the print works to him. Actually, that wasn't the only point of tension between us and our print partners. There was also the small matter of £20 million sitting as a cash deposit in the bank account of West Ferry Printing. As 50 per cent partners half that sum was ours and that too would be useful in reducing debt. I therefore went to the *Telegraph* and said, 'Hello, pleased to meet you, can we have our cash back?'

Enter, at this point, the big Canadian in ermine – or rather his emissaries: Daniel Colson, a clever lawyer; Jeremy Deedes who wore yellow socks and whose role wasn't quite clear to me (although his father was a great editor); and an Irish accountant who kept talking about 'fiduciary duties' (ironic, considering the trouble Black got into later).

What they told me was that because of these mysterious 'fiduciary duties', we could not have our money. I said that if it transpired that we had a fiduciary duty – whatever that was – we would write a cheque out. They didn't like this. In fact, they threw us off the West Ferry board (they were contractually entitled to do so since there had been a change of control). But taking that step put them in something of a bind. According to the contract, once we were off the board, they were immediately obliged to buy our half of the business for a price calculated by a previously agreed formula. That price, it emerged, was £68 million.

They ignored the formula and instead, assuming that we were desperate, offered to buy our share for £18 million. This seemed a little unfair, given that there was in any case £20 million of cash in the business. We consulted various very expensive lawyers and accountants. Everyone agreed that, according to the joint venture contract, we should be paid £68 million. We thought the Telegraph were now obliged to buy our share of West Ferry Printers for that price. There was a brief initial court hearing during which we were presumably seen as pornographers from the East End and Colson explained that he was a qualified lawyer of many years' experience and Conrad Black, being a Lord, was a pillar of society. In any event we were not victorious.

All that court decision meant, however, was that the Telegraph were not compelled to buy us out (lucky for us, in view of later developments). We therefore still had to find a way of working together. We had a meeting on a Saturday morning where I smoked a cigar, to which Colson objected. I said I owned 50 per cent and was smoking the cigar in my 50 per cent of the office. But I did offer him one too. He saved it for later.

We talked. We argued. Time ticked by. In the end, Colson had had enough. He said, 'I give up. You become the chairman of West Ferry, and you run it.'

'Well, in that case I want my share of the £20 million.'

'That's not possible.'

The meeting continued. By one o'clock I believe I had my hands round Colson's neck. 'I want my share of the £20 million!'

'If I agree that, can I go?'

'Yes.'

So the deal was done.

From there, the West Ferry business prospered. Perhaps, too, I added a little colour to the board meetings, including, regrettably, greeting the suggestion that our partners' business might be sold to Axel Springer with my version of Basil Fawlty's 'Don't mention the war' scene. Even more regrettably someone decided that my skills as an impressionist were so remarkable that they were worth making public, suggesting that I was anti-German. Well, I'm not: and those who know me will know how often I praise the attitude of German authorities to business as compared to some in England – for example, the city councillors at Luton, where we ultimately moved our printing operation.

That, however, was some years later, and only after a troubled period and near strike action by the print unions. Luckily, on that occasion, which came when the Telegraph group decided to break with West Ferry and move their printing to Murdoch's plant, I was able to explain to the unions that if they weakened the *Star* and the *Express* through industrial action, the only winners would be News International.

Anyway, after all our ups and downs, I rather thought, and hoped, that Conrad Black and I had achieved a working relationship. So did my friend Gerald Ronson, because once that big initial dispute about West Ferry was out of the way, he held a lunch at which he seated me next to Conrad so that we could make peace. (I did explain that Conrad had tried to steal my print plant, but Gerald said he was not a bad bloke really.) When we met, I told Black I was glad it was all sorted.

He said, 'I'm glad you think it is: you and your lawyer Mr *Rosenbloom.*'

I didn't care for that because my lawyer is actually Ian Rosenblatt and I thought Black was trying to make some kind of point by deliberately forgetting a name that he knew very well. Anyway, after these words he turned his back and spoke to the person on the other side.

At the end of the lunch he stood up. 'Good to see you, Conrad,' I said. 'Keep well.'

And I put my hand out.

He looked at me briefly, ignored my hand, and walked away.

16
CRUSADING FOR A FAIRER BRITAIN

At the same time as I was sorting out the business aspects of the newspapers, I was also obliged to come to grips with my responsibilities as the steward of a much-loved British institution. When I appeared before the Leveson Inquiry into press ethics in 2011, I tried to make the point that ethics are personal and law universal, but all I got for my trouble were uncomplimentary headlines from the broadsheets who misconstrued my meaning. So maybe I need to address that issue again.

My view is this: if running a newspaper means that you have to engage with politics – as Tony Blair rightly told me it does – it also means that you need a moral direction. I think I'd always known in my gut what the *Daily Express* was about. It was my parents' paper. It was everyone's parents' paper. It had represented the heartbeat of middle Britain for 100 years. Its second proprietor had been given a special place in the country's war effort against Germany. In fact we discovered, and still retain, Beaverbrook's official ministerial briefcase from the period. The previous owners hadn't exactly treasured it – in fact, I believe that at one point it was put in a skip.

Once again, I don't believe it is my job to edit the papers I own or to tell my editors what to say. So I'm always slightly surprised when I come across articles in rival papers that suggest otherwise.

What I do believe in, though, is a crusading paper that listens to its readers. *Daily* and *Sunday Express* readers, along with *Daily Star* readers, are highly committed to a set of values that define this country, its traditions and its history. The same is true of readers of the *Daily Star Sunday*, which we launched in 2002 as the feisty 'new kid on the block' against the ailing *Mirror* titles and the increasingly compromised *News of the World*. They tend to be people who are in work, who are aspirational, who want to stand on their own feet, who are kind-hearted towards those who can't work or fend for themselves, but unsympathetic towards those who won't. They want a proper NHS and a welfare state that will combat poverty but not discourage effort. They are concerned about law and order. Many are old enough to remember times when the country needed strong armed forces to protect us and they still wish for that level of security. They also wouldn't mind, within the context of a just and compassionate society, being allowed to keep as much as they can of what they earn. They like Britain to be British, distrust Europe, and hate being bossed around by people who don't live here.

I don't myself think these views are extreme – but they can certainly land you in hot water. My first experience of this came in 2002 when the then editor of the *Express*, Chris Williams, led with headlines saying immigration was running out of control. In fact it was, and in the years that followed everyone fell in behind the *Express* and admitted the truth of the matter, including the government. But at the time we were pilloried for what we said. I myself didn't comment on the issue publicly (though when I read our editorials it worried me, as a businessman, that government departments seemed to have so little idea of what was going on), but that didn't mean I was exempt from the criticism – or from the suggestion that I personally was stirring up racial hatred. In fact I have personal reasons for understanding the value of immigration: I am the grandchild of Jewish immigrants – asylum seekers even. My problem is with chaotic and uncontrolled immigration, just as I have a problem with any business or organisation that is not properly and efficiently run. But critics wouldn't – and still won't – accept the distinction. Far from foisting any agenda on the papers, however, I learned much of what I know simply by reading them.

It was about the time this big controversy started to make the headlines that we first put into words what we felt we stood for: we were 'Crusading for a Fairer Britain'. We had, after all, our crusader on the masthead. One of our rivals duly produced a cartoon version of him with a large cigar, and I have another in my office in which he sports distinctive spectacles. I cannot imagine who that was intended to represent. The point was we knew we had readers who felt they were being denied a voice. As a Jew, I know only too well the kind of politics that can emerge when people feel alienated from the government that is supposed to serve them, and I know the kind of evil that can insert itself into the vacuum when it appears that those in charge don't care. I'm reminded of the 'lost' young family man my friend the Tottenham MP David Lammy described in his book about the London riots of 2011, *Out of the Ashes*.

> I asked Scott why [he intended to vote for the BNP]. His response was matter of fact. Since the age of 16 he had worked as a labourer in construction. Now he had a wife and two children but could not find work to support them. Eastern European builders were getting jobs he felt should be his, with many working for less than the minimum wage, and he was fed up. He insisted he wasn't racist, but he didn't think it was fair.

At the *Daily Express*, the *Sunday Express*, the *Daily Star* and the *Daily Star Sunday*, we started to use the f-word a great deal. What was fair? Which government would deliver on fairness? Which politicians might turn out to be prejudiced and dogmatic? Who even understood what it was like to be Scott, or our readers?

I remember that during the first few years of my proprietorship Stephen Glover wrote in the *Spectator*: 'What next – will Richard Desmond soon be lecturing us on the decline of moral standards?'

Well, er, yes.

Because many of our readers are of a certain age, one of their core worries turns out to be the issue of fair pensions – and that was a topic I took up with Gordon Brown when he came to our offices looking for support.

The trouble with pensions is that no one understands them and the details tend to be very boring. That is why Brown got away with his earliest 'stealth tax' aimed at interest paid on dividends in pension funds: we all yawned, and didn't realise that it was costing us thousands a year. Yet, while their workings may be tough to comprehend, I'm only too aware of just how vital they are. At the age of 26 I had an accountant from Harrow called Howard Midgen who, when I got a tax bill, told me I had to put money into a pension. I told Howard to get lost (the expression I used was more colourful – but then I was only 26). I didn't want to pay the tax and I wouldn't need a pension because when I was 60 I would either be a billionaire or on a park bench. Howard explained that tax was not really something you had an option on paying, but that even I might some day get old, and it is not a bad thing to have a safety net. In fact in the course of my life it's often been the case that when it looked like business risks might not pay off, I have been able to say to myself – well, at least there's the pension to fall back on. A pension, then, is essential – as is knowing that the government won't at some point suddenly change the rules so that your life plan no longer works – as recent governments have in fact done for middle-income people.

During my argument with Brown on the subject, I called in our tax man who had just come to us from Price Waterhouse, and he proceeded to prove that Brown had got his sums wrong. Brown wasn't best pleased. I think, however, they made changes and at least they used the concept of A-Day so they did not take what you have already saved. I believe I am not alone in feeling that for successive governments to advocate self-reliance and saving, and then suddenly cap the amount you are allowed to save in a pension fund and hit you with a double penalty if you go over, is not a great incentive to be financially prudent.

In another 'crusade' to do with personal finance, the *Daily Express* fought to reform inheritance tax. Once thought of as a tax only on the rich, it had become – thanks both to Brown and to soaring house prices – a burden on a vast swathe of hard-working middle-income earners. Not for nothing was it dubbed the 'grave robbery of middle Britain', sucking ordinary people into a financial trap on the death of their loved ones. Some 400,000 readers joined our campaign, and in response the shadow chancellor George Osborne rang me to say that he would be making a speech in which he would pledge to raise the inheritance tax threshold to £1 million. He duly did so, and the favourable reaction he received scared Gordon Brown – by then the prime minister – away from calling a snap general election (which, had it gone ahead, might well have delivered a Conservative defeat). Everyone began to say that the Tories were returning to traditional Conservative values, and that their leader David Cameron was not just an old Etonian possibly dope-smoking twat. In fairness, every time I now see Cameron he acknowledges the importance of the campaign, and if the coalition deal with the Lib Dems in 2010 left Osborne unable to follow up on the pledge, it still remains an element of Tory policy.

So we fought for issues related to the well-being of middle-income British families. At the same time our 'anti-immigration' readers rallied to the cause when we took up cudgels on behalf of the Gurkhas, aided and abetted by Joanna Lumley who would more commonly have been seen in *OK!* magazine. The issue was whether they should be allowed British citizenship. On the one hand, the government thought Nepalese soldiers were good enough to fight and die for this country. On the other hand, it seemed to think that once they had finished their army service they should be treated like aliens and required to return to Nepal. Gurkhas have fought for Britain for 200 years and won 26 Victoria Crosses. More than 45,000 have been killed in combat and 150,000 wounded fighting for Britain. Some 40,000 *Daily Express* readers signed a petition that was then taken to 10 Downing Street. In the face of rising pressure the Labour government performed a U-turn and let ex-army Gurkhas settle in the UK and be granted British citizenship.

Daily Express readers also played the leading role in helping Bomber Command veterans raise the £4 million needed to build a memorial to their fallen comrades. Inspired by the paper's coverage, generous readers donated £500,000 and I added £500,000 personally. Even then, we had to put pressure on Cameron's government to help meet the costs of the dedication ceremony when the stunning memorial was unveiled by the Queen in June 2012. To ensure that what we were doing wouldn't upset people in Germany, I telephoned the Mayor of Dresden to sound her out; she assured me it wouldn't be a problem and even donated some trees to plant at the site. She reminded me I had had dealings with her city years before when I had contributed to the flood relief appeal there. Bomber Command suffered the highest casualty rate of any British-led unit in the Second World War, losing 55,573 of its 125,000 volunteers, average age just 22. It only took 67 years to get them a suitable monument.

Other successful causes included securing better laws on uninsured drivers and a 'take back our streets' crusade after London was torn apart by the 2011 riots. A rather less well-advised campaign was the one we fought to save Concorde from being scrapped. Fortunately on this occasion we were unsuccessful: BA chairman Colin Marshall told us privately that towards the end the old aircraft had been so patched together that everyone in the know said a fervent prayer whenever one took off.

We did what we could, in any case, and said what our readers wanted us to say as loudly as we could in the ears of the successive governments of Blair, Brown and Cameron (plus Clegg).

With Cameron himself, I enjoyed a friendly enough relationship but I sometimes wished he would be a proper Conservative – I suppose more like Mrs Thatcher. Also he was late to our first meeting – which is never a good thing with me. It was back in 2005 and Peter Gummer, Lord Chadlington, had arranged for us to get together. He organised a breakfast with the 'prospective' leader of the Conservative party. By that time the *Daily Express* was supporting the Tories, which had been the editor's decision because they were more in tune with our naturally conservative (small 'c') readers, and the Labour party was no longer Blair's New Labour.

The arrangement was that we would meet at eight o'clock at a conference centre near the Bank of England. Now, I don't like breakfast at eight o'clock. I have my breakfast at six o'clock. By eight o'clock you should be at work, or possibly at the gym, but in any event not having breakfast. That said, I also have a maxim that it is better to be half an hour early than a minute late, so I arrived with plenty of time to spare. There were around 30 people assembled at three tables. At ten past eight Cameron arrived.

I was invited, perhaps by someone with a sense of mischief, to put the first question. Remembering my terrible experience with Adam Cole, I put it very carefully. 'Mr Cameron, can I ask did you have any personal problems today?'

He answered no. I then asked whether his journey had been OK and whether his family were OK. He said, yes, fine.

I went on, 'Mr Cameron, you got us all here at eight o'clock. Now, you want to be leader of the Conservative party, so you are selling today.'

His eyes flickered as though he didn't quite understand what I was saying. I tried to explain. 'There are three types of people, those who sell, those who make, and those who account, and you are certainly not the last two, so you are selling. If I'm selling I always arrive a bit early so I can get off to a positive start, and if you arrive late, well, it's a bit insulting, so that's my first point.

'My second point, or rather question, is, are people ever going to like you? Because 99 per cent of people don't like Etonians since we think you are all privileged and a bit poncey and you've got those funny accents and you sort of look down on people.'

He did not think this would be a problem.

Since it was the time of the controversy over his smoking pot, I added, 'My third question is, why can't you admit you had a joint? I've had a joint. Peter here probably has.' (He did not disagree.) 'We all have a story to tell, it's part of life, so why run away from it?'

He gave his stock answer about it being personal. I was genuinely trying to help, but maybe he did not see that.

It was all very different from my first dealings with George Osborne. We'd been brought together by Howard Leigh, who is now Lord Leigh because I believe he contributed something to something. George, unlike David, was smart: he started off telling me what a great job I was doing for the Norwood charity and volunteered to speak at our Norwood annual dinner. His diary secretary got on the phone straight afterwards, and we made a date. I thought here is a man you could work with.

So Cameron and I didn't really click. Maybe it was because he had worked as a PR man for Michael Green, with whom I also didn't click. I was also unimpressed by his demeanour towards Mr Murdoch who seemed, as I have already mentioned, to have a fatal attraction for politicians. I'd often noticed that Rupert would hold cocktail parties where all the people who knocked him behind his back would come to drink his champagne while turning up their noses.

Cameron didn't do that. Instead, at one party we both attended, my supposed new friend and ally came up to me and, just as I expected to hear a friendly 'Hello Richard!', trod on my foot and pushed me aside in his rush to get to Rupert. He then did the same thing at a charity event at which Murdoch and I were present. He even trod on my foot once to get to Sly Bailey who used to run the *Mirror*. Maybe he thought he could be so sure of our support that he did not need to bother.

Before the 2010 election Cameron visited us for lunch in our boardroom with all our editors. But he seemed unable to relax with us. And, I have to say, he wasn't impressive either. I remember him rubbing his hands and saying it was good that the economy was going down because that would help the Conservatives win. He was perhaps half joking and, in fairness, if you buy a business you don't want it to be at the peak of its performance. But it struck me at the time as not being a very statesmanlike thing to say.

I emphasised to him that what our readers cared about was uncontrolled immigration, pensions, inheritance tax − in other words, issues that affect ordinary people. But he did not really take it on board and I believe that, in the final analysis, neither did Osborne. The reality is that one is a well-to-do PR man and the other is the playboy son of a bloke who made wallpaper; and while I mean no disrespect when I say that, the fact remains that neither of them has ever been broke, or worked in a cloakroom or a market stall or sold a balloon on Hampstead Heath. Even so, the *Express* decided to back them. It was a decision taken by the editors, based on what they knew our readers wanted. In any case there was little choice as the alternative was Gordon Brown.

So Cameron, for me, is no Thatcher or Winston Churchill. I met him on one occasion with the editor of the *Daily Express* Hugh Whittow and he said, 'I am a social democrat really.' I once went to see the Russian ambassador Alexander Yakovenko because I was trying to get support for an orphans' home I fund in Pinsk, Belarus. Alexander told me that at a G8 conference during the height of the crisis in Crimea, Cameron sought out Putin and demanded a one-to-one meeting. Putin had little time for Cameron so scheduled the meeting for two in the morning. Cameron turned up (I do not know if he was late), and said, 'Vladimir, I want to speak to you about your stance on gay marriage.' All well and good, but perhaps not what should be uppermost in a prime minister's mind when there's a war going on.

Well, I do not think I make a good politician, although I have always been fond of the tune of the same name by Cream. Life at the Express, in due course, found its rhythm, and maybe we did, and do, a bit of good. Yet while this was going on I also found another way to try to make the world a slightly better place.

17
THE
REAL
DEAL

The first few years of my time at the *Daily Express* were also important in expanding the *OK!* brand, creating *Star* and *New!* magazines to fight off competitors in the celebrity market, rolling out more foreign editions, and growing the Richard Desmond Charitable Trust because even I had to admit I was beginning to do well, and I wanted to be a good citizen too. I was working as hard as I had at 23, but despite the fact that those around me all agreed I looked like Harrison Ford in his earlier movies, I was no longer 23.

Despite my best efforts to make a difference in the world, however, I was still widely viewed as the maverick from Docklands, and I still had difficulty explaining to people what we were all about. I must give my communications man Alan Edwards the credit, or the blame, for my next step. It was his fault I ended up, in the early 2000s, in my early fifties, back behind a drum kit, with Roger Daltrey throwing water at me.

As I have mentioned, despite getting the cane for selling charity programmes in my schooldays, I still try to do my bit, and the RD Crusaders began with Roger Daltrey's charity, the Teenage Cancer Trust, which dramatically increases survival rates for teenage sufferers by securing them care in an upbeat environment with others of their own generation.

Roger was introduced (or re-introduced) to me by Alan Edwards in connection with raising money to build more TCT facilities. I used to go to Elton John's parties and because Roger had a big place in Sussex I initially suggested he got a marquee and did an evening with guests at £5,000 a table. Roger said he was not a tantrum-and-tiara type, he was a rock-and-roll vocalist and that would not be his scene. 'But,' he added, 'if I remember rightly, you play the drums, don't you? So put a band together and I'll sing in it.'

And then he left.

Now this would be grief. I know about bands. It's always grief. So I called my PA Allison in to dictate a nice note saying that it had been great to meet Roger but unfortunately I couldn't take up his band idea because I had a media group to run – and anyway I hadn't played drums for 30 years. Allison objected. She pointed out that I was always telling stories about these guys, so I clearly enjoyed their company. I should get involved while I still could, was her view. It might be fun.

'It won't be fun.'

'You'll enjoy yourself.'

'I won't.'

In the end I gave in, and we started to put a band together. I suggested that Roger's friend Zoot Money could be our organist. Then a few weeks later I was at Irvine Sellar's daughter's wedding and met a big fellow with Versace slippers whom Irvine introduced as Greg Lake, formerly of Emerson, Lake & Palmer. Now Greg, I know, is a great bass player. I told him about the new project.

'Well, I haven't done much charity work. Maybe I should. All right, I'm in. Here's my number.'

When it came to guitarists Roger suggested Russ Ballard, formerly of Argent, and asked if I knew him. I said I knew Bob Henrit and Jim Rodford from the band but Russ was always a bit of a superstar so I suppose I had been nervous of him.

'No – it's him who's nervous. *Very* nervous. You mustn't give him any stress . . .'

I said I was sure there wouldn't be any stress. For our other guitarist we went for the late Gary Moore who said he'd be happy to play 'Parisienne Walkways' – even with arthritis he was still one of the most powerful players going. Gary Brooker joined us on keyboards and of course for 'A Whiter Shade of Pale'. Sam Brown was on vocals. The sax player was Nick Newell who had always been nice to me as a kid. Roger got Simon Townshend ('as good as Pete') to help on the Who songs.

We put together a playlist. I championed 'The Letter' because it's funky, and we added 'Green Onions', 'Heatwave' and a few Who songs. When it came to selecting a venue we ultimately went for Ronnie Scott's, which seemed to have the right combination of prestige and intimacy. Our grand concert was booked for the night of Sunday 19 October 2003, with food supplied courtesy of Robert Earl of the Hard Rock Café.

The week before the concert I had constant nightmares. I dreamed that I tried to hit the bass drum pedal only to discover that it had disappeared. Or the snare would turn out to be broken. I practised every day and got so many blisters I went around with my hands covered in Elastoplast as if I had been carrying out some particularly perverse form of self-harm, which I suppose I had.

On the night, we did a sound check, and then I went for a long walk. I felt as if I were about to explode. When I returned the audience was there. I sat on the drum stool.

I thought, '*Get me out of here, I can't play!*'

But as this was Ronnie Scott's I realised the only way I could get out would be if I walked through the audience.

'Green Onions' started. I caught the rhythm. It wasn't too bad. It wasn't too bad at all.

And actually it turned out to be a great night. The gig and auction together raised nearly half a million pounds (about the same that Roger achieved at the Albert Hall). Roger was over the moon and said we should do it again. I said I reckoned I should quit while I was ahead. After all, I didn't even have a drum kit that was up to it, just Bill Bruford's old Ludwig kit – though it had been good enough in its day.

Later, I received a call from the Ludwig Drum Company whom I used to visit in the USA when I was selling pages for my music magazines.

'We saw you were playing an old Ludwig kit. Would you like a new one?'

Amazing. When you can't afford it you can't afford it, and when you can, they give it to you for nothing. So I agreed two more gigs for 2004 – as a Ludwig endorsee.

The aim on those occasions was to do more for Roger's Teenage Cancer Trust, and also to help the Norwood charity by raising money for a new care centre in north London. I aimed for £2.5 million. Two concerts on 18 and 19 October were planned for the Cirque at the Hippodrome – much larger and glitzier than Ronnie Scott's.

The idea was we'd perform for the TCT the first night and aim to get £450,000 from tickets, then reach £1 million the second night including an auction plus even more in donations from people who wanted to come on stage and sing with our stars. More rehearsals, more blisters.

This time our line-up had one notable addition – Robert Plant of Led Zeppelin. I had met Robert at Talk of the Town a few weeks before; he said he had heard about our concerts and had been intrigued, one thing had led to another and so here he was.

At our first rehearsal he said, 'Look – I've brought the music for you.'

'I'm not a professional musician,' I said.

He looked a bit surprised. My kit was the same as John Bonham's so he had assumed I could play like John Bonham. He tried to help by going through key signatures with me. Something would start out in 2:4 , then it would switch to 6:8 or 4:3 or 7:6. Oh dear.

'This is all a bit beyond me,' I confessed.

Zoot interrupted, 'Richard's fine, he'll *feel* it. I'll help him, trust me, it'll be fine.'

So Robert Plant trusted Zoot who trusted me that I wouldn't fuck up the drums. And somehow I didn't. I did notice, though, that whereas Plant still seemed to be a magnet for female fans of a similar age to those who would have chased him in the early days of Led Zeppelin, I didn't have the same effect. My conclusion was that it's the vocalist who enjoys most success in that area, or possibly the lead guitarist. The drummer, I decided, attracts a more specialised following.

Anyway, with ticket sales, the charities we helped were delighted, and Norwood suggested that my hard work on their behalf should be rewarded with more hard work on their behalf. Would I take over when the current president, Trevor Chinn, retired in a couple of years' time? I agreed. It was clear that the RD Crusaders were not going to stop any time soon.

And so the 2004 success was followed by further concerts over the next few years, each raising more money than the last. In 2006 we were even joined by my friend Lulu. I had done a great vocal duet with her at a Who concert ten years previously, although I have to admit that our contribution had been made from the safety of the audience.

Naturally, not every event went entirely smoothly. Musicians get tense at big gigs. Some you can't talk to before the concert; some you can't talk to afterwards; some need the same size dressing rooms as others; others need bigger; some have comments to make on others' musicianship, or how a particular song ought to be played. Some find the stage too high, or too low, or object because they are not getting their share of the limelight.

I had direct experience of the unpredictability of live music halfway through a Billingsgate gig when I was very perplexed to find Roger hurling bottles of water at me. I didn't know how to respond. Then I decided to toss a drumstick at him. He was furious. It later turned out that he used to throw water at Keith Moon during 'Won't Get Fooled Again' because when it fell on the snare drum the splashes made nice patterns in time with the beat. He had not reckoned on me returning fire, and thought getting a drumstick in the eye would spoil his rock-god good looks. Such are the misunderstandings that can arise at these affairs.

But from raising £1 million, we were now raising nearly twice that for the Evelina Children's Hospital appeal. I had, of course, still got a business to run and I arranged that I would pay the set-up of the Billingsgate concert, which was a major cost, and the following night we would play for a party for my staff and customers to celebrate ten years of *OK!* as a weekly title and my mum's 90th birthday, at which she made a great speech and got more applause even than the Crusaders.

For our 2008 line-up we managed to secure the services of Steve Harley from Cockney Rebel, Robert Hart from Bad Company, Rick Wills of Foreigner, Elkie Brooks and reality star Peter Andre (returning to his roots as a soul singer). We even had Mark Ronson, then at the height of his fame as solo artist and producer of Amy Winehouse and others. Mark, being a star, said he needed to bring his own bass player. Roger disapproved, pointing out that he wasn't sure who Mark was anyway, but I explained that when you were 35 you were bound to be a bit arrogant when it came to playing with old geezers of 60, and we just had to put up with it. Come to think of it, I added, playing with us would probably prove the high spot of his career anyway. Anyway when we started 'God Put A Smile

Upon Your Face' I stepped up the pace and poor Mark was soon sweating buckets trying to keep up. The moral of this? Never irritate the drummer.

And yet, thanks to Mark and everyone else – 2008 proved an extraordinary year. We raised nearly £5 million for Evelina, Marie Curie Cancer Care, Norwood, Fight for Sight and the National Hospital Development Foundation. Such fundraising proved a hard act to follow; I came up with the Health Lottery plan several years later. The band continued to play other gigs for some time. And I do not believe the last has been heard of it even today.

Meanwhile I still had a business to run and was busy turning our celebrity magazine into a global force. First we launched a Chinese edition, to be followed by ventures in countries that ranged from the Philippines to India, from Turkey to Vietnam, and from Mongolia to Venezuela. We even launched *OK!* in Madrid – really just to thumb our nose at *Hola!* owner Eduardo Sánchez Junco, with whom our rivalry continued unabated, even though by now *OK!* definitely had the upper hand.

On the domestic front, throughout the early 2000s *OK!* remained the home of Victoria and David Beckham. However, we had also discovered that reality TV was a great source of new talent. True to our strategy of adopting and growing our own stars, we became friendly with an ambitious model called Katie Price. Katie's boyfriend was the footballer Dwight Yorke. I suppose that makes her one of the original WAGs.

We actually took an enormous chance with Katie because she was best known as a Page Three pin-up, and there was no guarantee that she would appeal to the very female world of *OK!* readers. But Katie was outspoken and feisty, and she proved very popular. In time her affair with Dwight ended, leaving her to bring up her son Harvey, a baby who tragically was born with a number of disabling conditions. Katie tackled the challenge of raising a sick child with characteristic vigour and panache, combining her own zeal for publicity with a determination to raise awareness for kids in Harvey's condition and to get him all the help he needed. *OK!* readers liked her independence – they like a powerful woman who triumphs over adversity. And when she went on some TV jungle show, whose name I can't remember because it was not on Channel 5, and met Peter Andre, we had a new 'golden couple'. For his part, Peter Andre had a good voice and proved a valuable RD Crusader in several concerts (even though Roger had never heard of him). We were, however, driven mad by his occasional lack of focus. In the run-up to the concert we staged in Madrid to celebrate the launch of the Spanish edition of *OK!* he inadvertently set off with Katie's passport, and so had to dash home again. Then when he did turn up in Madrid he went walkabout just as we were doing the sound check: it turned out that he had gone clothes shopping.

There were to be other reality stars too, notably Jade Goody who went on to cause a storm by saying something inappropriate to Bollywood diva Shilpa Shetty on *Big Brother* (which *did* end up on Channel 5). When she found that she was dying of cervical cancer, she decided to share the whole experience with Lisa Byrne, our talented editor, and *OK!* readers in the hope that others would benefit by taking heed of the smear tests which she herself had ignored. I admired her courage, and although there was, sadly, nothing I could do to help her I did undertake to help her children when she had gone. I kept my promise.

Meanwhile, our long-running battle with *Hello!* rumbled on. It had, as I've already mentioned, started the day we bought Express Newspapers, when, with the pen more or less poised in my hand to sign, I was informed by managing director Martin Ellice that *Hello!* had run with photos of Michael Douglas and Catherine Zeta Jones's wedding: 'They've nicked the pictures,' he shouted down the phone. 'We have to injunct!'

To which my response was, 'Please – leave me alone!'

I have to confess that it was not a case for which I ever had much enthusiasm. I had a strong suspicion that our costs would outweigh any damages we might win. But I had persuaded Michael and Catherine to sell their wedding pictures to *OK!*, I had paid them £1 million for the rights, and *Hello!*'s behaviour had left a very bad taste in my mouth: they had tried to top our bid, and when that failed had sneaked their own man into the Plaza Hotel to take blurred pictures of the wedding reception.

Although we were able to secure an immediate injunction, *Hello!* managed to get it overturned, using evidence that was later found to be 'unreliable'. Then there was a hearing at which *OK!* was victorious and damages were awarded. Now *Hello!* appealed, and this time they won. Michael and Catherine were found not to have the right of privacy at their own wedding.

By this time I was a little irritated with the head of my legal department. He for his part, seeing the way the land lay, told me that since as a lawyer he could not be complicit in a murder, especially his own, he would make alternative arrangements for employment. Martin Ellice found a way to pursue the case using lawyers working on a 'no win, no fee' basis. The agreement I struck with Martin was that if we won he would be given an Aston Martin but if he lost he would personally launch and run a new edition of *OK!* in Siberia.

Meanwhile, because by nature I'm a peacemaker – and because Michael asked me to – I tried to make *Hello!*'s Eduardo Sánchez Junco see reason. Actually I have to confess I felt a certain affection for him. He was a straightforward, good-natured rogue. When on occasion he used to visit me in London, we would have 'fish and cheeps' and would discuss merging our two businesses. Of course, nothing ever came of that because he was – not to put too fine a point on it – impossible to do a deal with.

And he was also impossible during the case. At an early point in the proceedings when our costs already stood at £400,000, Michael said he would settle for £1 million from *Hello!* – his wife had been deeply upset by the whole business and nothing less would do. When I relayed this to Eduardo, he said, 'I will pay 1 million euros.'

'No Eduardo – you don't understand, this is not a negotiation.'

'I give a million euros!'

When we won the first round and he appealed, I again asked him to stop (costs and damages at that point stood at some £5 million), but he stuck to his guns. He did, however, send £2,000 worth of flowers to Michael and Catherine.

Finally, when the case reached the House of Lords we won, securing in the process a legal precedent for fair privacy laws. Eduardo lost around £13 million and I cannot see how *Hello!* can have been profitable from that day forward. I was nevertheless sorry when Eduardo died in 2010. He'd always said he did not mind about losing money, because the family had a big estancia and, if the worst came to the worst, they could always kill one of their cows and cook it. Apparently he referred to me as a chorizo, which, although it's a sort of spicy Spanish sausage, I took as a term of endearment.

So we emerged from the *Hello!* case victorious, but lawsuits, magazines, newspapers, global expansion, investments, *and* a roll 'n' roll band have a tendency to take their toll on you. I had always tried to look after my health. I went to the gym. I have always been more or less vegetarian since I do not like what has to happen to animals so they can be turned into food. I usually opt for fish, wholefoods and vegetables, and am known for trying to persuade my editors to include the miracle food porridge when they do diet features. But in the middle of one of the most adventurous periods of my business life, just after the first two concerts of the RD Crusaders, and as we were contemplating an American launch of *OK!* (Rupert Murdoch agreed to be our 'big brother' by a handshake, but then changed his mind), I had a problem.

I had started to notice that if I got very carried away, a little vein on my head would start throbbing. I saw a doctor, who suggested I consult an ophthalmologist but since I was none too sure what an ophthalmologist was I didn't bother. Had I known, and had I understood why when you visit an ophthalmologist they puff some air in your eye, I might have been less cavalier. That puff tests the pressure of the fluid inside your eye. If it's below 20 it's fine; 25 is not too bad. But more than that, and you're probably suffering from glaucoma, the biggest cause of blindness in the world.

Anyway, in the summer of 2004 Keith Harris of Seymour Pierce and I went out for lunch and the subject of whether you would rather be blind or deaf came up. I am sure everyone's had that conversation. I said better to be blind because then at least you could have a conversation, which is probably true. On the other hand, I decided upon reflection, you certainly don't want to be blind either.

Two weeks later, I woke up on a Sunday morning and saw the world through what seemed to be a veil of smoke. I set out on my bike, thinking that maybe some fresh air would clear the haziness up. It didn't. I watched the TV, put my hand in front of my left eye, where the problem was, and then put a bandage over it. I recalled that my mother had once begun to see spiders in her eyes and, having gone to all sorts of unhelpful people in Harley Street, ended up at the Whittington NHS hospital where they diagnosed a detached retina, said it could fall off any minute and packed her off to Moorfields Eye Hospital. Moorfields fixed the problem immediately.

So I drove straight to Moorfields accident and emergency and was seen within an hour. The pressure inside my eyeball was 45. The doctor said, 'This is very interesting, you've got acute angular glaucoma.' He called all his colleagues across to have a look. He asked whether I was of Indian or Chinese origin – it was, he said, very rare for a Caucasian to have this condition. I said I was glad it was so rare but could they sort it out. They gave me some eye drops.

The eye drops stung terribly and every time I used them I had to go to bed. So a few days later I went back to Moorfields and was referred to Professor Paul Foster, a giant of a man, but very gentle and very dedicated. He gave me different eye drops which seemed to work, but still required me to go back for a check-up once a month. Meanwhile I had my business, my band and the *OK!* launch in America to look after. The latter began with a legal battle over an editor whom rival publisher Jann Wenner had hired from us and we wanted to hire back. I flew to New York to meet lawyers and negotiate a settlement, but my flight got stuck behind an El Al plane with 300 Israelis aboard, all of whom then had to go through immigration, the airline lost my luggage and when I finally got to the hotel I discovered that something had gone wrong with my reservation. By the time I got home to England the pressure in my eye was back to 45.

Paul Foster said, 'This isn't good. If it gets to 50 the eye will burst and that will be it. I'd like to introduce you to a very nice chap, a surgeon, Professor Peng Khaw.'

Peng was all smiles. 'Yes of course. We'll just do a little operation – five minutes – no problem at all – we'll sort everything out.'

'And when should we do this operation?'

'We'd like to do it tomorrow . . .'

Hmmm.

It was the Easter week of 2005, and I'd just given up smoking – again. I went into hospital and was anaesthetised. As I was being taken to the operating theatre I noticed I was wearing a name tag. In my fuddled state I thought I was about to go on stage to perform. I hoped the bass drum pedal would be OK.

Just before we went in I said to Peng, 'Look, you don't really know who I am. To you I am just a bloke off the street. But I can be very helpful to you or I can be a complete bastard. If I go fucking blind I will kill you. But if it goes well you've got the best friend you could ever have, for the rest of both our lives.'

Later I talked to him about what I'd said, and he told me that he was quite used to that sort of behaviour. Everyone, he informed me, either pleads or threatens – even the kids.

I lay on my hospital trolley. It was then that I heard the voice.

'So, you idiot, you've worked 18 hours a day and seven days a week. You've ignored most things other than getting to where you've got. I hope you're pleased with yourself.'

I did not quite know how to answer this, but as I searched for a suitable response the image of my workplace came into my head. The voice persisted: 'Do you like your office – overlooking the Thames at the Tower?'

'Well, yes, I would say it's the best office in London.'

'And your newspapers and your magazines and your privileges and going to Downing Street to see the Prime Minister?'

'Yes.'

'Well, you'd better decide whether it's all been worth it.'

'What do you mean?'

'You'd better decide whether all your material achievements are really the most important things in life, and if they're not, just exactly what you're going to treat as your priorities from now on . . .'

The voice appeared intent on teaching me some kind of lesson, and I suddenly felt that I was about to face the toughest choice of my career. But before I could answer, the drugs took their full effect, and I knew nothing until I woke up. I then discovered that the 'five-minute operation' had actually taken nine hours. I had picked the wrong time to give up smoking. I needed a cigarette.

Later I went to Peng's offices at Moorfields. There was no air conditioning, it was hot, he was doing God knows how many operations each day – he never stopped working. He got his knighthood and he's about the only one I know who really earned it. He's fantastic. In the immediate aftermath of the operation he put me on about 80 eye drops a day and inspected me twice a day. Then it was once a day, then every week, every month, and so on. After nine years the pressure mounted again and I needed a further small operation – the treatment should have lasted for ten years but they told me if I hadn't smoked I might have got to eleven.

The one thing I did not understand was how Peng could work in the conditions he had to put up with. I asked him about it. 'It's so hot, it's so cramped. Beds everywhere. Kids everywhere. It's like the Victorian age.'

'Yes, well, I know. We're trying to raise funds for a new children's hospital, but . . .'

'It's done.'

'But . . .'

'No, you don't understand. It's done.'

And that was the origin of the Richard Desmond Children's Eye Centre at Moorfields. Peng thanked me and went on thanking me, which he had no need to do. He doesn't realise I got away cheap.

In fact, everything is connected, and I have been surprised a number of times by people who have since had friends or family treated at the eye centre.

I looked back as best I could to see if the kind of problems I had with my eyes ran in the family. My father had poor eyesight and my elder brother had some problems but there was no evidence of the same condition that I suffered from. The curious fact that acute angular glaucoma was usually found in people from Asia might have been because my family originally came from a part of Ukraine overrun by the Mongols. Some people have deduced from that that I am descended from Genghis Khan. It seems unlikely because apparently he was an aggressive fellow and I am very easy-going.

Unquestionably, the condition was made worse by the pace at which we were moving, and the mass of projects we were taking on simultaneously. I had been given a warning that I needed to slow down.

I decided to speed up.

18
BORN IN THE USA

The story of our acquisition of Channel 5 began with the usual combination of luck (if you believe it was luck) and fate (if you believe it was fate), and jumping on every opportunity (whether it seemed like an opportunity or not).

It did not begin with us making a bid for Channel 5. It began with taking on the American market with *OK!*.

Back in 2004 I was a guest of Matthew Freud and Elisabeth Murdoch at the BAFTAs. Following the awards ceremony I went on to the film producer Harvey Weinstein's after-party. Michael Douglas was there, whom I of course knew from the *OK!* exclusive for his wedding and the ensuing joint lawsuit against *Hello!*. I was impressed by Harvey's treatment of Michael: when you work with celebrities, you need to know how to be both respectful and firm, and Harvey was brilliant at combining these two qualities. I felt an immediate affinity with him.

'Harvey,' I said, 'I've been watching how you look after Michael. I think you're my new magazine partner in America!'

Harvey, however, reminded me that he had just lost $40 million on the Tina Brown vehicle *Talk* magazine, which had collapsed after just three years. Not surprisingly, he said he had probably had enough of the magazine business for the moment. He introduced me to

David Pecker of American Media (*National Enquirer*), but I did not take to David in the same way. We left it that Harvey and I would stay in contact. We certainly got on well, even though we're very different people: I try to be organised; Harvey is incurably chaotic.

My next 'partner' in America was Rupert Murdoch. At least that's what I initially thought. We met up to speak about the possibility of working together and agreed that it would make complete sense to do so. With *OK!* I had a winning brand and format. He for his part had a powerful existing US operation, and could contribute offices, distribution and advertising sales. We shook hands on the deal and I followed up with a letter. He didn't answer that, but shortly afterwards I received a call from Les Hinton, a top Murdoch lieutenant.

'You're going to be very angry with me.'

'Why would I be angry?'

'I have to tell you Rupert does not want to go ahead.'

I was later told that a handshake with Rupert did not represent a deal; it represented an option in his favour.

In the end we decided to try to make it on our own in the USA. We found offices, secured distribution, hired staff, and spoke to advertisers and celebrities. We started in traditional American style with a lawsuit with our rivals *Us Weekly* over the recruitment of an editor, and we launched with a party hosted by Jessica Simpson and my friend P Diddy. Jessica and P Diddy remained at opposite ends of the room for the entire party because each was too big a star to come to the other. P Diddy was also too big a star to be on time, even for his $250,000 fee. At my events I always like to stand near the entrance and shake hands with everyone I can as they come in. That way you know who's turned up – and who's late. By the time Diddy appeared I was getting a little tense. It was an important night for us, and I had a real go at him.

'Look – I'm paying you all this money, and you're 20 minutes late!'

'You're lucky I turned up at all.'

You need to know in life when to pick a fight, and when not to. We made friends over a cigar.

Jessica, too, was very warm. And as it turned out, it didn't matter that she and P Diddy would not move from their respective sides of the room: guests simply commuted between them and had their pictures taken with each star alternately. I made a speech, in which I said that as I didn't play golf my only hobby was *OK!* and that was why I was doing a US launch. One way and another a good time was had by all and I made a mental note that whether or not the American edition of *OK!* was thriving in ten years' time, something good, I was sure, would come of it.

Jessica was on the cover of the magazine that week. Later we did one with P Diddy. Everyone, including his people, said they admired our 'courage' in putting a black man on the front of our magazine. It was the days before Obama . . .

The early days of the magazine were a struggle. Our initial employment dispute needed to be settled quickly because New York courts being what they are, losing a case on a $100,000 appointment would have cost us $12 million and winning it would have cost $10 million. Then we had a problem with advertising. Following the usual Desmond model of securing the advertising before launching the title, we gained the reassurance of a 15-page per week advertising deal from Martin Sorrell's GroupM. Or so we thought. Sadly this proved to be about as bankable as Rupert Murdoch's handshake. Whatever GroupM's good intentions might have been, it turned out that those who had made the agreement with us later found out that they were not in a position to get their clients to deliver on it.

I think we also suffered from a degree of arrogance. Because our British *OK!* formula was so successful, we were convinced that it would work anywhere. Such utter self-confidence probably won us the initial buy-in of the American news trade. But readers were rather less convinced. To them our beautiful red and white logo had associations with downmarket *National Enquirer*-type magazines. Our luxurious eight- and ten-page treatments seemed heavy going and slow-paced. Added to that, our signature large format meant that the magazine didn't fit into the wire display stands universally used in the States. Some retailers ended up dumping the magazines in piles; others screwed them up and shoved them into the stands by main force. Such manhandling was scarcely consistent with the quality product we wished to offer.

So we got to work, changing our logo, changing our format, shortening our features. We adjusted to the cynical view of distributors that readers of magazines such as ours were 40 40 40, a statistic that referred respectively to their age, their income in dollars, and how many pounds overweight they were. That said, we continued to invest heavily in celebrity exclusives, following our iron rule that 'no wedding, engagement or baby will escape us'.

As with the UK edition we had our moments of setting the national news agenda. Britney Spears, for example, gave us a celebrated interview in which she talked of her demons more openly than perhaps any celebrity in any magazine feature had ever done before. Her sister, Disney star Jamie Lynn Spears, aged just 16, presented her new baby to the world through us, giving us in the process another million-plus-selling edition. Jessica Alba's and Matthew McConaughey's first babies were among the many others the public were initially introduced to via *OK!*, while the weddings of Pamela Anderson, Christina Aguilera and Eva Longoria were among the most sumptuous we covered. We were doing what we did best, and within a couple of years had built the brand into the seventh biggest news-stand title in the USA. True, it was not profitable yet, but nor had the UK edition been for the first few years, so we were prepared to be patient. We also did our best to live down the image of celebrity magazines as tabloid and irresponsible, while simultaneously ensuring that our readers were given what they wanted. One way and another it certainly felt that things were moving in the right direction. Of course, all this was at a time when the economy was booming.

Our American exclusives also fed our other licensees throughout the world, although just occasionally they presented an interesting cultural challenge. Our exclusive pictures of Demi Moore's wedding to Ashton Kutcher, for example, gave us a cover that featured a traditional Jewish ceremony, with the couple standing either side of a bearded rabbi. Our colleagues in the Middle East were delighted to have the exclusive but asked if they could use Photoshop to do something about the rabbi. In the interest of more tolerant international relations in that region, I refused.

The photo shoots also gave me the opportunity to meet more of Hollywood's finest. On one occasion I had the pleasure of being part of a line-up with several celebrity supporters – including Brad Pitt and George Clooney – of the Darfur 'Not On Our Watch' charity. It struck me at the time – and I've felt the same way when I've looked at other photographs – that Brad has a tendency to look as though he is somewhere else, or at least that his thoughts are. But he was very nice. I would very much like to say that that particular edition was a bestseller but I think readers found the picture too 'posed'. On the other hand, the fees involved meant that the charity benefited handsomely.

Obviously the Hollywood A-listers were our bread and butter, but there were times when our British celebrities managed to break through in America. The courageous and tragic end of Jade Goody, for instance, captured the public imagination worldwide.

John Mayall once made an album called *The Turning Point*. It's an album that has always stuck in my mind. I believe there really are turning points in people's lives, whether they realise it at the time or only in hindsight. What was about to happen forced a lot of people, myself included, to take a long hard look at themselves and their businesses.

Before 2007 I remember a world of private aeroplanes, private yachts, devious investment products that no one understood, bankers who lived like rock stars, investment houses that would lend anything to anyone because they got bonuses – and a generation of guys who had never known things any different. Richard Caring would buy a boat, Philip Green would buy a bigger boat, and then Paul Kemsley (the property investor and Tottenham director who once paid £10,000 to sit beside me in a restaurant and who always made bets with me that he lost) would rent a boat to go beside Philip's. Then everything collapsed: the whole financial house of cards came tumbling down. The last bets Paul made were on Lehman Brothers recovering. They didn't and Paul's 2008 £180 million fortune (if the *Sunday Times* Rich List is to be believed) disappeared. By 2012 he was bankrupt. For me, his story is representative of the whole period.

Fortunately, we weren't immediately affected. Our business was not based in the rarefied areas of banking and speculative investment that were hit first. But we knew the tidal wave was coming. We depended on the real world of people spending some of their wages in shops, and for that to happen they needed to have wages in the first place. I knew it could not be long before the storm hit us, and that, along with my eye problem, gave me a powerful reason to re-examine my life.

There was another reason, too.

On 24 January 2009 my mum, Millie Desmond, died, just a couple of months before her 93rd birthday.

Mum had always been deeply involved in my life. She had even been involved in my businesses – in the early days she did the invoicing. She read every paper and magazine we published – except *Chic* magazine, which, as she pointed out, was aimed at 'the older woman' (she was only about 80 at the time and preferred to get the latest news from *OK!*). All my editors were scared of her because she had a fearsome eye for typographical errors. At our events she met celebrities and royalty and took it all in her stride. I have already mentioned the knockout speech she made from the RD Crusaders' stage at *OK!*'s tenth anniversary party, which doubled as her 90th birthday party. She was a bright, energetic woman who made a point of keeping in touch with new developments in the world: it was Mum who taught me about shopping online using Ocado, not the other way round. Every Saturday of my adult life I would go round to see her.

It was a real source of pride and pleasure to me that my career enabled my mum to have things that she would otherwise only have been able to dream about. During our period in Docklands, for example, Nigel Broackes was kind enough to book her and her partner Harry Northwood on to a cruise on the QE2. It was one of the highlights of her life.

I know she was proud of me. After Harry Northwood sadly died, she would go to the Sobell Leisure Centre in Golders Green with Martin Sorrell's mum and the two of them would exchange news on how well their respective sons had done and how nice it was that they were such good mates.

Mum liked to talk. I pointed that out to her occasionally, but she told me that if she ever stopped talking, I would be sorry. Sometimes she talked so much that I nodded off, but I don't think that worried her. We would often eat together at the Duke of York in Barnet, a venue that had two things going for it: it was a nice place, and it was one of the few that Mum didn't find fault with (usually the decoration wasn't quite right, or the food or the service were below par). It was the same story with home helps, cleaners and carers. Fortunately I did manage to persuade her – or force her – to take on some support; when, as I had feared, she did finally have a fall, it was the cleaner whom Mum hadn't wanted who had the sense to call someone when she rang the doorbell and couldn't get a response.

After that, of course, I called and phoned even more often, although she told me I should not. 'You're just doing it out of a sense of duty,' she would say, and often she would deliberately not answer.

Having had to budget so carefully for so much of her life, she watched every penny. The cost of taking a taxi to and from the Sobell Centre, for example, became something of an obsession. 'So – when I went there, the taxi cost £11,' she would say. 'And when I came back, the taxi cost £11.50. So was the taxi driver coming back overcharging, or was the other one undercharging?' She knew Martin Sorrell's mother travelled to the centre by taxi, but then Martin was 'really rich'. I wondered whether to say that I could probably give Martin a run for his money, but decided against it: she would never have accepted money directly from me. Eventually, we invented a story that Jewish Care liked her coming so much they were happy to pay for her fares, and I settled the bills surreptitiously.

Mum's final years, then, were happy enough, I hope. But one Saturday, experiencing some backache she went to the hospital and there suffered a mini-stroke. I rushed in to see her, of course, but for the first time ever she wasn't talking much. I reminded her she had said I'd be upset when she stopped talking. She sat right up in bed, looked me in the eye and said: 'You know what? I was right. And I'm always right. And don't you forget it!'

The aftermath of Mum's death was unexpected. You might think that a parent's death would bring a husband and wife closer together, but this did not happen with Janet and me, and now we seemed further apart than when my mother was around. I felt a bit lost.

. . .

Something else happened around this time that also made me take stock. In February 2009 I went to the Oscars, as I was in the habit of doing. Afterwards, I went on to Elton John's party, which was definitely one of the biggest events there and boasted various stars with *OK!* links: Kiefer Sutherland and Sharon Stone among them. Elton was, as always, taking special care of everything and everyone. He said he'd chosen everything personally: the crockery, the cutlery and even, he made a point of saying, the waiters – to ensure there weren't any ugly ones.

Returning from Los Angeles on British Airways I found the terminal stuffed with more celebrities than you could shake a stick at. BA were apparently run ragged trying to look after all their individual requirements. As I've said, I was feeling a little bit lost so soon after the death of my mum, and I suppose I must have looked it because a nice blonde lady from BA took me from check-in to the first-class lounge, which was not part of her remit. She even indulged me when I wanted to stop off at the news-stand to see how *OK!* was doing. I suddenly felt like talking, and spilled out all sorts of things about my business, my US visits and my concerns. She listened sympathetically.

When we got to the departure lounge we discovered that most of BA's staff now seemed to be looking after Mr T, who is a large chap to look after and who was causing lots of confusion. My guide, however, sorted everything out and then took a picture of me and Mr T together. It may not have made the front page but it was nice to have a reminder of someone I took to straight away.

Finally, my guardian angel from BA escorted me on to the plane. She even gave me her phone number – a first for me, but then I suppose it was also a first to have chatted up a strange woman in an airport and taken her to inspect news-stands. And now as I sat down I encountered another woman I hadn't spoken to before: Jennifer Aniston.

Jennifer Aniston was a pretty constant feature on the front cover of our American issues, usually because it was being rumoured that she was getting married, or having a baby, or both. American readers liked gossip as much as they liked exclusives: that was one of the things we had learned in our first turbulent months there. Of course one of the biggest showbiz break-ups of recent years had been Jennifer Aniston and Brad Pitt, and our readers (who apparently preferred Jennifer to Angelina Jolie, whom they regarded as a home wrecker) desperately wanted Jennifer to get back with Brad, but would settle for her getting married to someone else or having a baby. I realised such speculation might not necessarily have endeared our title to Jennifer, but I felt I ought to come clean.

I introduced myself and told her I published *OK!* magazine.

'So, how do you live with yourself?' she asked.

'What do you mean?'

'Well – these magazines, these "tabloids". They print all kinds of stuff. What makes you want to start a magazine like that?'

I gave her the whole history of the company, starting with *International Musician and Recording World.* It's a long flight from LA to London.

She liked the idea of the music magazines. 'Why don't you go back to doing that?' she asked. 'That sounds really worthwhile.'

I tried to explain about the difficulties with specialist magazines, the publishing economics and the need to diversify and grow your business. She wasn't impressed.

'How would you feel if some paparazzo was going through your underwear drawer and taking pictures of your underwear?'

I objected that *OK!* did not go through people's underwear drawers and take pictures of their underwear. We liked to think of ourselves as celebrity-friendly. True, if we had sources who found evidence of some joyful event in a celebrity's future, we would want our readers to know about it, but our whole aim was to be positive and upbeat. And, of course, we helped keep famous people famous, getting them talked about and so in the case of say, an actress, ensuring that when film parts came up their name was remembered. That was the business.

'Well, there are some magazines that take pictures of everything and tell lies week in and week out.'

'I don't think I even read those magazines,' I said. 'Maybe you shouldn't read those magazines either.'

We talked for hours – we talked about music, and we talked about her then boyfriend John Mayer, a guitarist who would, I am sure, have read my music titles.

'Anyway, he's not my boyfriend. That's another example of tabloid lies,' she concluded.

Sometimes you have to accept you're not going to win. Jennifer Aniston was never going to be a fan. But at a time when – because of my health scare, my bereavement and my worries about the fallout of the financial crisis – I was re-evaluating my life and my business, our conversation had an impact on me. I'd always been driven and ambitious; I'd spent decades trying to build a successful company; but at the same I hated the idea that someone should be upset by what I did. My general philosophy is that if I can do something about what has annoyed them without hurting the business, then I will.

My conversation with Jennifer Aniston came at a time when we had some big decisions to make about the direction we were taking. It had become apparent to me, for example, that if we were to topple *People* magazine from its decades of dominance in the US market, we would all have to move to New York and focus exclusively on the American market. I asked the other directors whether they wanted to do that. There was not a lot of enthusiasm.

. . .

Meanwhile, back in England, I found myself fighting a battle on a more personal front. It is always tricky to know when you should just take criticism levelled at you, and when you need to hit back through the courts. I believe Mr Murdoch's attitude has always been – let them say what they like. Generally, I think he's probably right. But when the writer Tom Bower, who had been keeping tabs on me for a number of years, decided to take things a little further, I felt I had to react.

His early interest in me seemed to stem in part from Mr Bailey's encounter with the forces of darkness in New York in 1992. I should say now that I am very sorry about the whole affair, though I am still puzzled as to *what* is supposed to have happened, and indeed *how* it could have happened. Anyway, the whole matter received a public airing in a *Money Programme* documentary on me that repeated an old story that somehow I'd crossed paths with an investor who was also said to be a 'Mafia foot soldier'. (It came as something of a surprise to me to learn that foot soldiers in the Mafia are big investors – they must be on good wages.) Bower picked up on that, and seemingly planned to explore the issue in a Desmond biography.

In 2003, I was passing through Heathrow with my son Robert, at the end of a trip to see my aunt in Queens in New York for her 89th birthday. I visited the toilet (I believe in those days it was at least semi-legal to smoke in them), when I was suddenly hailed by a tall, shambolic fellow with a strange sort of smile.

'No – it can't be! It's you! It's Desmond!'

I had no idea as to the identity of this strange man and, not knowing what his agenda might be, had no desire to prolong the interview in the toilet. On returning to the outside world, though, I encountered him again, this time standing with his wife, Veronica Wadley, then editor of the *Evening Standard*.

'It's Desmond!'

'I'm sorry, but who are you, sir?' I asked.

'Tom Bower,' he replied.

'Ah, the writer. I see,' I said, comprehension dawning. 'Well, this is my son Robert. We've just been in New York visiting my aunt for her 89th birthday.'

'Oh,' said Bower.

If, in the course of his researches, he had seen the BBC's 2002 *Money Programme* about me, he might have been surprised that the same media magnate who had allegedly been threatened with violence via Philip Bailey (in the role of shocked messenger) was now stepping off a plane from New York.

There was, thereafter, no book about me from Bower, but there was a book about Conrad Black, and I was mentioned in a context that I did not find complimentary. To paraphrase, at one point I was portrayed as a timid fellow who was 'crushed' by the mighty Conrad in our dispute over West Ferry Printers, and at another I was portrayed as a very aggressive type who used the power of my newspapers to prevail against my enemies.

It seemed to me there was a pretty good chance a jury would find that one or other of these descriptions was inaccurate and damaging, especially as they contradicted each other. It also struck me that Black and I had mediated a settlement, so the fact that neither of us 'crushed' the other was a matter of record. I therefore sued Tom Bower for libel. The case came up in June the same year. It turned on two things: what had really happened to end my dispute with Conrad Black, and how controlling I was of the editorial side of our publications.

With Black the matter could have been resolved simply by asking him what he remembered of the way our dispute was settled, but unfortunately he was being detained in an American prison for shortcomings in corporate governance. I therefore wrote to him, and when the case was adjourned briefly, I even travelled to see him. What I discovered was that the Federal Correctional Institution, Coleman Low, Florida, is not Ford open prison. It was not quite chain gangs, but there were orange uniforms, shackles, and 14ft electrified fences. It was impossible to escape from. It was also, I discovered, impossible to get into. It was a very sobering experience.

So I couldn't get testimony from Conrad. But I could turn to his second-in-command Jeremy Deedes. I knew he had no particular reason to like or support me. On the other hand, I also knew he would be familiar with every detail. As it turned out, he was prepared to say that Bower's account was quite inaccurate and that my reconciliation with Conrad had indeed been a case of us both making a compromise.

All well and good. Unfortunately, though, while our barrister was cool and logical, the opposing QC, a Mr Thwaites, was more colourful and dramatic, dragging in such extraneous issues as the *Daily Express* stance on immigration. He also managed to get permission to cite an obscure argument that I once had with a hedge fund company called Pentagon. Essentially, I had had successful dealings with them for some years, had recommended them to others, and my son Robert had invested some of the money he had been given for his bar mitzvah with them. When they hit difficult times, I spoke on the phone – rather robustly – to one of their directors, saying that I felt they ought to pay Robert his money back, both because he wasn't much more than a child and because the sum involved was significant for him but could scarcely be so for them. I went on to point out that I was a very good friend and would make a very bad enemy. That didn't strike me as wholly unreasonable, but it's certainly not the kind of observation you want taped and then played back at a court hearing, which was, in the event, what happened.

Oh dear. The court action against Bower was not an unqualified success. However, I did not regret undertaking it because I wanted to send a signal that I would defend myself, using the courts if necessary, if I felt I had been wronged in print. It also began to dawn on me that if there was going to be a book about me, I might as well write it myself, since I have quite a lot of inside knowledge.

Things at home were going no better. Janet and I tried to get on, but nothing seemed to work. For the first time since we'd married, it seemed quite possible that we might not remain married.

And then, exactly a year to the day after my mum had died, we went out for a curry together and Janet announced that she had had enough of me and that she was leaving.

It's very easy to be bitter and recriminatory about a partner from whom you have split. But I think there's no point. I prefer to remember Janet as the girl who took me for a Chinese when the Pink Fairies didn't turn up.

What happened next not only led to the creation of a new relationship, but in a strange way brought the spirit of my mother back into my home as well. I was busy at work, but once away from the office I felt very much alone. One day, therefore, I decided to ring the very nice girl who had looked after me at LAX when everyone else was looking after Mr T. We had, as it happens, kept in touch after our first meeting, and I had learned that her name was Joy. Now, I said, I would love to see more of her.

As our relationship developed, Joy told me she was pretty sure she liked me, but she was not sure she liked England or that she would want to pack in her 12-year career as a senior manager at British Airways to spend all her time with me. But in the end she did. It was an enormous deal, utterly life-changing for both of us, but like most of my biggest decisions it felt absolutely right and natural, and I think it did for Joy, too. It was something that was supposed to be. After just a month of living together she became pregnant with our first child.

The baby turned out to be a little girl. Right back when Joy looked after me at the airport I had laughingly addressed her as my angel, so Angel seemed a natural choice of name. We gave her the middle name Millie, after my mother. She bounced into the world with her fist on her chin, looking round with her big blue eyes with an expression that reminded me irresistibly of my mum.

Like the original Millie Desmond, she never stops talking.

Which brings me back to the sequence of conversations that sparked my bid for Channel 5 – conversations that started because we happened to have launched *OK!* in the USA and I seemed to be spending a lot of time there.

19
GIVE
ME
FIVE

Times were about to change.

One of the luckiest dinners I ever had was in the company of Philip Green in New York. It took place on a Sunday night in the summer of 2007, just before the first rumblings of the financial crash. Owing to Philip's tendency to hand out $500 tips, he had quite a reputation amongst restaurant staff in New York, so when you went out with him you were besieged by waiters with unrealistic expectations. But something was said during our dinner conversation that made me suspect that the days of big spending might be numbered. At that meal we were joined by Ron Perelman, the owner of Revlon and a mate of mine because he's a fellow ex-drummer. We talked about business trends, and in the course of our conversation he asked me if I had anything in hedge funds. I said I did. Then everyone at the table began to shout at once, while Ron actually leaned across, grabbed the sleeve of my jacket with such excitement that he ripped it, and said, 'Get out! Get out now!'

I did. And it was just as well. Because as the world descended into financial panic, I at least didn't have to watch such investments as I would otherwise have had disappearing fast. Even so, my major investment was what it always has been, my own business. And that, certainly, was not immune from the global downturn. In America, as in the UK, I was spending a fortune on celebrity exclusives. And since celebrity magazines are at the luxury end of the market and so not top of people's purchasing list in Walmart, I found that our sales in the USA were starting to fall. True, everyone else suffered as well, but that wasn't much consolation: declining circulation means falling advertising revenue.

As the bad times hit, my directors and I found ourselves constantly commuting between London and New York. It soon became clear, however, that this was unsustainable: we needed more strength in our American management team. So we approached a former Wenner executive called Kent Brownridge, with whom I had had dealings before and who had struck me as professional, helpful and efficient. A series of meetings followed, at the end of which he agreed to join us and head up our American company.

Unfortunately, not only did he not produce the hoped-for improvements in profits, he seemed to have a management strategy very much at odds with our own.

But before we parted ways with Kent, he did play an indirect role in the first of a series of encounters that led me back to London and Channel 5. It all started when I was in Manhattan for one of my regular visits. Kent had arranged a car to get me from one meeting to another, but unfortunately it did not turn up at the appointed time. That made Kent so angry that he ran around saying that heads would roll. I was touched by his concern, but felt that his approach wasn't helping matters much, so I tried to calm things down by saying that I could easily walk around Manhattan. I would, however, I said, need a car to get me to the airport after my final meeting. We confirmed that a car would be ready and waiting at 4pm outside the Four Seasons Hotel.

At 4pm outside the Four Seasons there was no car. I'm on my own, I told myself, and whoever messed up on the car is doomed.

I began to walk down 58th Street, telling myself to keep calm, even though there wasn't a yellow cab to be seen anywhere.

And then I heard a voice calling me in a thick Israeli accent, '*Litchaard, Litchaard!*'

It was a guy called Ynon Kreiz. Some time before I had had dealings with the media owner Haim Saban, who had an early hit with the Japanese comic series Power Rangers (we published the magazine) and who had made a fortune by selling his stake in Fox Family Worldwide to Disney. Our first conversations had been about buying ITV together, then about Saban buying Northern & Shell (he said he would give me a big cheque and a big handkerchief I could use to cry into), and, of course, nothing came of either suggestion. But through Saban I had got to know Kreiz, who had once been his gofer. He hadn't been able to help then, but perhaps, I reflected, he could help me now.

'Are you going back to the airport?' he asked.

'No, I'm just walking up and down 58th Street with my suitcase for fun.'

He said he was heading for JFK and invited me to join him, for which I was very grateful. We talked about what had been happening since our last meeting.

'I'm with Endemol now – big company. Four billion, five billion, ten billion. Maybe we buy *OK!*'

'But *OK!* makes 40 million.'

'Pounds or dollars?'

'Pounds.'

'Hmmm. Maybe we buy *OK!* USA?'

'Well I invested 150 million dollars so you'd have to offer more.'

I added that I fancied creating an 'E channel', a celebrity TV channel that would capitalise on the success of *OK!*. After all, we had already had some success with *OK!* TV. Kreiz seemed very interested. At length we arrived at JFK and went our separate ways.

I was a little surprised to discover that despite all the billions of dollars Ynon had been talking about, he was travelling club class. Perhaps he believed in a modest lifestyle. Personally, I think flat beds are good.

The following Monday morning I told my directors about my conversation with Kreiz about E channels and *OK!*. We could look at doing *OK!* TV worldwide, I said, with Endemol handling content and production. We'd do it as a profit share and everyone would be happy.

Nothing happened.

A few months later, in January 2010, at the Presidents Club charity dinner, there was Ynon again. I seem to recall pointing out the contrast between his big talk and lack of action. Ynon, who trained in the Israeli military and whose hobby is kitesurfing, responded by getting my neck in an armlock. I stuck to my guns. True, I couldn't move, but I was confident that he wouldn't kill me in the middle of the Dorchester Hotel. Anyway, I didn't deserve to die as I still had a lot to achieve in my business.

A month after that Ynon called me and asked to meet at my house. When he arrived, he told me he had a potential deal on the cards that was just as good as the ITV deal we'd talked about years before: Channel 5. I told him that we had approached Channel 5 ourselves a few years ago and offered £500 million but that they had refused to sell.

He said, 'What if I told you it's for sale and I could get Channel 5 for less than £100 million? What if I told you I could get it for £60 million?'

'Well, if that's the case, I'm in. 50–50. I'll give you the cheque now. We'll sell the ads, Endemol will do production, and you will run it.'

After that I went with my team to Endemol's very creative offices at Shepherd's Bush. They were not, I have to say, the cleanest premises in the world: I had a shower afterwards. But we agreed a deal in principle and started to draft a joint venture contract. A few weeks later, though, my finance director, Rob Sanderson, told me things were not going well. Apparently Endemol had three share-holders – Goldman Sachs, Mediaset (owned by Berlusconi) and John de Mol, the eccentric Dutch format king – and they seemed incapable of agreeing on anything. I later met John de Mol myself and can easily appreciate why reaching an understanding would be a challenge. Rob also established that the company was completely debt-ridden. His view was that we should ditch Endemol and do the Channel 5 deal on our own. I said I couldn't do that because it had been Ynon's deal.

Five minutes later the phone rang. It was Ynon.

'My people are all arguing and they don't rate you. They want out. I offered to bet them £10,000 that if we don't do the deal you will and that you'll make half a billion pounds. Unfortunately, they're idiots and they've taken the bet.'

He added, 'I've got a Hamsa metal hand [the amulet commonly given in Israel]. I'll send it to you for good luck – I was going to give it to you when we did the deal.'

It was, I think, a critical moment for my group. On the one hand, I wanted to do a big deal that would give me scale and diversity. On the other hand, we were in the middle of the credit crunch and things weren't showing signs of much improvement. In fact everything was a challenge. In the USA we now had arguably the most well-proven American editor in the business, but our sales weren't going up. Our newspapers and magazines faced competition from the internet, and the old distinctions between still images, video, television and print journalism were becoming increasingly blurred. I was still committed to print – in fact I commissioned and built a brand-new print plant in Luton and at the time even thought that my 'big deal' might involve buying Murdoch's papers – but it was hard to know what the future held. What's more, although my company theoretically held £100 million in cash, some £60 million of that had been borrowed from HBOS, which, now under the control of Lloyds, made it clear that it wasn't happy with the conditions of the loan. Then again, I remembered Warren Buffett's line that you should be fearful when others are greedy and greedy when others are fearful. So I wanted the Channel 5 deal, but it wasn't necessarily going to be easy.

I went to Goldman Sachs and asked them to help us with our bid to Channel 5's owners, the German company RTL. We examined the business closely. I was pleased to note that Channel 5 did not seem to have much idea what they were doing. They had managed to get themselves into a stand-off with the Aegis advertising agency, where their inflexibility over terms lost them £50 million of revenue. Fortunately, from our print titles, we had an excellent relationship with Aegis so that would not be a problem. In programming terms, they had just massively over-invested in a 'shiny floor' entertainment show called *Don't Stop Believing* – which attempted the impossible by competing with the big talent shows on ITV and BBC. They had in my opinion neglected opportunities to produce smaller, edgy true-life documentary shows that would have both made financial sense and been popular. Management salaries were vast, and the culture seemed to involve a lot of dressing down, endless awaydays, evenings in wine bars, expensive restaurants and a 24-hour taxi for the CEO whose driver was also for some reason given a Sky subscription. I was not surprised RTL wanted to sell because all this was losing them a fortune, and they had the additional challenge of trying to sort out things from another country – a problem I knew a little about.

As far as we were concerned most of what was wrong could easily be fixed, but there was one major problem that made the business as it stood unsaleable and so unbuyable. While we were carrying out our health check, we discovered that, according to the terms of many of its contracts with programme producers, if Channel 5 changed ownership, it not only forfeited outstanding rights on the programmes it broadcast but would also be obliged to pay out the balance of any existing contract unless the rights owner approved the change. In other words, any buyer of Channel 5 might well have to pay the full cost of a series and yet not be allowed to broadcast it. Fortunately, RTL had excellent relationships with programme makers and sports people and were able to change their contracts with them before we concluded the deal.

I should have been elated when we signed, but actually I was tired. However, I went to the Channel 5 offices for the announcement, and we gave Channel 5 news exclusive coverage of the event, which was logical enough, even though no suitable Channel 5 signage for a backdrop to the piece could be found and we ended up having to improvise. But when they interviewed me, I found that the interviewer seemed less interested in what my plans for the station were than in whether I was going to fire her, which, I have to confess, I was somewhat inclined to do. The amazing thing is she's still there – but everyone has to eat and maybe I'm more tolerant than people think. I told her I was planning to buy *Panorama*.

Then I was offered a celebratory drink and said yes. A glass of water appeared. After that I was offered a tour of the building. Again I said yes. The offices were very messy with magazines and newspapers scattered everywhere, none of them mine. I also noticed that there was no one around. I was told that most of them had Friday afternoon off because the channel was doing so well.

I did, however, manage to find one highly paid executive and as was sometimes my custom on such occasions asked him what his proudest achievement had been in the current year. He said he had redecorated the office. Looking around all I could see were acres of lime green and lilacs and stripes. The place resembled a kindergarten. He said he had not got in any designers but had done it himself, which I could easily believe. I remember feeling very deflated when I got into the car. Luckily I had a holiday planned. My team told me they would sort it out. I believe they did.

So now we had a TV channel. We celebrated our acquisition with a lovely party one beautiful September evening in the canteen on the ninth floor of our building, which has a balcony overlooking the river, the Tower, and Tower Bridge. Our guests of honour were Roger Daltrey and Barbara Windsor. My friend Martin Sorrell of GroupM gave a very generous and supportive speech, although he did point out that his company was responsible for 30 per cent of our advertising share and that that figure could very easily be 32 per cent or 25 per cent depending on how well we behaved.

In response, I acknowledged that Martin was a very clever man, which is why he went to Haberdashers' School and I only went to Christ's College. But I said that the best thing about our working together was that it would make both our mums, who had known each other at the Sobell Centre, very proud. Sometimes it's good to address the person behind the businessman. I'm not sure my observation drew a tear, but I think it made the point that if we had to behave ourselves, so did he. And indeed we always have.

Is running a TV channel different from running a music magazine, a celebrity title or a newspaper? Actually, I think the fundamentals are the same, and in the case of Channel 5 I found that the preoccupations of our viewers were remarkably similar to those of our newspaper and magazine readers. But TV ownership does offer you one advantage. People are so keen to appear on television that you seem to acquire a lot of new friends. In fact you have to be careful not to do too many favours if you wish to avoid the embarrassing consequence of having to look at the ratings together. I tried to do what was best for my pals and for the channel, giving opportunities, for example, to Vanessa Feltz and Nick Ferrari. I declined, however, to help my old acquaintance Dale Winton when he proposed a format where he searched for a young boyfriend. I founded *Attitude* magazine and believe myself to be broad-minded, but that seemed a format too far.

The only blip I experienced immediately after the purchase of Channel 5 had to do with scrutinising an avalanche of costs associated with the disastrous *Don't Stop Believing*, which was produced by Elisabeth Murdoch's company Shine. I was still a television outsider and wanted to understand how you could get through £1 million for half an hour of TV and why Emma Bunton's hair cost so much. Elisabeth protested against the slight delay in payment that that entailed, despite the fact that for decades we had been regularly paying companies owned by persons who shared her surname. Shine's attitude spoiled what would otherwise have been a really wonderful round of press coverage – not at all like that which greeted the Express acquisition. Had I changed, or had the world?

And then along came *Big Brother*.

Within a few weeks of the deal Ynon wanted to come to my house. I thought it was to congratulate me, but no. Ynon was determined to agree a deal on *Big Brother*. And certainly, we had both envisaged there would be one. The trouble was, Ynon's deal was a little one-sided. Five years' lock-in with no mechanism for an early exit, and £40 million a year. According to Ynon that was a bargain because Channel 4 had been paying £60 million.

'Yes, but Channel 4 got rid of it!'

I wanted to do a deal but insisted I needed the flexibility to terminate the agreement before the five-year licence period was up, if necessary. It wasn't just a question of money: I needed an escape route if the ratings were bad or anything happened to make me unhappy. Ynon refused and relentlessly pushed for his terms. In fact, he pushed so relentlessly that I ended up with a headache. I tried to explain that if I accepted his proposal, I was jeopardising the financial health of my entire group. I had in effect bet £100 million by buying the channel, but what Ynon proposed entailed a further commitment equivalent to twice that much. I refused to submit myself to sleepless nights looking at the ratings of *Big Brother*. Anyway, if the proposition was so good, why bother to tie me in? His persistence was making me nervous. The show would be a big asset for us, but an old business maxim came to mind: turnover is vanity, profit is sanity and cash is reality.

I told him, 'People think Israelis are aggressive because they act like you. They have to send their tanks in straight away. You have to relax a bit. You have to have a little give and take.'

Ynon does not do 'give and take'.

The following morning a letter arrived confirming we had done the deal that we hadn't done. The struggle went on. I did, after all, want the property, and he did, after all, have no other buyer. Would he prefer to let the format die rather than offer a shorter term?

For many months Ynon stubbornly stuck to his guns, and neither we nor Ynon's number two Tim Hincks, who was speaking to our programme controller Jeff Ford, could break the deadlock. In the end I had a conversation with Mike Sherwood of Goldman Sachs, the owners of a third of Endemol. By this time it had been agreed that Ynon would leave the company; I believe the pay-off made him very happy and I still count him as a friend. Tim Hincks took over, and the contract was signed. And so we entered an era in which the reality TV of Channel 5 came to work in perfect harmony with our magazines and with the *Daily Star* in particular.

In our first year as owners of Channel 5 we raised its revenue from £250 million to £350 million and were therefore able also to increase its programming budget. We were hailed as saviours of the channel. That, more than anything else I had done, impressed David Cameron – he expressed amazement about what had been achieved and asked me how I did it.

'Well, I cut overheads, increased essential spend on production, and increased the revenues. Which I believe is what you ought to be doing for the country.'

We were also able to make more of *Celebrity Big Brother*, because it was essentially *OK!* territory and we were good at identifying the people who would please our audiences and then persuading them to work with us.

Vanessa Feltz was one of the 'inmates' whom I had a hand in introducing. Sometimes we got the process to work in reverse, taking TV celebrities and turning them into magazine stars. Sometimes we were successful, sometimes we weren't. Unfortunately, our attempt to make Heidi Montag and Spencer Pratt into a golden couple for our magazines was not one of our greater moments – I had forgotten my own rule that British audiences rarely truly identify with Americans.

With Julie Goodyear, the challenge we faced was rather different – nobody could persuade her to appear. Endemol tried hard and failed. I was therefore asked to have a stab. The meeting, I was told, would be at a hotel near Manchester. Oh, and Julie had asked Endemol's representative: 'Will he be coming in his helicopter?'

I pointed out I didn't have a helicopter. Endemol suggested I got one.

We flew up in a hired chopper and met Julie and her husband in their hotel suite (for which I was of course paying). She was smoking countless cigarettes, so, not to be outdone, I chose the largest cigar I had and, as the room slowly filled up with smoke, listened to her explain why she couldn't possibly do it.

I remembered my conversations with the Beckhams. I said she had to do it for the sake of her audience, her fans: they loved her; she could not let them down.

She said she was in her sixties and would not be able to cope. I pointed out that she was a beautiful woman in the prime of life and the Queen was in her eighties and still had a full diary. Julie liked being compared to the Queen. As we talked further I happened to mention my departed mum, and Julie said she consulted her own deceased mother on important matters. In fact she had a picture of her in her bedroom, and would I mind waiting while she had a quiet moment.

With that Julie and her husband withdrew and when she returned she said simply, 'You've got me.'

My mother also played a part in introducing me to Jim Davidson. Back in 1989 he'd been very pleasant to her at a Jewish Care event, as well as being genuinely funny. True, he was rubbish when I invited him to speak at my 50th birthday party but I think he may have had a couple of drinks. Anyway, I liked him and thought that *Big Brother* might revive his career. That his career needed reviving was proved when we invited him to our office and gave him the grand tour. Sure enough, as I had suspected, nobody below the age of 30 knew who he was.

That was in 2012 but then, suddenly, he had sex abuse charges levelled against him. The bold thing to have done would have been to use *Big Brother* as a platform to show who he really was and face down the allegations. But Jim was reluctant. Even when Roger Daltrey called and passionately urged him to go public on *CBB*, he declined. A year later, though, the charges made against Jim were shown to be false, he accepted the offer to appear, played a blinder, and won the show. I tried to follow through with a Saturday night show for Jim comparable to NBC's *Saturday Night Live*, but TV is a very slow medium, and by the time everyone had got their act together the moment was gone.

I feel I have to mention one other celebrity I had dealings with during this period – if you can call him a celebrity. An ancillary deal on Channel 5 gave us an opportunity to buy into the YouView project with BT, the BBC, ITV, TalkTalk, Arqiva and Channel 4. And this brought me into intimate contact – on one occasion almost too intimate – with my old acquaintance Alan Sugar.

YouView, or Canvas, as it was first named, was an extension of the old television Freeview, but operated via the internet. Essentially, it was a development of digital terrestrial TV designed to combat the dominance of Sky. I wanted to be involved in it, so that I could have a place at the table in decision-making that would affect the future of British media for years to come. And I have to take credit, or blame, but I believe on the whole it should be credit, for bringing Alan in as chairman. During his time with YouView he definitely lived up to his reputation for being a colourful character.

Back in 1984 when we moved to Docklands we, like everyone else, had to have Amstrads – for a while, they were the only word processor and they were definitely an improvement on the old IBM golfball typewriters. During this period I first saw Sugar at a Jewish Care dinner, where my wife and I sat at the back, leaving the lime-light to Gerald Ronson and his wife with chandelier earrings – I believe he was the richest man in Britain then – and Alan, who was also royalty and who was strolling around with his wife, who wore equally large earrings. At a subsequent Jewish Care event I intro-duced myself to Alan, but he was stand-offish because he was Mr Big. I often saw him on *The Money Programme*, which I never missed, and listened to his plans for expanding into white goods and other areas.

Later, as I mentioned previously, Jeremy Beadle re-introduced us and I was invited to a dinner at his house, which was very splendid and full of models of his aeroplanes and boats, and letters from Gordon Brown long before Gordon was chancellor (at the time I had never even heard of him). Alan then showed us his new Emailer machine, a device that would send emails independent of a computer. Jeremy, who loved gadgets, was very critical of it, which upset Alan. The punters would ultimately share Jeremy's view. Then I returned the invitation with a dinner at my house, where another guest was Roger De Haan, who owned Saga, the travel and insurance group.

I saw Alan on a number of occasions over the next few years. I remember being very struck by his explanation of why he had decided to take his business public: 'Well, with Jews, they always think that the Cossacks are coming on a Saturday, so they take the money out of the till on a Friday.' In other words he didn't like to leave his money on the table. Thanks to him, I was also introduced to the joys of emails and BlackBerries. I even rented his plane sometimes. On one occasion he offered to sell us Spurs magazine, but his estimate of its value was about three times over the odds, not an uncommon phenomenon among people who have small magazines to sell.

Eventually, we had a serious falling-out. I needed a plane to bring me back from Los Angeles and a new secretary, who did not know any different, found a quote that competed with Alan's price. He was offended, accused me of not trusting him in one of the rudest letters I have ever received, and cancelled the plane hire.

Time passed. Then out of the blue I was approached to host a new TV show called *The Apprentice*, taking the role for the British version that Donald Trump had in the American original. I called my then publicist Brian MacLaurin and asked him what he thought. He asked what I wanted to be when I grew up – a TV star or a businessman? I replied that when I grew up I want to be Rupert Murdoch, not Simon Cowell. I then called Philip Green to see if he was interested, but he said if I didn't want it why should he want it. He proposed Alan. So the call was made and Alan got the gig, although I don't think to this day he gives us the credit for setting the wheels in motion.

So far as YouView was concerned, it was Charlie Dunstone of Carphone Warehouse and TalkTalk fame who initially urged me to get on board. With the obvious exception of Sky, Charlie said, Channel 5 were the only mainstream broadcaster not signed up. It would cost £20 million to be a partner but we would get money back in advertising the new services and I would be sitting at the table with some important players. So for that reason, and for Charlie, I did it. Why not, for once, start off by being friendly with my competitors.

We had a few meetings, but it soon became apparent that while there was a lot of talk and a lot of pieces of paper with graphs and marketing and the like being circulated, there was one key element missing: we didn't have a set-top box. If you're setting up a business based on set-top boxes, that is quite an important omission. Two or three more meetings followed, by which point I may possibly have banged the table in exasperation (if I did, I apologise). I certainly expressed reservations about the then chairman, who was rather inauspiciously called Kip Meek. I said we needed someone in charge like Sam Chisholm, the tyrannical New Zealander who had piloted Sky through its first years. More than that, the person needed to know boxes.

I suggested Alan. I said he was not a personal friend, but I remembered hearing that when Rupert Murdoch did not know how to make a box he went down to visit Alan in Brentwood, and Alan managed to pick up a signal with a coat hanger. Had he not been afraid of Cossacks and wanted ready cash, he might have got a royalty deal that would have put his business on a par with Apple, because he could have negotiated a percentage on every box sold. Alan, then, it seemed to me, was the right bloke, though I did say that he was not the easiest of guys to work with. And I also pointed out that while he thinks he is a marketeer he's not: what he's good at is simplifying electronics.

So I called Alan. At that particular time we happened to be getting on. He had been a good source of advice during the spat I had with Tom Bower and was very kind at my son's bar mitzvah. To his credit, he submitted to the formal interview process, after which he was offered the job. He then decided he was not sure he wanted it and had to be persuaded by several of us, including me. I agreed to advertise on his Amscreen system, which with the generous salary on offer would give him a very meaningful sum. I also said this position might set him up to be the next chairman of the BBC. He liked that.

We got down to business. After half an hour of conversation he knew more about the box we needed than any of us. He loved the idea that you would be able to rewind programmes: I believe the correct technical term is 'backward looking EPG'. He then sourced the right hardware at the right price from the right supplier. We were good to go. Overall, I wasn't surprised that people's attitudes to him varied. Some found him difficult. David Abrahams, the CEO of Channel 4, on the other hand, addressed him as Your Lordship and asked him for autographs.

My role in all this was to be Alan's counsellor – until the day we had a new problem. The business disagreement was over the share that I should get from advertising. The original understanding had been that Channel 5 and ITV would split revenue equally, but because the Channel 5 audiences were smaller, Alan felt ITV should get more. The more personal disagreement had to do with the whys and wherefores of a particular charity event Alan had been invited to.

Fortunately or unfortunately, our showdown took place in front of a large audience on the open floor of the offices YouView rented from me.

I started out arguing with Alan about the charity do, and then, in what may have been a bad bit of timing, moved on to talk about our dispute over advertising revenue. I had a compromise solution, I said, that would benefit everyone. Alan responded by asking me what I was fucking talking about, was I an idiot or something.

I said, 'Alan – the meeting's over, goodbye, there's the door.'

He left the building.

Richard Halton, the CEO of YouView, could not understand Alan's attitude because he said that when he had suggested the same idea, Alan had been in favour and had thought it would be me who argued against it.

Then there was a banging on the door – Sugar was back.

What happened then would have made good footage on any-one's television channel. Alan is a small person and by now was quite a thin old man. But he squared up to me and proceeded to prod me with his right hand saying that I couldn't talk to him like that, that he was the chairman and was doing us all a favour, and that everyone else was useless. Mixed in with all this was a large number of expletives which I myself, naturally, would never use.

He pushed me and then put his fist up to my face.

Now, the only person who ever frightened me was Kerry Packer. Alan is no Kerry Packer. I was determined to keep calm. I retreated and let him advance until we reached the window. His face was purple. I think I worried that he might have a heart attack.

He shouted, 'I'm not one of your fucking yes-men – I don't have to fucking agree with you, you don't pay my wages!'

I thought, well, if he punches me, it won't hurt.

I decided it was time to use his line. I replied, 'Actually, Alan, I do pay your wages. And actually, Alan, you know what? Fuck off, you're fired.'

Afterwards the other shareholders were 100 per cent supportive, though Charles Dunstone was worried we might be subject to pro-ceedings for unfair dismissal. I said if this happened I would sue him for assault.

I must admit I expected a note or maybe a cigar. But up to the time of writing, not a word.

Still, without Alan's involvement with YouView I maintain we would never have got the box out. Today the platform is a huge success and it has sold 2 million boxes. And Alan was clearly part of it.

But television has a funny effect on some people. The more I got inside it, the more I realised that.

20
SALE
OF THE
CENTURY

There was a lot going on in my neck of the woods in 2013 and into 2014. The media was under intense scrutiny, with ever-growing demands for regulation. Online rivals Google were continuing to grow and diversify at a seemingly unstoppable rate. Meanwhile, in the background, the economy was undergoing a 'fragile' recovery.

With all these factors in play, the question that was uppermost in my mind was this: could Channel 5 get to where ITV was, and if not, what should we do with it?

Initially, I have to say, we had no thought of selling. We were busy developing our discussion show with Nick Ferrari, and we were planning documentaries on topics which we knew from our newspapers were dear to the hearts of the British public. Besides, we were doing well with the programmes we already had, in particular with what many people were calling the 'best *Celebrity Big Brother* ever' (even people outside the *Daily Star*, which had always dubbed itself the show's 'official newspaper').

But while these various projects were important to us, I wasn't convinced that they would break the duopoly on big entertainment shows which the BBC and ITV enjoyed. To do that, I decided, I would need the services of an ex-A&R (artists and repertoire) man called Simon Cowell.

I had known Simon for some years. There was no common ground between us in terms of business interests, and while I admired his skills as a talent scout I have to admit – as a good blues man – that I couldn't help looking at the music he represented as cheesy pop. I had first come across him some years before at an event for Nordoff Robbins, a music therapy charity, but I don't believe we spoke then. However, when I met him properly around 2004 at a do Philip Green had arranged for BHS homeware I felt an immediate rapport. Simon and I spoke together about knighthoods, music and television. He was very charming.

After that I encountered him on various occasions, and eventually received an invitation to stay at a house he was renting in the south of France with his former (but somehow not departed) girlfriend Sinitta. The house was perhaps a little modest by some people's standards, but not bad for an A&R man.

While I was there I got a phone call from Philip Green: he was in his boat not far away – would I like to come on board? I said I couldn't really, as I was Simon's guest.

'Oh, that doesn't matter. Bring him too!'

'I'll have to ask him.'

It was two in the afternoon and Simon had just got up. He was busy taking thousands of vitamin pills and smoking thousands of cigarettes, as well as eating all kinds of healthy food. I mentioned Philip's invitation. We both agreed that we weren't that keen on visiting a yacht in harbour, because not only would we need a launch to get out there, but once there we'd be slightly trapped. But we suggested a little grudgingly to Philip that we could meet up at the VIP club in St Tropez. We thought it would be a short get-together.

Simon was being charming, as usual. 'You're the cleverest businessman I know,' he said.

I flattered him back, though at the back of my mind was the

thought that I didn't really know that much about his career. I knew he was a manager of the old school: one who spots kids early on and signs them up for the long term, just as Larry Page and Dick James did back in the day. I also knew, of course, that he had a TV show, but I wasn't sure who the show actually belonged to – I had a vague idea that it might have something to do with Simon Fuller, the Spice Girls' original manager and Cowell's A&R rival. One thing was for sure, I decided: it was not my world. So when Simon then suggested a deal whereby I could have 50 per cent of his company Syco for £100 million, I didn't leap at the chance. I asked him what exactly it was that he owned, since Fremantle did the production and Sony had some kind of option – I wasn't quite sure what I would be getting for my £100 million. Either Simon did not clarify sufficiently or I did not understand the clarification, but I ended up without a strong inclination to pursue the offer.

We passed the afternoon in the company of Sinitta and Simon's ex-sister-in-law, along with some middle-aged ladies Simon had invited. For some reason Simon didn't seem to want to spend time with his guests, so he went off for a lie-down, leaving me to talk to the middle-aged ladies. Dinner was fixed for eight. I therefore made sure I was ready at half past seven. And then I waited. Finally, at a quarter to ten, long after the time I like to eat, Simon appeared. If I wasn't exactly delighted at the delay, I have to admit that we did then go to a lovely restaurant in St Tropez where we passed a very relaxed evening. From time to time Simon would step out for cigarettes and be accosted by fans. He was very gracious to them, which is the only way I have ever seen him behave.

We arrived at the VIP club at midnight and shortly afterwards Philip ambled in with Mrs Philip, their children and – Harvey Weinstein. (An interesting combination for me: I had actually introduced Harvey to Philip because Harvey's designer wife had wanted to get her T-shirts into Topshop, but on that occasion Harvey's failure to see Philip's point of view had proved so stressful that I had ended up needing an hour in private with one of my directors who has a talent for psychotherapy.) Anyway, our evening at the VIP club went well, even if the simple food did come in at 1,000 euros for four covers, and the drinks cost us about 1,000 euros a round. Ouch. We left at 2am. On the way back to Simon's house I recall him explaining his business philosophy, which is to use the music that means most to people on his shows – in other words, the sort of songs that people play at weddings, funerals and other life events. It all made a lot of sense to me – his taste in bands might not be mine, but I understand the power of music to engage people's emotions and even change their lives.

I was up at eight the following morning. Not another soul in sight, except the gardener. A little later Harvey phoned and asked if we could meet for lunch. I explained yet again that as I was Simon's guest I couldn't make arrangements without consulting him – and that certainly ruled out lunch, I said, as Simon didn't get up until one o'clock. Harvey insisted that Simon wouldn't mind at all, and since he seemed to know Simon better than I did we agreed that we'd meet at Club 55 at one o'clock. Sinitta and others agreed to come along, and the hypnotist Paul McKenna did too, but the other member of our party, Harvey, was irritatingly late (as I had predicted he would be). Apparently, he had been dealing with something the *Independent* had run and he wanted me to sort it out. In case it has escaped the reader's notice, I do not own the *Independent*. More stress. More psychotherapy.

St Tropez, I concluded, is like that. It's full of wealthy people visiting expensive places to meet other wealthy people who never seem to be quite where they are supposed to be when they are supposed to be. My preference is for Mallorca. Nevertheless it was interesting to spend some time with Simon and enjoy his hospitality. I felt that we understood each other pretty well and that we would probably do business together at some point – even if he kept rather unconventional hours. (He didn't seem to mind that all his guests had disappeared off together for lunch.)

After I purchased Channel 5 Philip Green called me up. Philip had had a long association with Simon but by this time he was beginning to describe himself as his 'business manager', which appeared to mean he was in charge of looking for new deals.

Philip was very cordial. 'You know I am always the first to congratulate you,' he said. 'I'm not an envious bloke!'

I was slightly confused by this, since before the purchase he had taken me aside and advised me not to buy the channel. I had done well enough, he had said, and there was no point in pushing things further. Still, it is always nice to be congratulated on a deal.

'Have you heard from Cowell?' Philip asked.

I hadn't, but I soon did. Five minutes after I finished talking to Philip, Simon called to congratulate me, saying he was very jealous and then suggesting that we should work together. I learned that Philip was going to set up a meeting. For some reason, though, it didn't happen, though Simon and I continued to chat and Philip for his part promised we'd do something when 'Simon's contract with ITV ended'. I recall advising Simon not to collaborate with Tom Bower on a biography he was writing of him. Perhaps Philip thought otherwise, because the book did eventually appear. Having read it, I think that Simon would have done well to have taken my advice.

Anyway, by this time I had a fair idea of what ITV were paying Simon and I knew I could afford him. I managed to secure a meeting with him, at which I offered various options, including the idea of him 'renting' Saturday nights from Channel 5 in an Ofcom-compliant way, with me selling the advertising. It was a creative approach, if I say so myself, and Simon liked it. We started to talk figures.

The next thing to happen was that I received a call from Philip asking for a secret one-to-one at which we could further explore a deal to bring Simon and his shows to Channel 5. I duly turned up to discover, rather to my surprise, that Karren Brady was also there. I have to confess I wasn't terribly impressed. One-to-ones don't usually involve three people, and in any case I never really understood why Karren is feted as a great business icon.

One of the points we discussed was how much advertising revenue *The X Factor* generated on ITV, since that would help me arrive at a valuation for the show itself. Karren Brady came up with a figure significantly higher than I knew it must be. I was irritated. I said to Philip that if we were discussing the costs of making a suit or designing a dress I would defer to him, so perhaps he could extend to me the same courtesy when we were talking about advertising, a business I had been in for 40 years. They refused to accept the figure I came up with, so I left.

Eventually I had a meeting with Simon himself, at which I offered him the role of creative director of Channel 5, for whatever he was currently being paid by ITV, and said that he could buy 30 per cent of the channel from me. I had paid £100 million for it and reckoned it was now worth £200 million. He could therefore have a 30 per cent stake for £70 million, and at the same time would have a channel to fund his new productions. Nothing, however, came of this.

Even so, despite all these ups and downs and near-deals I still felt that Philip, Simon and I were friends and that it was worth pursuing our tortuous discussions. The ITV deal was due to come up for renegotiation in March 2014. I knew they could not speak seriously to me before that but assumed that once they had ITV's best offer they would come to me and ask if I wanted to make a counter-offer. But in autumn 2013, with several months still to go, I learned through a third party they had renewed with ITV. I did not bother to call them. I have to confess, though, that I was a little hurt they did not let me know directly.

Some weeks later, Karren Brady telephoned to tell me officially that they had signed the deal.

In some ways, I still regret that no deal with Simon materialised. From my point of view, it meant that I lost my shortcut for transforming Channel 5, which was a pity. From his point of view, I can't help thinking he lost an opportunity to transform himself into something even bigger. But that was his decision. Nevertheless, he continued to be supportive in other ways. He took an interest, for example, when I was building up the Health Lottery (of which more later), hosting a celebrity tea party that publicised it and the good causes it helped. By that time Channel 5 was being hailed as a very valuable business and I could not help reminding Simon that had he listened to me about acquiring a 30 per cent stake he would have multiplied his money substantially. He just smiled his charming smile. I came to the conclusion you just can't be cross with him. He's a lovely bloke and a great entertainer, though maybe not a great businessman.

My secretary Allison tried to console me by pointing out that with my early hours and Simon's late hours and his inclination to be late, it would never have worked anyway, and that I would have needed more hours of therapy than even my adventures with Harvey had prompted. And one of us at least would have ended up having a heart attack.

In my business life I have often looked to link up with a partner, but nothing has ever quite clicked. I thought at times it might be possible with Murdoch, then with ITV, then with Simon. Perhaps I have always been on the lookout for a big brother to fast-track what I was doing. Perhaps I also expected too much from people, and was then unfair to them when I was disappointed.

. . .

Yet even if Channel 5 didn't get sprinkled with Cowell stardust, it did become a very prosperous business in the course of 2013 and 2014. I had a solid team and a feisty programming controller. I had a stable base of programming and one standout show, *Big Brother*, which also worked well with my print products. There was no reason, really, to sell the channel.

Except for a couple of things. I had become aware that there were people out there with strong reasons to buy – who had the resources to achieve immediately what, with my lack of a world-class programming partner, I would probably take a number more years to do.

That may sound a little surprising coming from someone who was prepared to be in it for the long haul when he launched *OK!*. So why, if I could be so patient with print products, was I not prepared to hunker down in the British television industry for a decade-long build?

And that leads me to my other reason: the level of regulation TV has to endure. In the first place, it is closely scrutinised by politicians, and so to some extent subject to political whim. Then there's the fact that the ads that can and cannot appear at different times are controlled, and those controls seem only ever to tighten. To make things even more frustrating, the terms of the programme suppliers, the UK production companies, are also regulated. There are quotas for particular kinds of programmes you have to buy from particular kinds of suppliers, and even quotas from particular regions (for example, you are obliged to buy a certain proportion of your output from outside the M25 area). The regulatory authority Ofcom originally laid down these terms for production companies and their trade association (PACT) to protect small production outfits from giant, predatory broadcasters. But even though many of these small production companies were then aggregated into giants that were bigger and more profitable than the broadcasters, the regulatory environment remained highly restrictive. I felt, therefore, that the rules worked too strongly against the broadcaster. Whereas with a newspaper or a magazine you are, to a large extent, limited only by your own imagination or by the market, in TV the ground rules favour a status quo dominated by a few large established players. And it's very hard to challenge it.

As it happens we had a very harmonious relationship with Ofcom. But I couldn't be confident that Channel 5 or other broadcasters might not be subject to changing political attitudes. One reason for my concern can be expressed in three words: the Leveson Inquiry.

From my perspective, the events that led up to Leveson were pretty straightforward. Certain individuals had broken certain laws which at the time the authorities had not bothered to enforce. Then there had been a change of heart and a number of people, mostly at News International, started getting their collars felt. A police investigation was set in train, and existing laws started to be brought to bear.

And then the political dimension crept in. David Cameron had made the huge mistake (against my explicit advice) of employing ex-*News of the World* man Andy Coulson as his head of communications. That *News of the World* link took things straight to the heart of the Murdoch empire, and now a storm blew up over Murdoch's massive past influence with prime ministers and others. At the height of the hacking scandal, Cameron justified his hiring of Coulson to me by saying he was 'very good with tabloids', which I suppose is a bit like Bernie Ecclestone saying Hitler did some good things for Germany – it kind of misses the point. Cameron, in any case, did what the British Establishment always does when there is a public-opinion crisis: he set up a very expensive inquiry that would last long enough for everyone to become bored with the subject.

My own position in all this was made uncomfortable by the fact that my newspapers had left the PCC (Press Complaints Commission). To be honest, we had never really wanted to be members in the first place. I have always had a healthy scepticism of trade associations which dates back to my early encounters with the MIA (Music Industries Association) and PMA (Piano Manufacturers Association). In my experience, such organisations always seem to involve some old chap whose own business has gone broke but who is the friend of someone who is prepared to help them, and they are always preoccupied with conferences and meetings in places like Bournemouth. In other words, so far as I am concerned, they are pointless. When I was a magazine publisher, the PPA (Periodical Publishers Association) didn't want me and I didn't want them, so that worked out very well. But when I became a newspaper proprietor, we were asked to join the Press Complaints Commission, and because we were under the spotlight and needed to show we intended our stewardship of the papers to be correct and responsible, we duly joined. From my perspective it was a total waste of time, and I know that I wasn't alone in thinking that: a lot of people felt it wasn't fit for purpose and simply indulged industry cronyism.

My low opinion of trade associations was confirmed by my experience of the NMA, the Newspaper Marketing Agency. Stan Myerson had told me that the advertising agencies liked it, so in addition to being a member I agreed to have a meeting with some of its representatives. That meeting went all right, but afterwards they informed me that they wished to double our membership fee. I objected. We met again. I asked what they had done to justify the money they were asking for, and they proceeded to give a very impressive account of what they had achieved and what they could do in the future. I said I would give them half of what they wanted and would hand over the other half if they delivered on their promises. They didn't, of course, and it then turned out that their figures on the advertising revenue they had attracted for the industry as a whole were wrong anyway. We pulled out.

Actually I wanted to pull out of the PCC at the same time. On this occasion, though, I was dissuaded by James Murdoch, Rupert's son. He felt that if the Express left it would destroy the organisation.

What brought matters to a head was press coverage of the disappearance in Portugal of Madeleine McCann. The McCanns had engaged the services of a public-relations firm who worked with us and the rest of the press over the course of what must have been appallingly difficult months for the family. The McCanns did not, I am sure, like some of the stories we were being given by the Portuguese police, but their PR people accepted that if the little girl was constantly featured on the front page, it would maximise the chances of her being found.

During the spring of 2008, however, the McCanns appeared to change tack. Instead of being given press briefings, newspapers found themselves receiving writs. We had relied quite heavily on what we had got from the Portuguese authorities, so when the McCanns now complained we paid them damages and apologised very openly. Others paid and apologised less openly.

And now Christopher Meyer, the head of the PCC (which is a reactive body and which had therefore been deafeningly silent during the period all the newspapers were running regular stories on the case) suddenly took it upon himself to appear on television, where he proceeded to criticise Peter Hill, our editor, who was himself on the PCC complaints committee.

I rang Peter straight after the broadcast. 'I suppose you want to fire me,' he said.

'No – I want to fire the PCC.'

We did.

A little later David (Lord) Hunt came to see Paul Ashford and me. He, like us, felt that the PCC wasn't operating properly and wanted to put something better in its place. A lawyer by training, he had in his time been blown up by the IRA with Margaret Thatcher, been involved in enterprise zones, had been everywhere and done everything. He was also a proper bloke, and incidentally vice-president of the Holocaust Education Trust even though he was not Jewish, so that gave him a brownie point with me. Paul and I pushed for a body where serving editors would not police one another. If there was to be regulation, we said, it should not be done by a cosy club of insiders. By the time I came to give evidence to Brian Leveson this view was starting to become widely accepted.

The arguments I made at the Leveson Inquiry, however, proved more controversial. My view is a straightforward one: newspapers should be bound by the law of the land. If a newspaper does something illegal, then it should be prosecuted. If what it's doing is not illegal, it should not be prosecuted. I also happen to believe that it's risky to start mixing ethics up with questions of legality: ethics are a matter for the individual (the *Daily Mirror* reported this as me not knowing the meaning of ethics). Above all I worry when politicians want to penalise a nearly 200-year-old industry that has been a cornerstone of British culture and the British economy and brings information, education and entertainment to tens of millions. I can completely understand why there should have been public outrage when it was reported that the telephone of the murdered schoolgirl Milly Dowler had been hacked by *News of the World* journalists, but I dislike the political capital that was made out of it. And I can't help feeling there might be a desire on the part of the political class (particularly in the aftermath of the scandal over MPs' expenses) to have a press that does not make trouble for them. One reason Britain is great is because our national newspapers are good – even the *Guardian*. (In fact I quite like the *Guardian*. Sometimes I watch

Al Jazeera and I quite like that too.) I believe in free speech. If we don't have free speech we don't have anything.

My experiences with the regulation of newspapers, then, were not happy ones, and I didn't feel optimistic about the future. And if I worried about newspaper regulation, then I had cause to be even more concerned about the future direction of television regulation. As I've said, it was already tightly controlled. Who could tell what might happen in the future? What's more – and from a business point of view this made matters much worse – highly regulated television had to contend with the internet, which nobody felt like regulating because it looked too much like hard work. It wasn't exactly a level playing field.

As it happens, we had a few meetings with Google. Their people were invariably very clean, very tall, very American and very smart in every sense. They operated like this: at the first meeting they flattered you and told you they wanted to fund everything you did and participate modestly in the rights. In the second meeting the terms changed and started to look a little less favourable. And by the fourth or fifth meeting you weren't going to get anything from the deal: they just wanted to cherry-pick your iconic brands. Google answer to no national authorities, submit to no regulation, and have 'interesting' tax arrangements – although, of course, they never break the law.

With the prospect of such online companies entering television, and with Blinkbox, Netflix and others moving in on film as well, the future looks far from certain, and all the early warning signs were there while I agonised what to do about Channel 5. I remember witnessing a negotiation at the Cannes Film Festival between Jeffrey Schlesinger of Warner Bros and a lady from Netflix. Jeffrey plainly did not want to sell her the film rights she demanded, and didn't like the way she was pressuring him, but equally she clearly was not going to take no for an answer and was going to continue upping the price until he agreed. As an executive of a public company he had a responsibility to do the best deal he could for those rights, but new kinds of arrangements with new kinds of players might ultimately change the economics of an entire industry, as they already had with music.

So all the while that our takeover of Channel 5 was being acclaimed as a great success, with revenues up and exciting new programming, I knew the landscape of broadcast media was changing and would continue to change. Did I really want to be in it for the long term?

Moreover, I was beginning to receive enquiries. The first was a call from Barclays, who had helped us with the sale of *OK!* USA several years earlier. They said they were acting for Discovery: would we sell Channel 5?

I said no, I was enjoying running it.

Behind the scenes, though, we discussed our options. Rob Sanderson, my finance director, wanted to know how we would make the quantum leap we needed to make: perhaps, we said, we could look for new tie-ins, buy new sporting rights (perhaps in partnership with television newcomers BT), or invest heavily to build up news shows. We could explore further reality TV formats or create game-changing news debate shows.

Rob pointed out that what Barclays was proposing could yield us £450 million – not bad, bearing in mind we had made close to £100 million already during the course of ownership. A £550 million return on a £100 million investment in less than four years was not to be sniffed at. That made me think. Even if nothing came of it, I concluded, it's sometimes worth getting your house valued even when you're not planning to sell it.

So Rob and Richard Martin, our commercial director, started on a round of meetings and lunches. By July 2013, Barclays said Scripps, whose brands included HGTV and the Food Network, were also very interested. We had two strong potential buyers, both of whom had more scale than we did.

Meanwhile, elsewhere in our group cash was tight. We were building a newspaper print plant in Luton that would reduce annual costs on our papers by around £11 million and simultaneously free up our Docklands site for an exciting development I had in mind, but I had to loan £65 million of my own money to the business to fund the enterprise. We were not a *Daily Mail*-type business which ran comfortably on up to a billion of debt on the basis of buying market share. We were sensitive to the fluctuations of cash flow from the timings of certain programme series, in particular *Big Brother*. We needed liquidity.

In June 2013 when the Crusaders played at the Royal Television Society's Cambridge conference I talked about my future plans with Russ Ballard and Greg Lake, both respected friends. Both said the same thing. 'You've climbed the mountain, why are you looking for another one?' Joy was 39, Angel was just 2. There was so much we could do together as a family. Maybe Russ and Greg had a point.

On the same evening I gave the keynote speech to the RTS itself. I talked about the power of agencies and said I was not ready to take on Martin Sorrell because I did not have ten-stone testicles, a reference to the very upmarket Channel 4 programme of that name.

The reasons to sell Channel 5 seemed to be mounting up.

In November, I bumped into an old acquaintance – Sir Harry Solomon, formerly of Hillsdown Holdings – while he was running on Hampstead Heath. Harry had gone out with my big sister when she was 17 and I was a little boy. The way he remembered things, I was a pain in the neck and wouldn't leave them alone. I find that hard to believe.

I was concerned that, at his age, Harry should be running so vigorously. I'd recently been in a restaurant in New York when an elderly man had come in and been greeted with a round of applause because he'd just completed the marathon. He'd then ordered his meal (which seemed to consist of very little except lettuce leaves) and collapsed forward on to the table. An ambulance had to be called. I don't know what happened in the end – I don't think he paid the bill anyway – but seeing Harry bright red in the face from his efforts reminded me of the incident and made me feel I had to do something.

'Look,' I said. 'I've known you since I was 5 years old and I'm worried about you. It looks like you're pushing yourself too hard. You're in your seventies. You think you're on a mission but you need to ease off. You've never got time to rest and have a little chat. Please – stop running.'

'You're right,' he responded. And then he gave me some advice in return. 'I'd actually been meaning to call you,' he said. 'I sit on a number of boards, and one of them is this production company. They talk this digital claptrap the whole time and there's none of the old camaraderie. Your business acquaintances don't become your mates any more. I thought of you, and I wondered how you're coping with that? You built your business up because you understood about personal relationships.'

This gave me pause for thought. He had articulated something which I'd been feeling for a few years, without consciously realising it. 'You're right,' I said. 'Things are changing.'

'One of the reasons I got rid of Hillsdown was I had a customer who accounted for over 10 per cent of my revenue,' Harry went on. 'One customer over 10 per cent can really ruin your business if they start being awkward or getting difficult on price. Can I ask you whether you have any customers on Channel 5 approaching that level?'

'I have one customer at 30 per cent, one customer at 20 per cent and one customer at 15 per cent.'

Harry's eyebrows went up. 'Hmmm. Who's the 30 per cent customer?'

'Martin Sorrell.'

'Do you trust him?'

'I trust him to do the best for himself and his shareholders.'

'If you don't mind me saying – I would sell that business.'

The next time we spoke he was enjoying a holiday in the Lake District – walking, not running this time, so maybe what I had said had struck a chord. But his words stayed in my mind, too.

The last quarter of 2013 was good for Channel 5. Instead of making the £45 million before interest and taxes we had anticipated, it looked as though we would make more than £60 million. Maybe, we thought, the valuation for the channel could be as much as £600 million.

Now we put together a 'book' (a comprehensive information memorandum, in accountant-speak), and outside interest started to mount. At one point BT talked in terms of taking control of 50 per cent of the group. They were engaged in a battle with fighting Murdoch and felt this would give them a key advantage: together we could buy properties like *The X Factor* to make ourselves really competitive. Then BT's boss Gavin Patterson switched their tactic to a simple acquisition. It was a pity we were doing so well, he said, because now he'd have to pay more, but he would nevertheless definitely be bidding. He took me out for lunch and while his conversation was peppered with a lot of maybes, it all felt very positive.

Sky was simultaneously telling Barclays that they'd more than match the highest bid: they had to have this deal. Sky director Sophie Turner Laing privately confirmed that intention to me and raised the possibility that they could pay with ITV shares. They had perhaps 10 per cent of ITV with a value of perhaps £600 million. The transaction would make me the biggest single shareholder in ITV. I could definitely enjoy that.

Comcast, NBC, Sony, Time Warner and others joined the party. Some suggested we might instead consider going public. Things were hotting up.

Opening bids were received in March 2014. There were a couple of less than credible offers on both the high and the low sides. The rest ranged between £650 million and £415 million, the lowest being from Viacom. We debated whether to strike them out. However, Daniel Ross of Barclays advised us not to do so. He said he knew them, that they were good people, that they had the cash and a proper investment rationale, and that their financial director, Wade Davis, was a good and honourable bloke. I had still not definitely decided to sell, but I could see, as I reviewed each potential buyer, that each of them could make more out of the channel than I could.

And so we moved to second-round bids. There was no real reason why they should be different from the indicative first-round bids, but then those weren't binding, so who knew? I was acutely aware that the sums of money involved were life-changing for me, and that any deal would inevitably transform the media business I had spent so long building. Not knowing how it would all turn out made me tense. One day I remember being almost too frightened to get up; I had a feeling of dread about what the day would bring — something that had never happened to me before. I had a bad vibe. We went to the pub, which I never normally do, drank beer and ate calamari and chips, which I don't drink or eat.

Then we had a call from Discovery, by then bidding in tandem with Sky, to say their bid was not going to be as much as they had thought but that we shouldn't be disappointed: there would be 'scope for further movement'. The figure they then came up with was £420 million – a poor offer compared to the others. What's more, the bid was made after a piece appeared in the industry magazine *Broadcast* (based, presumably, on some sort of strategic briefing) that seemed to suggest that they'd already bought the channel. I could only assume that that was intended to discourage other bidders. Other reports quoted a figure of £350 million for Discovery's purchase of Channel 5. Even Discovery's boss, David Zaslav, was talking about the channel as if he owned it – which I thought was not quite consistent with the confidentiality agreements.

I told Barclays that I didn't like the way Discovery were behaving and that we should stop negotiating with them. Barclays said I would be turning down £420 million. I said I didn't care. My directors and I discussed the option of waiting a year and doing a public offering for Channel 5, and we got Barclays to call Discovery and Sky to tell them they were now out of the process. The finance director of Sky got rather irate and laid into Barclays, implying we would never get a sale and that when we had failed, they would come back and buy Channel 5 for £50 million less than their current offer. I think there was some suggestion of a bad write-up on the front page of the *Wall Street Journal*, too, and all because poor Barclays had pointed out politely that Discovery's bid was not high enough. In fact I knew the *Wall Street Journal* part was bluff – Rupert Murdoch was aware that I had inkwells too. Still, I hate a bad loser.

Meanwhile, as confusion and rumours circulated everywhere, other second-round bids threatened to be less robust or less immediate than the indicative bids that had kicked off the process. Viacom alone remained consistent. After a short negotiation their offer was £450 million, clean. They would sign within three days.

OK. Done. They got a bargain, and everyone was happy. And it didn't go on the front page of the *Wall Street Journal*.

The next day the boss of Viacom, Philippe Dauman, whom I

had not previously met, called, thanked me and praised my team. I thanked him and praised his. I shared some ideas for the channel with him and said I envied him because he had the programmes and the clout to do what I hadn't been in a position to do. He said he envied me banking a cheque for £450 million when I had already had £100 million back in profits.

The deal was supposed to be passed by the European regulators in July. Shortly before the deadline I was taking Angel to her first school when I suddenly felt inexplicably irritated and tense. Sure enough, later that day I received a phone call telling me that due to press speculation that Sky would be selling the advertising on Channel 5 (even though Viacom had confirmed they would handle ad sales in-house), there would have to be an EU investigation to ensure nobody was getting a dominant market share of advertising. That meant another two months' wait as hundreds of lawyers earned fortunes filling in millions of forms to prove that we hadn't got a dominant market share. Incidentally, the same conclusion could have been reached in two minutes by a primary-school pupil. Given that Channel 4 had £1 billion, ITV £2 billion and Sky £500 million of advertising revenue, it's hard to see how our £400 million plus Viacom's £100 million could add up to a dominant share in any case.

But that's why I love the EU. Maybe *Daily Express* readers are right.

During that interim period I met Gavin Patterson from BT. As a salaried corporate employee rather than a business owner himself I suppose he might have felt slightly envious of someone who might be about to bank almost another £500 million. In his position I think I would have been. But that's not what I got from him at all.

'Do you realise what a great strategist and marketer you are?' he said.

'No,' I said. I wasn't being modest – I really don't see myself in that light. I just get things done, one after another.

'Timing – everything – perfect!' he continued.

'Thank you very much, Gavin,' I said, genuinely touched.

'What will you do now?'

I told him my thought.

'You should go to Cambridge and do an MBA,' he said, seemingly even more excited about all the options open to me than I was.

'Well, Gavin, maybe I should.'

'Or you could buy a huge farm somewhere!'

'Errr, yes, or I could do that.'

People have different ideas about what to do with success. But quite clearly, it was time to turn my thoughts to what I did want to do next, and what I intended my legacy in business and in life to be.

21
THE FUTURE AND THE PAST

So, if you have done more than you ever thought you would do, and reached further than you ever thought you would reach, what happens next?

After the sale of Channel 5 I was repeatedly congratulated on my success. I'd certainly made a lot of money out of that deal. But I have often noticed there are people who always 'think rich' whether they are or not, and people who always 'think poor' whether they are or not, and I know that I belong to the second category. For people like me the idea that you could lose everything never entirely goes away. Maybe it goes back to Alan Sugar's idea that one day the Cossacks might come. My mother was the same; remember that despite her devoted son being reasonably successful in business and determined to give her everything he could, she still thought she could not afford to take a taxi.

But after Mum died and Janet left I found a new family, and maybe some new values – or perhaps old values rejuvenated and renewed. And one day I found myself saying to Paul Ashford and Martin Townsend, 'You know, I wonder if there might be more to life than driving yourself mad, driving other people mad to get somewhere you're not sure you want to be in any case?'

I had a similar conversation with Russ Ballard, rock-and-roll singer and poet. His reply was, 'You need to find time to smell the roses.'

So that's what I tried to do. I started to cut down the hours I spent working. I went for more walks on Hampstead Heath. I spent more time with Angel. I also made time to explore links with the past, often with my son Robert. He had become interested in his roots, and had started to enquire about our family.

One day he asked me, 'Dad, exactly where in Ukraine are my great-grandparents buried?'

'Well, actually, Streatham,' I replied. Robert was right that his great-grandparents were Ukrainian but despite his academic brilliance seemed to have forgotten that my mum had often spoken to him about going to visit their grave. Of course, to me as a North Londoner Streatham is almost as much of a foreign country as Ukraine, but Robert's interest in our origins tripped something in my mind and prompted me to organise a visit (accompanied by my cousin Alan Hordyk) to the cemetery so that we could pay our respects. Once there, we stood beside the grave of the two Ukrainian Jewish immigrants, Louis and Golda Chachewitz (at some point the family changed their name to Harris, probably to avoid prejudice), we said Kaddish, the Jewish prayer of thanksgiving, and thanked Louis and Golda for making the journey that they did, so that we could have the wonderful lives that we did. It was a very moving experience for me, and I think for my son too. The graves were modest and they were unkept. I believe Robert spoke to the attendant there, and £500 in readies changed hands. In the future Louis and Golda can be sure of one of the best-maintained plots in that cemetery.

The past – our own, other people's – never entirely lets us go. And now Robert became really serious about connecting with his Jewish roots. This was rather ironic, because as you will remember, Robert was the Jew who would not have been allowed to be Jewish had we followed the views of the Orthodox community. I was a proud father, so years later I let my Orthodox friend know about Robert's academic success and told him how, having felt a little isolated at first at Cambridge, he had found a home at the Jewish Society there, and how he had then gone on to support World Jewish Relief, as well as local Jewish relief and related charities. I explained how he created memorial websites for the Holocaust (being a computer whizz), and cycled alone from Britain to Auschwitz in Poland, using his personal blog to remind people of what none of us should ever forget. I suppose I thought my friend would say, 'Ah, you were right and I was wrong.' But he didn't, which I think is sad.

I retained my interest in charitable causes, an interest that I think stems from seeing what happened to my dad when he was struck by ill health. From my twenties onwards I'd helped out with the Boys' Clubs and the Variety Club, and then later, with the help of Brian MacLaurin, I'd set up the Richard Desmond Charitable Trust which gave money to some hundreds of good causes. My big idea of the noughties had, of course, been the RD Crusaders and I was delighted when our 2008 fundraiser pulled in upwards of £14 million for half a dozen charities. But I did begin to wonder how sustainable the venture was. Apart from anything else, it gave me blisters (during our concert periods I had to buy a lot of sticking plasters). And, of course, some members of the band – not me, of course – weren't getting any younger. How many more times can you expect a 65-year-old to play 'Won't Get Fooled Again'? I also started to feel that charity events in a credit-crunch era were problematic: fund-raising events, dinners and auctions became embarrassing at a time of general austerity because even if some individuals could afford to give, they were held back by a worry that they might look flash.

So I needed to find something a little more solid by way of a charity platform.

Now, if you are a computer genius like Robert, you do that by launching a charity website. If you are an artist you fundraise through art. I'm a businessman. I therefore decided that the answer was to create an organisation.

A few weeks after we acquired Channel 5, Stan Myerson heard from the advertising agency Walker Media that they'd been working on something called the Health Lottery but that the owners could not get the backing for it that they needed. Stan brought the three geezers in: the CEO Martin Hall, an accountant and a salesman. I liked the salesman, but then I usually like salesmen. I also loved the idea that this was a (seemingly) viable business that could donate millions to charity as its primary purpose. If I could make it work it would support good causes at a local level.

Once you'd got through the hundreds of pages of statistics the charity's champions had prepared, the concept was a simple one: the lottery would sell 5 million tickets a week which, once retail margins, operating costs, prizes and the like were subtracted, would leave £50 million a year for local health causes, defibrillators, care centres and exercise classes – all the things that are fundamental to building healthier communities but which the cash-strapped NHS is often unable to provide. Handling the donations would be a series of 'people's health trusts' under a very good chief executive called John Hume. Professor Jennie Popay, a leading academic who specialised in health inequalities, would act as chairperson. The concept had been worked up into a major media campaign and I loved the TV treatment, which was colourful, energetic and lively.

The Health Lottery people told me that research clearly showed that they would reach their 5 million tickets a week target even without the support of the supermarkets. This, it seemed to me, was just as well. My previous experience of an exciting new concept linked to a good cause had been *Green* magazine, and from that I had learned that fine words and good deeds don't necessarily go together. On the other hand, I also thought it would be incredibly difficult to reach the target of 5 million a week if we *didn't* have the supermarkets on board. I was confident that since the top guys in all of them were my mates and my trading partners they would help me, as I had always helped them.

In fact it turned out that the reason the team had written off the supermarkets was that they had already sold the concept to them on a previous occasion when the lottery had then failed to launch, and the team felt embarrassed to go back and ask again. I didn't have any such reservations, and gave myself a week to deal with the matter. We started on Monday with Tesco and finished on Friday evening with Asda. In the case of the latter I actually refused to leave until we had a deal. At heart I was still Mr Page, and Mr Page does not go home until the sale is made. In those five days we got deals with all the big supermarket chains. True, it still took over two years for Sainsbury's and Asda to be completely online, but they did hurry up when I threatened to come and spend a Friday night with them again. Apparently their difficulties arose from technical issues, but drummers don't care about that sort of thing. Tesco, Morrison and Lidl were the best – and grasped the concept the quickest.

Everything was working out. For £30 million seed money, and with the support of 360-degree coverage from advertising in papers and magazines, it looked as though we'd have a continual revenue stream going straight to the charities. Fantastic! We decided to start things off with a bang, spending £2 million of our advertising budget in the first two weeks alone on ads with ITV. In those first two weeks we sold 2.5 million tickets. That meant there was a sound business there, and one with the potential to grow. You couldn't ignore the fact, though, that it was still only half what we had hoped for.

At this time I still had Channel 5 to think about, and since that could make or lose money very quickly on a detail of programming or a big acquisition, I still had to devote most of my time to it. That meant that for a while the Health Lottery was left to its former management, who had joined us en bloc. But I felt that if it wasn't taking off quickly, and was losing a couple of million a month, at least the charities were benefiting.

'Well,' I said to Richard Brasher, then head of Tesco in the UK, 'at least this is something I can't be criticised for!'

'You watch,' he replied. 'You will be.'

I suppose when you are an outsider, you will always be an outsider.

Within a week of our launch Camelot, the Canadian-owned company who run Britain's National Lottery, went berserk, just as the national newspaper groups had when we entered their territory a decade previously.

Camelot sell £7 billion worth of tickets a year and the Health Lottery was selling around £100 million: in other words, our yearly turnover was considerably less than their turnover in a week. We therefore scarcely constituted a threat. Furthermore we were properly licensed by the Gambling Commission. We were adding to the funding of good causes. And demonstrably we weren't even affecting Lotto revenues. Even so, Camelot were determined to undermine us. They hired a PR agency and various lobbying firms. Martin Hall later said that he got less grief when he was selling crisps than from running a charity lottery. I felt as though I was being caned for selling programmes for charity all over again, although it didn't hurt as much as it had when I was a child. On the other hand, at least then the caning had stopped after a while.

Camelot took legal action against the Gambling Commission for giving us a licence. The judge found that the Gambling Commission, and we, were acting entirely correctly, and Camelot's case was thrown out with £2 million costs awarded against them. The judge advised them to talk to Parliament, not him, if they wanted laws changed. Dianne Thompson, the then boss of Camelot, took this literally and proceeded to try to round up politicians. Unfortunately for her, most of them were rather pleased with what we were doing because we were helping to fund health causes in their constituencies. The rules for contributions and for prizes were different for us because Camelot was a state monopoly, but nobody could dispute that our existence raised extra funds without undermining their business.

Meanwhile, I supported the charity whenever I could. I recall visiting a community centre we were funding in Hatfield, with the Conservative party chairman Grant Shapps, and finding myself conscripted into a crocheting class. My attempts were only minimally successful, and I was obliged to promise that I would return for further training, in order to become (according to the YouTube recording of the event) 'the best crocheting media owner in the world'. I don't know how hot the competition is on that one – though perhaps Mr Murdoch has been practising secretly. On another occasion Boris Johnson joined us for a site visit in inner London where he tried out a child's swing at enormous risk to himself and everyone around him. We then moved on to cooking classes, preparing Pacoras, which involves naked flames and hot oil (by mayoral decree the normal health and safety rules were temporarily suspended) – all done in the semi-darkness of a February evening. I would have felt safer behind a drum kit.

Ed Miliband also pitched in, joining me with a spade and a rake for a Conservation Volunteers 'Green Gym' project in his Doncaster constituency. The idea was that people should band together on work that benefited the local environment and also provided outings, exercise and companionship to those who might not otherwise have access to such things. We made a pretty effective workforce with our spades and shovels and implements of destruction. It's just a pity that the guys who were supposed to be repairing the M1 at Junction 10 were not in our league – I had been held up for three hours on the journey and was nearly a no-show as a result. Andy Clarke, CEO of Asda, had to keep Ed talking while I, with my horror of lateness, used a mobile phone to try (unsuccessfully) to find a helicopter to pluck me off the motorway and get me there on time. Perhaps I should suggest to Hailo and Uber that they add helicopters to their services.

I derived a great deal of personal satisfaction from the work of the Health Lottery charities. We were able, for example, to help provide funding for some Hasidic Jews with learning and caring problems. They were so Orthodox that even my own Norwood charity did not have the flexibility to adapt to their needs. We even helped a bunch of (very probably illegal) asylum seekers who were in a bad way. Well, I felt, you had to do something. I just hoped that *Daily Express* readers would understand if they ever found out – they have good hearts.

However, while all this was going on, Camelot were mobilising the Enemies of Desmond against the Health Lottery. In April 2012, four members of the House of Lords wrote to *The Times* to warn that, if allowed to continue to operate, the Health Lottery would 'have potentially disastrous consequences for the National Lottery and the good causes it supports'. The letter echoed the court papers lodged by Camelot (although it was careful not to mention Camelot by name). It accused the Health Lottery of 'general unlawfulness' and claimed that the noble Lords' 'grave concerns' were shared by 'MPs and peers across all parties', as well as a string of organisations across the voluntary sector, none of them named. The first signature was that of Lord Grade, with whom I had once had a falling out over his support for a charity event; suffice it to say that I was not now his biggest fan. The other signatories were Lord Clement-Jones, Lord Faulkner of Worcester and Lord Burns, chairman of Channel 4.

Ben Webster, the then media editor of *The Times*, who had been handed the letter by the letters editor, noticed that it bore the fax number and identification of Pagefield PR company. A few phone calls later, it emerged that the letter had been organized by Camelot. What's more, certain rather key pieces of information had not been divulged in the letter, such as the fact that Lord Grade and Lord Burns had both held senior positions at Camelot and the National Lottery Commission, and that as chairman of Channel 4, Lord Burns was a direct competitor of Channel 5. A little scrutiny of Pagefield's website also showed that its advisory board was chaired by none other than Sir Christopher Meyer, an old mate from the not fit for purpose PCC.

I was told by Jeremy Hunt, the minister then responsible, that if we had had an impact on the National Lottery's takings he might have been concerned. However, Camelot's sales had actually increased since we'd got going, so he was quite happy, and even confirmed this in writing. That seemed to draw a line under any serious political objections to our idea, if indeed any ever existed, although it didn't stop Camelot sniping.

Unfortunately we were still losing money. Martin Hall withdrew from the fray in a most gentlemanly manner – along with some of his original team. We tried to make savings wherever we could. At the time the Health Lottery ads were being done by my Channel 5 production team and I accused them of wanting to make *Ben Hur*. They were paying Melinda Messenger a fair whack a week for a few seconds' work. I said that was outrageous. They said no, she was a big star. I said yes, a big star on *my* Channel 5 *Cowboy Builders*. In the end Natalie Cassidy from *EastEnders* got the job for a much more modest sum (she gave me a beautiful engraved cigar cutter). But I knew that reducing costs wouldn't in itself turn the business round. We needed to grow revenue. We needed a bit of luck.

And then we got lucky. Camelot announced that they were doubling their price – something you can do when you have a monopoly and something that also explained why they had been so sensitive about us entering the market. The increase from £1 to £2 finally went through in September 2013, and at a stroke our sales went up by 50 per cent, as, of course, did our charity donations. Such was the nature of the legislation that protected Camelot that we weren't allowed to compete on equal terms, but at least we now had a chance.

I decided it might be worth talking to Camelot themselves and trying a radical idea on them. So I rang Dianne Thompson, Camelot's chief executive, and Andy Duncan, its managing director, and, despite the fact that both our companies had perfectly good offices, we agreed to meet at the Corinthian Hotel. We all decided we liked each other.

'I remember, when we met at a do with the Queen, and I was trying to raise £50,000 for a charity, you said you would give me five thousand to get me going,' said Dianne.

'Well, that's the sort of chap I am . . .'

'When I worked for Channel 4 you invited me to a Led Zeppelin concert,' said Andy. 'I had the night of my life.'

I remembered that too. I also remembered that when Andy worked for Rolls-Royce and one of their salesmen got me to agree to change my car, Andy hadn't followed through on the deal. Well, I suppose at least I saved some money. And, in any case, we had all decided that even if we did have a little issue about lotteries, we liked each other very much.

That made it easy for me to put my proposition to them. 'Look, it's nice that we all get on, but what about this: suppose you took over the running of the Health Lottery – or even bought it? The good causes would benefit and what costs me £20 million to run as a stand-alone would only cost you three or four to run as an add-on.'

They seemed interested, and Andy said, yes, he thought three or four million to run it sounded about right.

'Maybe we should get some financial people involved?'

'That would be good.'

A meeting was therefore set up with Macquarie Bank. Unfortunately it was then cancelled when a journalist called Mark Kleinman, a little bastard (I use that word in its most complimentary sense) who used to work for me and who has the knack of always getting the story, found out, and the matter became 'too high profile'.

And maybe Dianne and Andy just didn't like me as much as they said they did.

Meanwhile, thanks in part to my son Robert, I had become increasingly interested in finding out more about my family background. Together we began to make journeys that, with the weight of my business concerns over the years, I had never really believed I would make, and to trace a heritage I only half understood.

As for most people, my knowledge of the Holocaust and the culture of persecution that shamed Europe in the early part of the last century had come from books, documentaries and films – perhaps also some encounters with survivors. But now it suddenly became much more personal. My late mother's parents had left Ukraine in the 1900s, and their hard life in London's East End meant that both died prematurely in the 1930s. But what about the family who were left behind?

It was Alan Hordyk who initially suggested a trip to Ukraine to explore our ancestry, as well as a visit to Auschwitz. And it was Robert's persistence that made it happen. With his strong Jewish identity, he felt that at 22 the visit was long overdue. I'd once visited Poland on business and been moved by sharing a religious service with members of the Jewish community there. But I still saw that whole region as very distant. 'Education from books is not enough,' my son said. 'You have to see things for yourself.'

So a group of us set off for Krakow. Our departure date coincided with the run-up to the French elections, in which 17.9 per cent of voters backed far right Marine Le Pen. Extreme nationalist groups were also expanding in the economically devastated southern Europe. Suddenly, the events of the 1930s did not seem as remote as they once had.

On reaching Krakow, we were met by Jonathan Ornstein, director of the Beit Chayil Jewish Community Centre, which is funded by World Jewish Relief (a charity to which I had been donating for about 30 years and which had planned our itinerary). We went straight to the Centre for a Shabbat evening meal. There was no security around the synagogues and the Centre — nor, apparently, was it necessary. Robert noted that the gates to Beit Chayil are left open, something that would be unusual in other cities. 'The community has already faced the unimaginable. They have nothing left to fear,' said Jonathan. 'We are building a new future for the Jewish people in Poland. We are looking forward.'

From Krakow we went to Auschwitz. The camp's first commandant, Rudolf Hoess, testified at the Nuremberg trials that up to 3 million people died there. That figure was later revised to 1.3 million, 90 per cent of them Jews. Those not killed in the gas chambers died of starvation, or as a result of forced labour, infectious disease, individual executions and medical experiments.

It was May, but it was unseasonably hot when we arrived on the Saturday morning. Many of the visitors were in T-shirts and casual clothes. The informal dress gave the initial, incongruous impression of a holiday outing. The buildings were clean, stark, well cared for. We saw the former houses of the guards, the sheds for the inmates, the gas chambers, and the ovens where the bodies were burned. It took 40 minutes to kill someone, and then up to 48 hours to process the bodies. After that there was nothing left: no evidence; no memory.

We were shown the railway lines which brought the victims here, many still believing the deception that they were going to a new settlement. We learned about the elaborate logistics necessary for murder on such an unprecedented scale. We thought about the kind of mentality required to bring this about, and the millions who would have had to collude to make it possible. Auschwitz is not a holiday outing. It is a grim reminder of what human beings are capable of, and of atrocities that we must ensure are never repeated.

On Sunday, we left Krakow for Kiev, a clean, lively city with busy streets, as well as a picturesque medieval tower and a synagogue, but relatively poor and heavily dependent on Russia for its energy supplies. Between 350,000 and 500,000 Jews live in Ukraine today, making it the third largest Jewish community in Europe. Just outside Kiev is Chernigov, the region my grandparents called home, where half the population was Jewish at the beginning of the 20th century and where, after all those mass executions, almost no Jews live now. No trace of my family or our name remained there. Our guides did tell us that a man in his nineties who shared my family surname had died recently, but they also pointed out that the surname was a common one.

In neighbouring Kharkiv, home to some 14,000 Jews, the WJR's community centre was full of friendly faces. The children at the centre had a band, and since someone had heard I was a drummer I got put on bongos.

The next day we travelled to the Babi Yar Holocaust memorial site. It is estimated that between 100,000 and 150,000 died in this ravine in a series of massacres carried out by the Nazis. Reciting Kaddish there was the most moving experience of our trip. Today, people walk over the dead, oblivious to it all. But as I looked down into the ravine I felt the horror of what had happened, and wondered what it must have been like for the thousands who marched there, knowing they were going to be shot. I tried to imagine how it would feel if we suddenly got the order to abandon our homes and march across Hampstead Heath carrying a single bag of possessions, and with the sound of gunshots in the distance.

Later we visited a synagogue and a cemetery. It was sickening to see that vandals had daubed there: 'Ivan the Terrible was right'. (Ivan the Terrible was the nickname of the concentration camp guard and sadistic torturer later identified as John Demjanjuk, who died on 17 March 2012, before his trial could be concluded.) We saw other examples of anti-Semitism on our trip, too. There were swastikas felt-tipped on walls around the homes of clients visited by World Jewish Relief. Disgusting. Personally, I would be very nervous living in Ukraine as a Jew. You would feel as though you permanently had to look over your shoulder. The charity is doing what it can, but old prejudices have not entirely died and life is tough there.

We left Kiev's Boryspil Airport on Monday. I made Robert promise that if I'm not around in 20 years, he will take his young sister Angel on the same trip. He said he would happily accompany her and, if necessary, push me round in a wheelchair.

That was the first visit I made to the former Soviet Union, but it was not the last. I was overwhelmed by the resilience of those I met, and the work that is being done to create a more secure future. On one of my visits, to Belarus, I met the heroic Rabbi Moshe Fhima, founder and head of a unique school for rehabilitating and inspiring young people. To me he is even more remarkable because he's originally from Manchester and only intended a three-day visit when he came to Ukraine 21 years ago.

That particular visit came about because I had met Rabbi Barry Marcus at Lloyd Dorfman's daughter's extremely lavish wedding, and he had told me all about Fhima. Perhaps I could help raise funds for him. I talked to Trevor Pears, the property guy who had contributed so generously at my last Crusaders event, and he said he would contribute if Ian Livingstone did. I therefore contacted Ian Livingstone with a suggestion that he should offer £75,000 (on the basis that Trevor would feel he had to match), but he said he would only do that if I did, too. Between the three of us, therefore, we raised the best part of a quarter of a million for Rabbi Fhima's institution in Pinsk. We then all agreed it might be an idea to find out exactly where Pinsk is. I was chosen to make the trip, the argument being that I would be able to spend at least some of my time checking the news-stands to see how Russian *OK!* was doing. Rabbi Fhima kindly agreed to drive 250 miles to pick us up at the airport in Brest.

I said that Rabbi Fhima is heroic, because there really is no other description for what he does and for what he has achieved. He showed us around his establishment of Beis Aharon. It's a school and orphanage, but it also has a yeshiva, a synagogue, a mikvah and a soup kitchen serving the whole of Belarus. Fhima built the entire enterprise up little by little, and had a story for how he came by every candle and every piece of furniture and every book. He was overflowing with applicants for his school, and showed me the field where he was planning the next school would be. He had me climbing ladders to inspect the roof. There was a reason for this – local legislation forbade him from putting in stairs and additional rooms in the roof area. His solution was to put the rooms in anyway and to use ladders to access them – if the authorities visited, they could just be hidden. He has told me it is fine to record this detail as Belarus planning officials are unlikely to buy my book.

The schools are spotless, the library immaculate, and all of the students are well behaved – a testament to Fhima's teaching. The most important rule is that you have to contribute. 'Only the very young children and the elderly are excused from helping,' he said. 'Everyone else has to do something.'

There were times during my meeting with Rabbi Fhima when I thought he was the ideal person to run this country: modern Britain, I thought, could do with people of his vision, his energy and his commitment. As we left he pointed out a building and said it was the local office of the secret police. He said that since I was an interesting foreign visitor he would, no doubt, be taken in there so they could ask questions about me.

'It's quite scary,' he told me, 'because when you go in they put you in a little room where you can't, sort of, move. But it's all part of the game.'

As with my other visits to eastern Europe I returned home full of mixed emotions. The world can be a cruel place. Yet it can also be inspiring. The next day I was back to my media group and my Health Lottery, juggling costs, looking at deals, trying to get my messages across, meeting all kinds of people with different schemes and agendas. I found myself asking, 'Is this the real world, or was that?'

2014 was a good year for me. The digital side of my newspaper business was booming, up 300 per cent year on year, although the print side was downsizing as more people moved across to internet platforms. The Health Lottery was a third bigger than it had been during the previous year. But I was spending more of my time abroad, relaxing and learning to 'smell the roses'. And like anything else that you are not used to, it really was a learning process. At the same time I was also becoming more concerned about the world around me.

Just as I had rediscovered my family roots in Ukraine, that country was torn apart by insurgency and outside intervention. I read in my own papers about the tragedy of flight MH17 and the impotence of Western politicians to find a solution. Iraq disintegrated further into crisis with Islamic fundamentalists cutting a swathe through its territory and that of neighbouring states with beheadings, abductions, rapes and forced conversions. It was a similar story in Syria, where Christian communities in particular were targeted. Violence in Gaza erupted anew; Israel's response was criticised; I heard of boycotts on 'Israeli businesses and Jewish businesses backed by Israel'. Some of us thought again of Kristallnacht and all that followed. In the previous year there had been 200 registered incidents of anti-Semitic crime in the UK – as for unregistered ones, who knows? My own charity, Norwood, had its shop targeted with anti-Semitic hate material, and its voluntary helpers intimidated. I was beginning to meet people who no longer wanted to reside in the UK. I even had such thoughts myself.

In September 2014 the Health Lottery organised a donation to Conservation Volunteers in Tottenham, north London. As is often the case with our projects, we were pursuing health goals below the radar, creating a set-up where individuals could receive the support and care they needed in a sustained and consistent manner that offered more than visiting medics or popping pills could. In Tottenham, the focus was on offering a community solution to those with mental health problems. I had to do some digging again, but no crocheting or cooking, at least. There to greet me was my friend David Lammy, the MP who had just thrown his hat into the ring for Mayor of London. I have already mentioned his thoughts on creating opportunities for people who feel alienated from the political system; I had read his book and developed a respect for his political judgement. (Incidentally, and paradoxical though it may sound to mention Nigel Farage in the same breath as David Lammy, it's the fact that so many of Farage's supporters similarly feel locked out of the establishment that led me to conclude that he

– and they – deserve a voice: that it is right to make life a bit less comfortable for the big parties; that they should be reminded how many ordinary British people feel. From my point of view, this has nothing to do with being right wing and a lot to do with resisting arrogant cliques (which I don't like).)

I found myself saying to David Lammy, 'Is the world getting worse, or is it me? Does this country really have anything to offer that would make someone like me want to stay here?'

'Where would you go instead?'

'The Caribbean? Bermuda?'

'Well, maybe I could come and visit you.'

'So you started as a black kid living in Tottenham in a single-parent family, and now here you are – an MP. Same story with me, I started out poor. What makes us do it? Where does the motivation to pull ourselves up come from?'

He thought about it for a while.

'I think we did it to look after our mums,' I said. That's what he and I, with our very different backgrounds, had in common. We had both effectively lacked fathers in our households as we grew up.

You try to succeed for those closest to you. When your grandparents struggled to escape adversity and persecution, when your parents put you on the right road and you have made something of your life, what remains? I think perhaps you need to use what you have to give meaning to their sacrifices by trying to make the world a better place for future generations – your own children and those of others.

David Lammy and I made our way through the urban garden that was growing fruit and vegetables of every kind, tended by people who had been less lucky than we had, and whom the Health Lottery funding was giving a chance to spend time in a tranquil, healing environment. It felt good to have helped make something like that happen.

That garden, and countless other local projects across the country, is the ultimate reward of my Health Lottery. At the time of writing, it has given away £93.8 million in prizes and £64.3 million in good cause donations. The only person who hasn't made any money out of it yet is me. It lost me £28 million in 2011, £19 million in 2012, and £16 million in 2014. I suppose, though, you could argue that the trend is encouraging! And at the same time I don't have to pretend to be a rock-and-roll star any more.

I believe that Dianne Thompson, the ex-CEO of Camelot, has gone off to run a hotel on the Isle of Wight. But I did finally work out why my adversaries reacted in so disproportionate a manner to what I was doing.

The last time tenders were sought for the British National Lottery, Camelot was the only company to bid. Why? Because to be a bidder you had to have experience of running a national lottery – in the UK. You also had to have experience of selling lottery tickets to retailers in the UK. And you needed already to have a licence from the Gambling Commission to sell lottery tickets in the UK. Strangely enough there was only one company which could fit those criteria at the time – Camelot. Now there are two.

For their information I definitely will go for the National Lottery when the licence comes up, and I think I stand a good chance of getting it because I'm smarter than Andy Duncan, I'm British and I will give profits back to charity.

22
HOPE

The real deal is the one you make with yourself.

The title of this book was inspired by the moment when turbo-charged Sex Pistol Johnny Rotten leapt on stage and announced the band as 'the real deal'. Actually, at that particular time, in the late seventies, I was too busy to pay much attention to punk, besides which I was running a musicians' magazine and we thought that punks couldn't play (we liked Ritchie Blackmore and Phil Collins). But when I saw a video of Johnny Rotten's performance recently, I realised that he was doing what the best musicians of every generation do – breaking the rules – and his phrase stuck in my mind.

As I sit here in 2015 there's a lot I feel I can be pleased about. My business is doing well; in material terms I have pretty much everything a sane person could dream of wanting. Admittedly I don't have boats and aeroplanes – not to mention Caribbean islands – but I don't envy those of my mates who do. I've been on plenty of boats and aeroplanes which have been incredibly luxurious, but I haven't found them comfortable, nor are they the best places to get just a nice cup of tea and some good food. (The exception is perhaps my mate Jamie Packer's converted ocean-going tug which he needs as a base for his global business and where 'the only rule is there are no rules'.) In other words, I don't find expensive stuff for its own sake necessarily satisfying. I was once asked what my greatest enjoyment in life was, and I answered, 'A nice cup of tea in a nice environment.' On that occasion I was probably thinking of my own house next to London's Hampstead Heath.

But while I feel comfortable, I do find myself increasingly wanting to try to make a difference in a world which, in some ways, seems to be changing for the worse and not for the better. My rock-and-roll contemporary Richard Branson comes to mind as a great example of an entrepreneur who has used his success to advance worthwhile causes. For example, he led the foundation of a group called the Elders, originally presided over by the late Nelson Mandela: it consists of influential people who no longer hold public office – and who therefore have nothing to prove and no constituency to appease – working for the good of the planet. The project goes hand in hand with Branson's commitment to environmental issues and his view, unless I am misrepresenting him, that many of the world's most pressing problems will be solved through technological means.

I admire Branson's work, but he and I tick differently. I'm not a techie like him. I am at heart just a drummer. And because I believe that the world's worst problems are to do with human nature, my view is that they can't be solved by what we invent but by changing how we behave.

Take the internet, for example: the most amazing global technology of our era. It magnifies everything that is good and noble in humanity – but also everything that is petty and vile. It isn't intrinsically good or bad in itself. As I write, video footage of the beheading by a British-born member of ISIS of the journalist James Foley has 'gone viral'. The internet is an amplifier: you just get out what you put in, only more so.

So when I support a cause, I want to get to know about the human element, to meet the people involved. I want the human detail, as with Rabbi Fhima and his candles. I want to listen to what people have to say.

I've been told I'm a good listener. Perhaps it's connected with having to listen for my deaf father from such an early age. Whatever the reason, it has served me well, and listening is perhaps my number one recommendation for success in business and life.

Do I have any other recommendations? What would I tell someone starting out at the bottom the way I did when I was 15? I suppose I would say: always know what you're aiming for and keep it in mind at all times. Keep to your word and stick by your mates. And remember you also have to give something back to the world – if you don't, then what's the point?

I once met a wonderful couple. They were happy, active and both nearing 100 years of age. They told me the key to a good life was to have food on the table, a roof over your head, and not to worry! To that I would add: have hope for the future, because something new is always going to turn up.

In the spring of 2014, while Joy visited her family in Newport Beach, I went on a trip with Robert to Israel. It was good to spend time with my oldest, especially as I had recently been focusing so much on Angel.

The two of us visited Jerusalem pretty much as tourists. We went to the markets, to Temple Mount, and to the wailing wall. We also visited Masada and Yad Veshem, the Holocaust History Museum. And I also stopped off at some projects I'd been invited to look at, and contribute to – for example, some pioneering medical projects in which Israeli universities are involved.

Eventually our tour brought us to a city called Tzfat, in the mountainous region of Upper Galilee. It's the birthplace of Kabbalah – a Jewish mystical tradition. I attended a meeting there, and then decided to go for a stroll. The guide suggested we could visit the old town. We climbed a hill, and there in front of us were cafés, ice-cream places, and various galleries and studios. Suddenly I caught sight of a sculpture outside one of the studios. It was of a woman carrying a baby boy.

Now, I am not a great art man. The only real work of art I have is a piece by Bob Dylan. It isn't particularly good art, but it is by Bob Dylan. In the same way I am proud to own one of Elvis's old pianos: it's not a particularly good piano but it belonged to Elvis. I also have a Picasso pot which Matthew Freud gave me for my 50th birthday and which I thought was worth tuppence halfpenny. (Actually, according to Mr Picasso's grandson – whom I know because he is our neighbour at our holiday home in Majorca – it's worth 50,000 euros.)

In other words, while I like art, I'm not crammed full of it. My creative side is more attuned to music. But that statue in Tzfat stopped me, held me and would not let me go.

I stared at it and started shaking. Tears welled up in my eyes.

The manager of the studio appeared and invited me inside. Did I know who the sculptor was? No, I didn't. He told me it was an artist called Nicky Imber. Would I like to see a video? Yes, I would. We watched the video, which described how Imber had been in Dachau for nine months, three days, and two hours. He had escaped by dressing up as a Nazi guard, using his artistic skills to disguise his face with dust and cake mix.

The curator showed me a few miniature versions of the statue. They were good but, well, not quite the same as the original.

'You really want the one outside, don't you?'

'Yes, I think so.'

There was no negotiation. The studio was a non-profit organisation and Imber had laid down the prices they could charge before he died in 1996. We discussed delivery details. I called Joy and told her I had a weird experience. I had found a statue that was connected to the Holocaust but that conveyed a positive message, and, I felt, something more. I also said that I had felt I had to buy it. It bore an inscription which speaks about hope for the future after the horrors of the past, and about the universal idea of a mother's love.

A few days later, when Joy was still in America and I was back home enjoying *The Sweeney* (I am only allowed to watch it when she is not there), she rang me. She had not been feeling well, she said, and had needed to visit a pharmacy. While she was there a sudden thought had struck her, and she had purchased a pregnancy test kit.

She told me the test had been positive.

I thought of the statue. 'It will be a boy,' I said with certainty.

The scans, which were done around the time the sculpture arrived, confirmed my prediction. Then on 3 January 2015 my second son was born. We decided to name him Valentine because we liked the name. It was only afterwards that Joy looked it up and discovered that it means brave and bold – in keeping, I feel, with the motto on which I have built my business. Joy, Star, Angel, Valentine – all positive names. Like many other Jewish children, Valentine also has a Hebrew name, which was given to him at his *bris* – or circumcision – ceremony in February. That name is Tikvah, which means hope, and which was also the title of the statue I'd bought. When Joy's brother Michael recently told me about the Italian maternal grandmother who made challah bread, he also mentioned the grandfather, Vincent, who disappeared in northern Italy in the early years of the Second World War, along with the rest of his family. Apparently, sensing that his life could be in danger, he gave a ring to his sister, who in turn gave it to Kay, who in turn gave it to Michael, who in turn gave it to me. His father, Michael informed me, was called Valentino – something I had no idea of when we gave Valentine his name.

Recently, then, I have been spending a lot of time with my family. But I am also looking forward to building my business in new ways and directions. I plan to make a real difference to London, the city in which I grew up and which has shaped my life. In particular, I have been working on a large-scale project to regenerate and develop the site of our old West Ferry print works to provide new housing for all types of people, as well as a secondary school. It is early days so I cannot say for sure whether there will be a Desmond Quay, an Angel Close or a Valentine's Way, but you never know. Perhaps instead the many people who played a part in getting me to where I am today (whether they meant to or not) ought to be recognised, although I would argue that O'Mahoney Wharf, Guccione Mews, Stevens Street and Hollick House do not trip off the tongue so easily.

Those, then, are my plans. But my experience has shown that sometimes the most exciting developments are the ones you never planned, the ones that came about because you kept your eyes and ears open for new possibilities, and if a door opened, you let your gut instinct tell you whether to rush through it into a new adventure.

I hope I still have time for many of those . . .

INDEX

Index

Index